THE NEW BEST OF FINE WOODWORKING

Working with
Power Tools

The Editors of
Fine Woodworking

The Taunton Press

 **The Taunton Press**

The Taunton Press, Inc., 63 South Main Street, PO Box 5506, Newtown, CT 06470-5506
e-mail: tp@taunton.com

Editor: Paul Anthony
Jacket/Cover design: Howard Grossman
Interior design: Susan Fazekas
Layout: Cathy Cassidy
Front cover photographer: © Phillip Dutton
Back cover photographers: (top row, left to right) Dennis Preston, courtesy *Fine Woodworking*;
Asa Christiana, courtesy *Fine Woodworking*; Mark Schofield, courtesy *Fine Woodworking*;
(bottom row, left to right) Asa Christiana, courtesy *Fine Woodworking*; Matt Berger, courtesy
Fine Woodworking

The New Best of Fine Woodworking® is a trademark of The Taunton Press, Inc.,
registered in the U.S. Patent and Trademark Office.

Library of Congress Cataloging-in-Publication Data
Working with power tools / the editors of Fine woodworking ; edited by Paul Anthony.
      p. cm.
  ISBN-13: 978-1-56158-872-5
  ISBN-10: 1-56158-872-5
  1. Power tools. 2. Woodwork--Equipment and supplies. I. Anthony, Paul, 1954- II. Fine
woodworking.

TT153.5.W67 2007
684'.08--dc22

                                        2006103140

Printed in China
10 9 8 7 6 5 4 3 2 1

The following manufacturers/names appearing in *Working with Power Tools* are trademarks: Biesemeyer®, Black & Decker®,
Bormax®, Bostik®, CMT®, Cool Blocks®, Craftsman®, Delta®, Delta® 40-680, Delta Machinery®, DeWalt®, DeWalt®
DW788, Dremel® 1800 Scroll Station, Dremel® Moto-Tool, Elu™, Enco® Manufacturing, Esta®, Everlast Saw and Carbide
Tools, Inc.®, Excalibur®, Freud®, General®, Grizzly® GO537, Highland Hardware℠, HTC® Products, Inca®, Jet® Cabinet
Saws, Kraemer Tools, Lee Valley℠, Leeson®, Lexan®, LPS®, Masonite®, Mitutoyo®, National Supply Source℠, Nordfab®,
Olson®, Oneida®, Oneida Air Systems®, Plexiglas®, Porter Cable®, Porter-Cable® 55K Plate Joiner, Powermatic®,
Quick-Fit®, Rockler®, Rout-R-Lift®, Scotch-Brite®, Silencer®, Stanley®, Starrett®, Stellite®, Styrofoam®, Suffolk
Machinery℠, Teflon®, Timberwolf®, TopCote®, T-Square® Blade Guard System, Underwriters Laboratory®, Uniguard®
Blade Guard, Unisaw®, Vise-Grips®, Watco®, Wood Slicer®, Woodcraft®, Woodworker's Supply℠, Xacta® Lift, X-Acto®

Working wood is inherently dangerous. Using hand or power tools improperly or ignoring safety
practices can lead to permanent injury or even death. Don't try to perform operations you learn
about here (or elsewhere) unless you're certain they are safe for you. If something about an operation
doesn't feel right, don't do it. Look for another way. We want you to enjoy the craft, so please keep
safety foremost in your mind whenever you're in the shop.

Acknowledgments

Special thanks to the authors, editors,
art directors, copy editors, and other
staff members of *Fine Woodworking*
who contributed to the development
of the articles in this book.

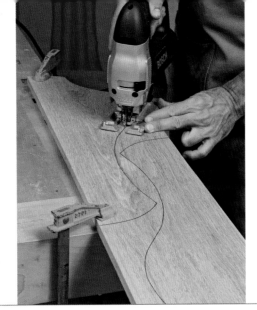

Contents

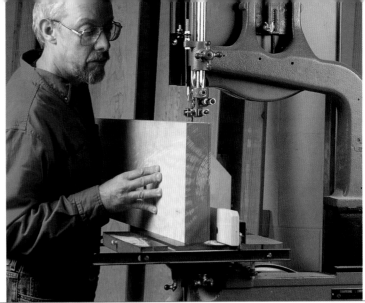

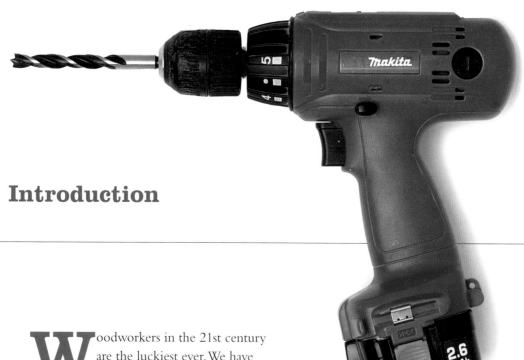

Introduction

Woodworkers in the 21st century are the luckiest ever. We have available to us a selection of power tools and machines that would have amazed our woodworking forbears a century or two ago. In addition to powerful high-tech tablesaws, jointers, and planers, we rely daily on electric drills, routers, jigsaws, sanders, and other portable power tools.

It's tempting to romanticize working wood in simpler times, quietly handplaning boards, cranking away at a bit and brace to drill holes, or leisurely cutting joints with handsaws and chisels. But the truth is, building furniture and cabinets solely with hand tools was hard, sweaty work. You can bet that woodworkers of the past would have jumped at the opportunity to power plane boards or cut joints with a tablesaw or router. If you think they wouldn't have traded in their sharkskin "sandpaper" for a random-orbit sander, then you are an incurable romantic indeed. Just like us, those guys were looking for the quickest, most accurate way to get the job done.

For all the power tools we have these days, though, we often don't use them to best advantage. They may not be tuned up properly or outfitted with the best bits or cutters. Or we may simply be handling the

tool or workpiece incorrectly. Furthermore, many tools require jigs of some sort to perform specific operations. There's a lot to know.

Fortunately, you'll find much of what you need to know in this collection of expert advice culled from the pages of *Fine Woodworking* magazine. Here, some of today's top woodworkers share their techniques, tricks, and approaches for choosing, using, and tuning power tools to bring out the best of your woodworking talents. Regardless of whether you're new to the craft or are already on your fifth router, this book is bound to help vault you forward in the world of woodworking. More power to you!

—Paul Anthony, editor

Portable and Benchtop Machines

Portable power tools like biscuit joiners, jigsaws, and circular saws have long had a place in the woodshop. In fact, they are often the first tools that a budding woodworker buys. Although they may be relatively small, these aren't "beginner" tools. Suited to specific purposes, they hold their own alongside their bigger brothers, the tablesaw, jointer, and other machines.

There's also a plethora of benchtop woodworking tools, including scrollsaws, spindle sanders, miter saws, and grinders. Tablesaws, jointers, planers, and other hardy pieces of equipment are now available in benchtop models for those who can't afford or accommodate the larger stationary versions.

In this section, we'll focus on a few of the more common and useful portable and benchtop tools, such as jigsaws, biscuit joiners, scrollsaws, and oscillating spindle sanders. You'll even find out how to put the humble portable circular saw to use in making cabinetry and furniture.

Biscuit Basics

TONY O'MALLEY

When I started my first job in woodworking in 1984, the biscuit joiner, also called a plate joiner, was just arriving on the shop scene. The company where I learned the trade still was using rabbet and dado joints to assemble plywood case goods. It's a tried-and-true system, but one we abandoned forever after discovering the manifold benefits of biscuit joinery.

First, by using biscuit joints instead of rabbets and dadoes, every joint is a butt joint, which makes calculating dimensions from a measured drawing much less painful and error prone—no more adding and subtracting to account for dadoes and rabbets. Second, biscuit joinery allows you to move a stack of freshly cut parts directly from the tablesaw to the workbench, where all of the joinery work can be done (maybe not a big deal in a one-person shop, but a definite advantage in a shop where co-workers are waiting to use the saw). Third, there's no need for dado blades and the finicky process of getting the fit just right. Fourth, biscuit joinery eliminates the frustrating task of sliding large workpieces across the saw to cut joinery. Sure, you can avoid these last two problems by cutting rabbets and dadoes with a router and T-square guide, but

biscuiting is much faster. Fifth, assembling a case with rabbets and dadoes, no matter how finely fit, always requires some extra effort to get the case clamped up squarely, the joints just seem to lean a little bit on their own. A biscuit-joined case, in contrast, almost always clamps up squarely right from the get-go (assuming your crosscuts are square, of course).

But the biscuit joiner's usefulness goes far beyond joining carcases. From strengthening miters to joining panels, from assembling face frames to attaching them to cabinets, this versatile tool can be a major player in your shop's lineup. As a colleague recently observed, the biscuit joiner may be the most significant tool development for the small-shop woodworker since the invention of the router.

I should point out that dovetails and mortise-and-tenon joinery remain the best approaches for solid-wood furniture construction. But the biscuit joiner can handle all of the joints in a basic plywood cabinet—from the case to the shelves or dividers to the face frame, the base molding, and even a drawer—with the exception of the door, which requires traditional joinery for additional strength.

What to look for in a biscuit joiner

Most of the time, the base of the machine can be used as the reference surface for making a cut. In most machines, this positions the slot in the center of ¾-in.-thick stock. However, a fence mounted onto the face of the tool provides more versatility in positioning the slot. So it is very important that the machine cuts a slot parallel to both its base and its fence; otherwise, joints won't line up properly.

Not all machines are created equal, and it's worth the time and effort to check that a new machine is accurate and to return it if it's not.

Joining cases and boxes

When joining parts to form a case or drawer box, the first step is to mark the slot locations on all of the parts. Often, this can be done simply by aligning the two pieces as desired and then drawing a small tick mark across the mating edges. However, for casework, where there are several of the same type of piece—sides and shelves, for example—it helps to develop a system (see the photos on p. 8).

How Many Biscuits and Where? Biscuit joints in case goods supplant conventional joints like the dado, the rabbet, and the splined miter. These are long joints, and it seems logical to cram in as many biscuits as possible, but it's not necessary.

Biscuits are manufactured by compressing the wood slightly so that upon gluing there will be a predictable amount of swelling. This swelling makes the joint at every biscuit stronger than a conventional wood-to-wood bond. My loose rule of thumb for case material is to use one biscuit for every 6 in. of width.

This is fully adequate, especially when using screws instead of clamps to pull

QUICK CASE JOINERY. A biscuit joiner makes fast work of assembling plywood cases. Laying out and cutting the basic slots is easy, especially when using simple alignment jigs.

THE BASE IS A CONSTANT REFERENCE

Try to rely on the base of the machine as the reference surface. This generally is a better approach because the distance between the blade and the base does not change, whereas the fence is movable.

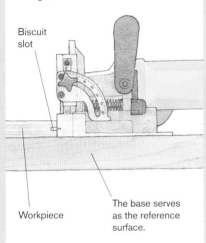

Biscuit slot

Workpiece

The base serves as the reference surface.

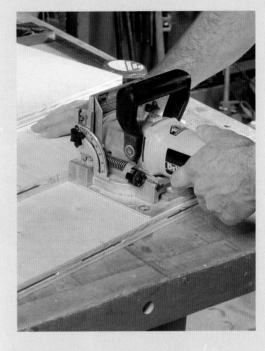
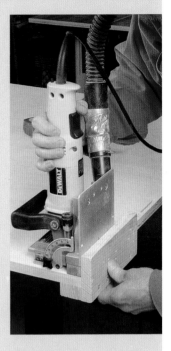

THE STANDARD POSITION IS SHOWN AT LEFT. To cut the mating slots, the workpieces or the tool (right, with the help of a jig) must be positioned vertically.

THE FENCE OFFERS FLEXIBILITY

Make sure your fence is reliable, and be sure the base isn't getting hung up on the benchtop or another workpiece below.

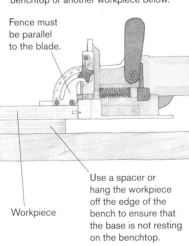

Fence must be parallel to the blade.

Workpiece

Use a spacer or hang the workpiece off the edge of the bench to ensure that the base is not resting on the benchtop.

FENCE ADDS CONVENIENCE. If the fence is used for both cuts, the workpieces can remain flat without the need for jigs.

Laying Out Biscuit Slots

HOW MANY BISCUITS?

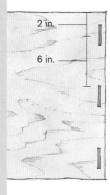

A good rule of thumb for carcase construction is to use at least one biscuit for every 6 in. of width. Locate them close to the front and back edges to keep the corners aligned, unless screws are used for assembly.

LAYOUT TRICKS. For this carcase, only the center of three biscuits must be marked. To locate the outside biscuits, line up the edge of the tool with the edge of the stock. Mark the pieces as a group, first on their ends (left), carrying the marks onto the faces where necessary (right).

Two Ways to Locate Dividers and Shelves

CUT SLOTS FOR A SINGLE SHELF OR DIVIDER ALL AT ONCE. After laying out all of the pieces and cutting slots in the divider or shelf, clamp the case parts together and use a long straightedge as a fence for the tool.

A JIG TO LOCATE MULTIPLE FIXED SHELVES. For a symmetrical series of shelves, use a piece of sheet stock that reaches to the center shelf. A small cleat at the end locates the jig accurately each time.

DRAWER-BOX CONSTRUCTION

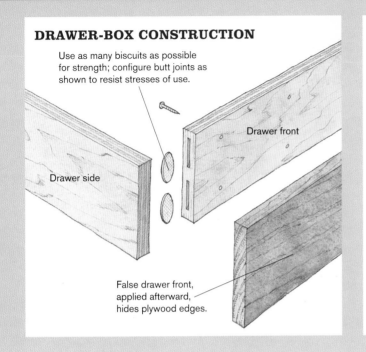

Use as many biscuits as possible for strength; configure butt joints as shown to resist stresses of use.

Drawer front

Drawer side

False drawer front, applied afterward, hides plywood edges.

CARCASE CONSTRUCTION

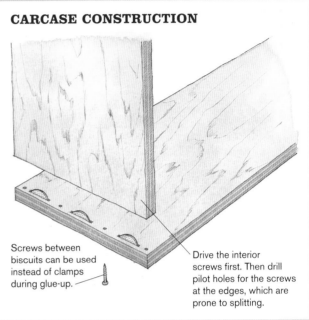

Screws between biscuits can be used instead of clamps during glue-up.

Drive the interior screws first. Then drill pilot holes for the screws at the edges, which are prone to splitting.

together the cabinet during glue-up. When I can't use screws to clamp and reinforce the joint—when the sides will be exposed —I don't use more biscuits; instead, I position the end biscuits as close to the edge as I can.

Whenever Possible, Use the Base of the Tool as a Reference To cut biscuit slots along the edge of a workpiece, you have two choices: You can use the machine's fence or the machine's base to position the slots. Whichever you choose for any given joint, you need to use the same reference for both sides of the joint. Remember, too, that the reference surfaces on the workpieces should be the outside face and edge because they must end up perfectly aligned.

For most biscuiting tasks, you can rely almost solely on the base of the machine as the reference surface. Even on inexpensive biscuit joiners, the base usually is parallel

to the blade. However, some fences are less reliable than others in terms of being perfectly aligned with the blade and staying locked in position. It's also easy to rock most biscuit joiners out of alignment when using the fence on the edge of a ¾-in.-thick panel; cutting those same slots with the base of the machine flat on a bench is a more stable and reliable approach.

When using the base as a reference, a biscuit joiner automatically places the center of the slot ⅜ in. from the bottom edge of the stock. To change that dimension, use thin stock such as hardboard to shim the machine or the workpiece to the proper position.

When joining box sides, cutting slots in the ends of panels is simple using the base, but cutting the opposite side of the joint— into the face of the panel—requires either holding the part on end or laying the part

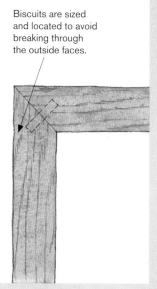

STANDING MITERS
To use the trusty base as a reference, clamp two pieces with their inside faces together, aligning them carefully. Then the biscuit joiner can rest in the 90 degree notch to cut slots in both miters.

Biscuits are sized
and located to avoid
breaking through
the outside faces.

flat and orienting the machine vertically. For tall pieces the latter option is easier; so make a simple L-shaped guide to keep the machine perpendicular to the workpiece (see the photo on p. 6).

Building and Attaching a Face Frame

Biscuits can be used both for joining face frames and for locating a face frame on a cabinet. When assembling a face frame, use the largest biscuit that the stock will accommodate. In most situations, you don't want part of a cutoff biscuit showing at the corner of the frame. So narrow face-frame stock may require using the small biscuits designed for face frames (they require a

smaller cutter). On wider stock, one of the standard three sizes should work fine.

Just a Few Biscuits to Locate a Face Frame When attaching face frames to cases, I generally rely on the long glue joint for strength, using a few biscuits to keep the frame from sliding around during the glue-up. A complete row of biscuits up and down every side would be overkill and would make it harder to fit the face frame to the case.

First, cut the slots in the case sides. This can be done before or after the case is assembled. Then glue up the face frame and lay it on the case to check the fit around the edges. Sometimes I build the frame to create a 1/8-in. to 1/4-in. overlap on the out-

FLAT MITERS
Clamp down workpieces
for safe and accurate results.
Be sure to keep the tool pressed
firmly in place throughout
the stroke.

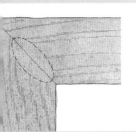

Locating biscuits closer
to the inside of the miter
allows the outside edges
to be profiled or molded.

GLUING MITER JOINTS
End grain can drink up glue, starving the joint. Prevent this by
brushing a thinned wash of glue on the joint and letting it glaze
over before applying glue at regular thickness. Don't forget to
put glue on the biscuits as well.

side of the case, which is fairly typical of
kitchen-cabinet construction. Other designs
require that the face frame be flush on
the outside. Still other times I allow a very
large overlap for scribing a built-in cabinet
to a wall. If there is overlap, use plywood or
medium-density fiberboard (MDF) shims
to raise the base of the biscuit joiner the
appropriate amount when cutting the slots
in the face frame.

Mitered Joints

Miters provide clean-looking joinery in
numerous situations. However, having an
equal combination of end grain and long
grain, miters need more than glue to hold
them together for the long run. Biscuits are
the perfect way to reinforce them.

There are two different types of biscuited
miters, and plywood cabinets use both of
them. Face frames often feature flat miters
for a picture-frame effect. And base moldings usually have standing miters at their
corners. Of course, both types of miters are
used elsewhere in woodworking—in boxes,
frames, and other moldings—and biscuits
can be used for these, too.

Biscuiting Flat Miters Once the stock
has been mitered, determine which size
biscuit will fit best. Be sure to factor in any
shaping that may be in store for the assembled frame (rounding over or rabbeting,
for instance). Usually, it's necessary that the

BISCUITS KEEP PIECES FLUSH

NARROW FRAME PIECES REQUIRE SMALLER, NONSTANDARD BISCUITS. The Porter-Cable® 55K Plate Joiner includes a smaller blade for joining pieces as narrow as 1½ in.

DETERMINE WHERE THE BISCUIT WILL BEGIN AND END. Allow extra room at edges that might be molded later, which could expose the biscuit. Mark the center of the slot and then transfer the mark to the mating piece.

biscuit be concealed in the stock. Remember that even a #0 biscuit is better than no reinforcement at all.

Biscuiting Standing Miters The outside corner on a base-molding assembly is a typical situation for a standing miter reinforced with biscuits. I also use biscuits to reinforce mitered case corners, instead of the more conventional continuous spline. With base moldings, the bottom edge of the stock won't show, so you can use a larger biscuit and let it extend out the bottom. A bigger biscuit gives you a deeper and stronger joint, and the excess is easily trimmed with a flush-cutting saw or utility knife.

The main layout principle is to position the biscuit slots off center, closer to the inside of the miter; otherwise, you risk cutting through the face of the stock.

BISCUITS ALIGN THE FRAME AND CASE

For an overlapping face frame, offset the biscuits. The stiles on this shop cabinet will overhang the sides by ¼ in., which must be factored in when locating the biscuit slots.

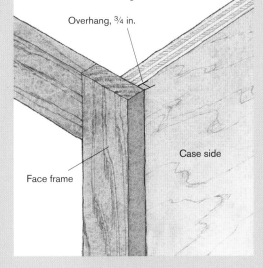

Overhang, ¾ in.

Case side

Face frame

USE THE TOOL'S BASE AS THE REFERENCE. Cut the slots in the case as usual, but place a ¼-in.-thick shim under the tool when slotting the face-frame stiles.

ONLY A FEW BISCUITS ARE NECESSARY. These serve primarily to keep the frame and case aligned during glue-up. Use plenty of clamps to distribute pressure. The glue-up will go more easily if the piece is on its back with room all around for clamps.

The best technique for biscuiting standing miters depends on the size of the stock and the configuration of the fence on your machine. Some fences offer a fixed 45° position, while others are adjustable. Some fences have a solid face, while others are an open frame. And the thicker and wider the stock, the more bearing surface you have for the fence to register on.

TONY O'MALLEY is a cabinetmaker in Emmaus, Pennsylvania.

Choosing and Using a Scrollsaw

BY PAUL SCHÜRCH

The scrollsaw holds extremely fine blades under tension, allowing it to do jobs that no other motorized saw can do. Unfortunately, many woodworkers think that a scrollsaw is only for hobbyists who make fretwork, bookends, whirligigs, and knickknacks. As a professional furniture maker, I've found the machine much more useful than that, and I believe it makes a valuable addition to any woodworking shop.

I use a scrollsaw to rough out dovetails, to cut mortise-and-tenon templates; to make small mock-ups of furniture I am designing; and to make cuts particular to marquetry, such as cutting "packets" of multiple layers of veneer. I've also cut material such as shell, bone, sheet brass, pewter, and copper for decorative hardware and inlay. It is even possible to cut ⅛-in.-thick glass for a curvy door panel using a barbed diamond-wire blade and to perform detail sanding and polishing using small belts attached to the scrollsaw like a blade.

It is true that most scrollsaw users don't focus on furniture making. But decorative fretwork and intarsia (a picture made of various woods, of various thicknesses) certainly qualify as woodworking. Some professionals also make a living gluing pictures onto seven-ply, ¼-in. aircraft-grade plywood and scrolling beautiful puzzle patterns. If these areas interest you, there are clubs devoted to scrollsawing, and scores of books and magazines that contain useful information, project ideas, and patterns.

Inlay, Marquetry, and Beyond

For inlay and marquetry, a scrollsaw is indispensable. These machines give you an easy and accurate means of cutting highly detailed inlay pieces to add to your furniture. Whether it's a bellflower on a period table leg or a mother-of-pearl square to be used as a decorative element, the process is straightforward. Draw the design onto the inlay material—usually between ¹⁄₁₆ in. and ¼ in. thick—and cut it out on a scrollsaw with the table set at a slight 2° to 4° angle, beveling each edge of the material inward a bit. This is called a conical cut. Then place the inlay onto the background, scribe around the outline with a knife, and hollow out the recess with a small router and a small chisel. Clamp and glue the inlay firmly into place, and then level it with the background after the glue has set. The bevel-cut edges will ensure a tight fit with the surrounding wood.

With a decent scrollsaw, you can step past inlay into the world of marquetry, which involves making detailed pictures by

TOOL TEST

Turn to p. 20 for a review of five
midpriced scrollsaws, all suited
to a wide range of tasks.

joining multiple pieces of
veneer. Panels of marque-
try can elevate the look
of your furniture and
case work. Except for one
machine, which takes only
pin-style blades, all of the
midrange saws tested on
pp. 20–21 will perform
the basic marquetry
cuts well, including
the packet, contour, conical,
window, piece-by-piece, and boulle
methods.

For packet cutting, my preferred marquetry method, a good scrollsaw and a
very thin blade make the job as easy as
stacking and pinning together all of the
veneers to be featured in the final picture,
spray-gluing a drawing onto the stack, cutting out all of the pieces in one shot, and

then pulling the pieces apart and taping
them into place. A #2/0 blade leaves only
a 0.010-in.-wide kerf, which tends to close
up in the final pattern. For more information on marquetry techniques, go to my
Web site (www.schurchwoodwork.com).

Scaled mock-ups of furniture are very
helpful in the design process, allowing a
3-D preview prior to drawing and building
the actual piece. Models also are great for
selling a design idea to a client. A scrollsaw is ideal for the detail work involved in
building a model out of thin materials. The
pieces can be put together very quickly
using hot-melt glue.

I sometimes use a scrollsaw for cutting
dovetails, roughing out the pins and tails
before trimming them to the line with a
sharp chisel, if need be. Other times I make
the initial sawcuts with a dovetail saw and
then use a scrollsaw to cut squarely across

Scrollsaw Uses in the Shop

MARQUETRY

**INDISPENSABLE FOR MARQUETRY. A scrollsaw
can cut through a thick packet of veneers (see
p. 15) with a very thin blade, cutting out all of
the pieces for a picture in one shot.**

JOINERY

**PERFECT FOR DOVETAILS. After the initial
cheek cuts are made, the tiny scrollsaw blade
makes it easy to cut across the bottom of a
dovetail socket and quickly remove the waste.**

MOCK-UPS

**AN EASY WAY TO TEST DESIGNS. With a
scrollsaw, small, intricate pieces are eas
to cut quickly and assemble using hot-
melt glue. This 1/10-scale model is a read
ing podium.**

the bottom of each socket, removing the waste. If the blade is tensioned properly, the cuts will be accurate and need very little cleanup. I've seen other woodworkers make the initial cuts on a tablesaw, then use a scrollsaw to remove the waste.

Once you have a scrollsaw, you'll find that lots of odd cuts become easier to make. I've used one to create matching templates in ½-in. plywood for routing odd-shaped mortises and tenons where large furniture components join. The matching inside and outside templates are attached temporarily to the mating workpieces, where they can guide a flush-cutting router bit. I use this technique often when joining solid-wood legs directly to a top piece. On period furniture, I've used a scrollsaw to cut out carving blanks for applied decorative elements.

Setting Up Your Saw

It's important for first-time users to realize that scroll-saw blades break regularly, especially thin ones. A #2/0 blade, for example, will break in 5 minutes or 10 minutes when cutting ½-in.-thick material. A broken blade can make a startlingly loud noise, but it doesn't necessarily mean you are doing anything wrong.

For best results, the blade should be tensioned to roughly an octave above middle C on the piano, or until a clear musical plucking sound is reached. If the blade is too loose, it will make a *thunk* sound when plucked and will tend to deflect in use, distorting the cut, fatiguing the blade, and causing it to break early. With too much tension, the blade will snap more often or slip out of the blade clamps.

Sources

SCROLLSAW BLADES
Wildwood Designs®
800-470-9090
www.wildwooddesigns.com

Woodcraft Supply
800-225-1153
www.woodcraft.com

BARBED DIAMOND WIRE
For cutting glass and other very hard materials
Alpha Supply
No. J0510B
800-257-4211
www.alpha-supply.com

FRETWORK

ENDLESS OPTIONS FOR PIERCED WORK. Schürch made this jewelry-box tray by cutting out small openings in solid wood and laying that fretwork onto a felt-covered plywood bottom. He detailed the carved leaf after the main vertical cuts were done.

INLAY

INLAY BECOMES STRAIGHTFORWARD. Tape the design to thin material and cut out the inlay. Then scribe around the inlay piece to lay out the recess. When cutting fragile materials like this abalone, make a zero-clearance plate from a piece of veneer.

Scrollsawing Tips

ADJUST FOR DRIFT TO CUT A STRAIGHT LINE

I have found that the toughest techniques to master are cutting straight lines and going around sharp corners. Many blades are milled in a way that can leave the blade slightly sharper on one side, so it tracks like a dull bandsaw blade. To cancel out blade drift when following a straight line, adjust the angle of the workpiece when pushing it into the blade. For best results, work in a series of short pushes, making small corrections as you go. As the blade dulls, the drift gets worse; keep blades well tensioned and change them often.

HOW TO TURN A SHARP CORNER

When cutting marquetry or finely detailed fretwork, negotiating sharp points and corners can pose a challenge. Essentially, you need to pivot the workpiece around the blade while the saw is running, reorienting it toward the new direction. This is accomplished by cutting up to the corner, then slightly pressing the workpiece against the side of the blade. This method stabilizes the workpiece without any unwanted

cutting. Now maintain that pressure as you pivot the workpiece into the desired position, shifting the pressure onto the back of the blade as you go.

MATCH THE BLADE TO THE TASK

Scrollsaw blade sizes range from the smallest #8/0 (pronounced eight-aught) to the largest #12 (sometimes called #0/12), with the most common for woodworking between #3/0 and #8. Thinner blades have more teeth per inch. The orientation of the teeth also is important (see chart on the facing page). For more blade information, check out the excellent chart at www.olsonsaw.com/scroll_chart_1.html.

AN ESSENTIAL BLADE KIT

These are the six blades Schürch uses most often, with the Olson® item numbers in parentheses.

- #12 skip tooth (453): Heavy-duty blade for cutting straight lines in thicker material such as plywood.

- #5 precision ground, reverse tooth (495RG): Used for straighter-line fretwork.

A Few Modifications

I recommend making changes and adding accessories to any scrollsaw. A wider auxiliary table placed over the top of the standard table will support wider work. To turn the saw on and off, a foot-pedal switch (the electrical type that stays on only when the pedal is depressed) takes the panic out

of scrolling detail work and stops the noise when the blade breaks. Also, I tape zero-clearance plates of thin cardboard, plastic, or veneer on the saw table to support fragile material and keep small pieces from dropping through the throat.

I don't like the blade guards on a scroll-saw, they only get in the way, so I remove

TOOTH PATTERNS

STANDARD TOOTH **The basic, cut-anything blade.**

SKIP TOOTH **Runs cooler in harder material.**

REVERSE TOOTH **Bottom few teeth are reversed to reduce tearout.**

PRECISION GROUND **More aggressive and straighter cutting. Available in #5, #7, and #9, in skip tooth or double/reverse tooth.**

DOUBLE TOOTH **Slow cutting, but smoother results.**

CROWN TOOTH **Cuts on both upward and downward strokes; slow, but minimizes tearout. Good for plastic.**

SPIRAL **Cuts in any direction but leaves rougher, wider kerfs.**

- #5 skip tooth (446): Thinner depth than the precision-ground #5; turns tighter corners. Good for more detailed fretwork as well as for dovetails.

- #2/0 skip tooth (440): Schürch uses this one for marquetry and other very finely detailed work; kerf is only 0.010 in.

- #1 metal-cutting (479): For metal, shell, and bone.

them. In the classes I teach, with students ranging in age from 8 to 85, I've never seen more than a minor cut on any scrollsaw with the blade guards removed.

PAUL SCHÜRCH, a furniture maker and teacher in Santa Barbara, California, specializes in marquetry.

Blade Source Tool Test: Midrange Scrollsaws

With the average woodworker in mind, I tested five midrange scrollsaws with throat depths between 18 in. and 22 in. Each saw has enough throat capacity, power, and accuracy to handle all of the tasks described in this article, and each costs less than $600★. (Unfortunately, Craftsman® was not able to supply its latest 18-in. model in time for testing.)

I put the machines through a variety of tasks, and all made acceptable cuts. For each of these saws, it is important to find an ideal midrange speed for any given task, a sweet spot that is the balance between speed and smoothness. If you don't push a saw past that point, you will minimize vibration and produce the best cuts.

One of the most important factors for efficient and enjoyable scrollsawing is the ease of tensioning and changing the blade, especially if you plan to try fretwork or other pierced cutting where the blade must be untensioned, removed, threaded through the workpiece, and reattached often. All of these saws come with quick-release blade clamps, which are important, but not all have access to their tensioning system at the front.

Also important is the ability to change speeds quickly. Some saws have easy-to-reach adjustment knobs at the front, offering an infinite range of speeds, but two have pulley systems that take more

SCHÜRCH USED EACH SAW TO MAKE A VARIETY OF CUTS **in a variety of common materials. He graded the smoothness of cut by feel and by looking at the cuts under magnification.**

DELTA® 40-680
800-223-7278
www.deltamachinery.com

THE DELTA IS A SOLID PERFORMER, but the belt system forces you to turn off the saw and reach under it to change speeds. (The PS Wood also has a belt system.)

PS WOOD MACHINES 21-IN. SCROLLSAW
800-939-4414
www.pswood.com

THE REMOVABLE BLADE CLAMPS ADD 2 MINUTES to the blade-changing process, requiring a special jig built into the side of the machine.

time and effort to adjust and offer a limited range of speeds. I also prefer saws with a larger stroke, which uses more of the blade's teeth and prolongs blade life.

I evaluated the stability of each saw's upper arm and table, looking at how wobbly they were and how easily they could be knocked out of adjustment. If either happens while cutting through a packet of veneers, for example, the crooked cut will leave big gaps in the finished marquetry. I can't recommend scrollsaws that accept only pin blades. These perform well for rougher work but have limited abilities for finer detail.

My choice for the best overall scrollsaw is the DeWalt®, a quiet, smooth-running, well-designed machine at a reasonable price. It is very solidly built. The trunnions supporting the table are strong and allow full tilt in both directions. The upper arm lifts up, making it easier to thread work onto the blade from above, which is helpful for pierced cutting.

My choice for best value goes to the Dremel®. It also is a smooth performer, with important adjustments at the front of the saw. While it tends to bog down just a bit more often than the DeWalt, the Dremel is a great value at its price and includes some helpful attachments, such as a small disk sander on the side, a work light, the ability to take either pin-end or plain-end blades, and the option of attaching a rotary, flex-shaft tool onto the motor.

Please note that all price estimates are from 2005.

Model	Average price*	Throat depth	Blade types
Delta 40-680	$480	20 in.	Plain end
DeWalt DW788	$390	20 in.	Plain end
Dremel 1800 Scroll Station	$240	18 in.	Plain end and pin end
Grizzly G0537	$130	22 in.	Plain end
PS Wood Machines 21-in. Scrollsaw	$600/ direct	21 in.	Plain end

DEWALT DW788
800-433-9258
www.dewalt.com

THE DEWALT, LIKE THE
DELTA AND DREMEL,
has its tensioning lever up
front (jutting out at top),
making it easy to release
the blade.

**DREMEL 1800
SCROLL STATION**
800-437-3635
www.dremel.com

LIKE THE GRIZZLY AND
DEWALT MACHINES,
the Dremel's speed-control
knob is up front, allowing you
to improve the cutting action
while under way.

GRIZZLY GO537
800-523-4777
www.grizzly.com

THE GRIZZLY MACHINE TAKES
ONLY PIN-STYLE BLADES,
which require a bigger pilot
hole than plain-end blades,
making then unsuitable for
the finest pierced work.

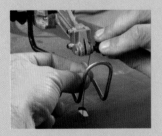

Table angle	Stand	Strokes per minute	Stroke length	Ease of changing speed	On/off access	Stability of table and arm	Smoothness of cut
Left 45 right 15	Included and necessary	400–2000, 6 speed	$7/8$ in.	Very good	Fair	Excellent	Excellent
Left 45 right 45	Optional	400–1550, Variable	$13/16$ in.	Very good	Very good	Very good	Excellent
Left 45 right 7	Optional	500–1700, Variable	$13/16$ in.	Good (plain end) Excellent (pin end)	Excellent	Very good	Very good
Left 30 right 2	None	425–1300, Variable	$5/8$ in.	Fair	Good	Fair	Fair
Left 40 right 30	Included and necessary	170–1370, 5 speed	$15/16$ in.	Fair	Poor	Fair	Good

Oscillating Spindle Sanders

BY BERNIE MAAS

Smoothing concave surfaces can be a chore. If you've tried sanding these areas by hand, you know what I mean. A belt sander works well on outside curves, but it can't follow a concave surface. However, a spindle-mounted drum sander will take the pain out of cleaning up after the bandsaw and jigsaw.

Maybe you've made do with a sanding drum mounted on a drill press or a radial-arm saw. Though inexpensive, this type of drum-sander attachment has several disadvantages. First, the size of the work is limited by the distance between the spindle and the machine's support column. Second, stock removal is slow. With the sanding drum always buried in the work, the abrasive is quickly clogged and glazed. Finally, high spindle speed accelerates the heat buildup and glazing. If you have to sand a lot of interior curves, you'll want a benchtop oscillating spindle sander.

Pick Drums to Fit the Work

An oscillating spindle sander is an ingenious marriage of a drill-press-like quill and cam or crank that allows the sanding drum to move up and down and spin simultaneously. This cyclic motion speeds stock removal by bringing more abrasive into play and allowing some of the abrasive to exit the work

briefly for cooling. With a rate of about 60 to 75 oscillations per minute, the reciprocating action minimizes deep scratching. And because the spindle sticks out of the machine's table, like a shaper, there is no structure above the table to limit your work.

All oscillating spindle sanders accept several different diameter drums. When I lay out interior curves, I try to size each radius to fit one of my array of sanding drums. Usually, I aim for the largest drum that fits. The bigger the drum, the smoother

the finished curve. Larger-diameter sanding sleeves, with greater abrasive area, also last longer. Sanding drums are available in standard diameters, from ½ in. to 3 in. Because the sleeves fit over the drums, the actual sleeve outside diameter is about ⅛ in. larger than the nominal diameter.

To mount a sanding drum, simply slip the abrasive sleeve over the drum and then slide the drum over the spindle. The retaining nut should be tightened just enough so the sleeve doesn't slip. Overtightening the retaining nut can distort the sleeve.

THAT'S A BIG DRUM. Use the largest drum that fits the work and the correct-size insert for stock support. Large drums produce the best finish in the least amount of time. Some work may require using several drums of different diameters.

ANATOMY OF A SPINDLE SANDER

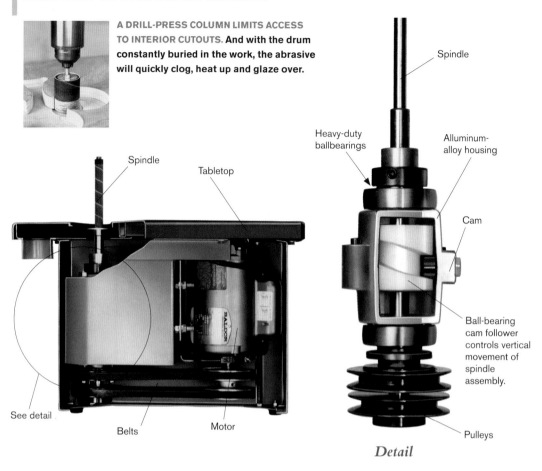

A DRILL-PRESS COLUMN LIMITS ACCESS TO INTERIOR CUTOUTS. And with the drum constantly buried in the work, the abrasive will quickly clog, heat up and glaze over.

Spindle

Tabletop

Spindle

Heavy-duty ballbearings

Alluminum-alloy housing

Cam

Ball-bearing cam follower controls vertical movement of spindle assembly.

See detail

Belts

Motor

Pulleys

Detail

There are many sizes of table inserts available to close the gap between the drum outside diameter and the table opening. A table insert is critical for stock support and helps vacuum draw for under-the-table dust collection.

A Few Tips on Using the Sander

There's no steep learning curve to this machine, but here are a few tips. For the best control, feed against the spindle rotation. Feed pressure should be tangent to the drum, not radial. What's that mean? As you feed, don't push heavily toward the center of the spindle; instead, feed with even pressure both against the drum and in line with the edge of the drum. Pushing toward the center of the spindle produces a washboard

surface that is difficult to remove. To reduce heat buildup, work the entire piece from one end to the other, back and forth, allowing one area to cool down while sanding another.

Also, take care in approaching inside corners, where the drum can catch and whip the work out of your hands. Snagging the edge of holes or interior cutouts is possible if the work is cocked. Pick a drum that gives sufficient clearance with the opening.

Take the usual safety precautions for rotating machinery. Stop the machine before placing the work over the spindle. Keep your hair back and avoid dangling clothing and jewelry. Wear eye protection and keep your hands away from the drum.

BERNIE MAAS is a professor in the art department of Edinboro University, Edinboro, Pennsylvania.

A Circular Saw in the Furniture Shop?

BY GARY WILLIAMS

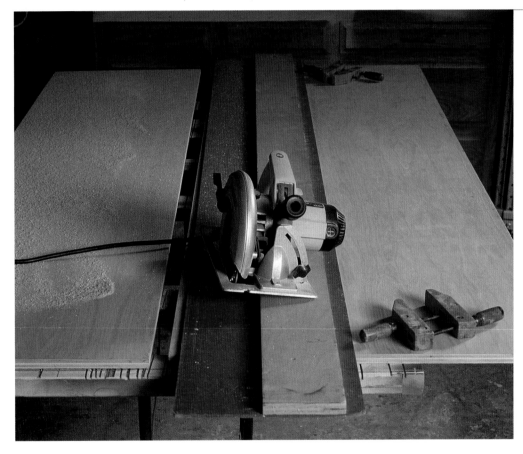

Contractors couldn't live without the portable circular saw, but we of the warm, dry furniture shop tend to leave it on the same shelf as the chainsaw. Great for building a deck but far too crude for quartersawn oak. Necessity has a way of teaching us humility, however.

I've been a sometimes-professional woodworker for nearly 30 years, but somehow I have never managed to attain the supremely well-equipped shop. I work alone in a no-frills, two-car garage that I share with a washer, a dryer, a water heater and a black Labrador. My machines are on the small side, and I lack the space for large permanent outfeed and side extension tables for my tablesaw. Perhaps you can relate. Under these conditions, cutting a full sheet of plywood can be a very challenging operation. Even if you have your shop set up to handle sheet goods with ease, perhaps you've run into similar difficulties cutting plywood and lumber accurately on job sites and installations. The solution?

May I suggest the humble circular saw. Cutting lumber and plywood with a hand-held circular saw is nothing new. You've probably done it before, with varying degrees of success. You get that 4x8 sheet up on the sawhorses, mark your cut line, rig up some kind of straightedge and cut. Trouble is, in the instant before the cut is complete, gravity happens, and you are presented with an entirely new challenge. Now you have two pieces that either want to collapse in the middle or fall off the end. Meanwhile, the scrap you used as a straightedge bowed a little during the cut; and it wasn't quite long enough to begin with, so the last few inches of the cut were done freehand. And as to the cut produced by that blade you last used to cut creosote-soaked fence posts. . .

I've developed methods of tuning the saw, supporting the workpiece, and guiding the cut that combine to make slicing up sheet goods and unwieldy planks of solid wood with a circular saw so simple and the results so clean that I don't even daydream about the big shop and the behemoth tablesaw anymore.

You Must Tune the Saw

If you're going to make joint-quality cuts with a circular saw, there are rules:

Rule No. 1: Start with a good saw, one that can be properly adjusted and that has good bearings to prevent the blade from wobbling.

Rule No. 2: Install the best 40-tooth carbide blade that you can find.

Tuning the Saw

To make joint-quality cuts with a circular saw, start with a good saw and a good blade and keep them well tuned.

PARALLEL BASE AND BLADE. Use a dial indicator to check that the blade is parallel to the edge of the saw base. Adjust the base to correct any error.

SQUARE IS ESSENTIAL. Use a machinist's square to get the blade at 90°. A flat base like this one makes it easier to check for square and more likely that the cut will be square, too.

Rule No. 3: Always check the blade tilt with a machinist's square before starting a job.

Rule No. 4: Make sure the blade is exactly parallel to the edge of the saw's base. Use a dial indicator if you can. If you can't adjust the base, see Rule No. 1.

Use a Cutting Table to Support the Work

The backbone of my system is a sacrificial cutting table with folding legs. Picture that unwieldy sheet of plywood lying serenely on a dedicated cutting table, waiting to be operated on like a patient in surgery. When each cut has been completed, both halves of the sheet will still be lying there, awaiting further disposition. Nothing caves in or falls off the end. Each cut makes a shallow kerf in the table, and when you've chewed up one table, you simply make another (for

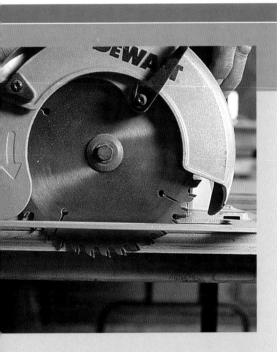

DON'T WORRY ABOUT WHAT'S BELOW. Set the depth of cut so that a full tooth of the blade extends below the workpiece. You'll be cutting right into the surface of the sacrificial table.

me, a matter of a couple of years). The table is cheap, easy to build and lightweight, and you can store it in a narrow space when you're not using it. The table's open-grid format serves three purposes: It keeps the table light; it keeps it clean (sawdust falls through, and you can't pile junk on it); and it allows a clamp to be used anywhere on the table surface.

It doesn't take a 4-ft. by 8-ft. table to handle a full sheet of plywood. I build mine a little under 3 ft. by 7 ft. This size is comfortable to work on and easy to store. If you have to cut a foot or less off one end of the sheet, you can slide it over so that the far end hangs over a foot or two. Same thing with width. As long as there is enough table to support more than half of the piece, it's not going to fall off.

There are various ways to assemble the grid. If you have a regular workbench large enough to lay out all of the pieces on, you can use a couple of bar clamps to snug the assembly together while you insert screws. Alternately, you can lay the pieces out on the floor and use a wall to give you something to push against while driving the screws. I use fir 2x2s for the long rails and 2x4s for the crosspieces. I drive 3-in. drywall screws to connect them, and I drill clearance holes only for the screws at the ends of the long rails, where there is some danger of splitting the wood. If you work on the floor, you can assume the grid won't be perfectly flat, but that's okay. As long as it's not far out of flat, it should perform well.

You can place your tabletop on sawhorses for use or just put it on a bench or table, but I'd recommend fitting it with folding legs. Folding banquet table legs, available in many woodworking catalogs, are fairly inexpensive and add a tremendous amount of convenience.

To get a heavy sheet of plywood or medium-density fiberboard (MDF) up on the table, there's a simple way to save your back (see the photos on p. 29). Place a couple of wood scraps on the floor and tilt the table down so that the edge of the tabletop rests on them. This gives you room to get your fingers underneath. Then set the plywood on edge on the blocks as well. Lean the plywood against the tabletop, reach underneath and tilt up the table and sheet together.

Make Dedicated Cutting Guides

The difficulty in using a straightedge with a circular saw is that you have to offset the straightedge from the cut line to account for the width of the saw's base. My first approach to simplifying this process was to rip a strip of Masonite® the exact width of this offset. I would lay this spacer down next to the cut line and then snug my straightedge up to the spacer. It didn't take long to figure out that it would be more convenient to attach a Masonite spacer to the bottom of the straightedge.

Now I simply lay the Masonite base of a cutting guide right on the line, clamp the guide to the workpiece and cut. One bonus is that the saw glides smoothly across the Masonite instead of on my workpiece. And another is that the Masonite backs up the cut, minimizing splintering of the veneer in cross-grain cuts.

I keep several of these guides in the shop, in different sizes and configurations. Together with the circular saw and the cutting table, they make dissecting large panels a breeze. I recommend at least three different guides: an 8-ft. guide for cutting sheet goods in the long dimension, an easier-to-wield 4-ft. version for shorter cuts and a 90° guide for perfectly square cuts (see the photos on p. 30–31).

To make a guide, begin by cutting an 8-in.-wide strip of ¾-in.-thick plywood for the fence portion. Next, measure the saw's footprint—the distance from the blade to the edge of the base on the side under the motor. Then make the Masonite

The guide is always placed on the good side of the cut marks.

base. Its width is 8 in. plus the saw's footprint plus ½ in. or so extra, which will be trimmed off. The plywood for the fence should be of good quality—something with good inner plies, such as hardwood or marine plywood. The edge that the circular saw will be running against should be free of voids, if possible. For the Masonite base, tempered is best, ⅛ in. or ¼ in. thick.

To assemble a straight guide, lay the plywood fence, best-side down, on the table, and lay down the Masonite strip with the best side down on top of the plywood. Drill and countersink clearance holes in the Masonite, about every 6 in. along the length of the assembly. Clamp the two boards and screw them together, being careful to get the screws fully countersunk.

Your next move will be to trim the Masonite base. If you haven't bought a good sawblade yet, drop everything and do it now—your guide will be trimmed to match your exact saw and blade combination; you don't want to make a guide with one blade and use it with another. When you get back from the store and put your good carbide blade in the saw, check the blade for square and parallel according to those iron-clad rules on p. 26. Then clamp the guide to your cutting table and trim off the excess Masonite by running the saw down the length of the assembly. Now the guide is ready to go.

The key to making the right-angle cutting guide is getting an accurate 90°. I use a scrap piece of plywood as a form when I join the two legs of the guide. I use a factory corner (checking with a square to see that it is 90°) or cut one corner square.

Using a guide is a snap. The only thing to remember is that the guide is always placed on the good side of the cut marks—that is, on top of the piece you're going to be using—so that the saw kerf is in the waste.

Setting Up the Table

A boon to the small shop, a folding cutting table can be stored in a space several inches wide and can be set up in about a minute. To load a sheet of plywood, tip the table onto a pair of scrap wood spacers. Lift the ply onto the spacers, and lift the ply and the table together.

Using the Guides

Simple two-part cutting guides—with a Masonite base attached to a plywood fence—make it possible to get accurate cuts with minimal layout.

LONG DIVISION. The long, straight guide makes quick work of ripping a full sheet of plywood. When the cut has been made, the halves of the sheet stay put, supported by the cutting table.

Nonstandard Cutting with the Guides

Once you've used this cutting system for a while, you will no doubt see other applications for it. Here are several that have come up in my work since I first made these guides.

Straight-Lining Crooked Boards The 8-ft. guide offers an easy way to straighten the edge of a long, waney-edged plank. Use scraps the thickness of the workpiece to space the cutting guide off the table. Clamp the guide to the table. Then tuck the crooked edge of the board under the

guide's Masonite base just far enough that the waney edge disappears. Then clamp the plank to the table and rip.

Mitering What if you need to rip a wide mitered edge to make a large box? All you need is another cutting guide. Make one with an oversize base, just as you did with the others, and then trim it with the sawblade set to 45°.

When you are ready to cut the miters on the workpiece, mark the cut on the edge of the piece with a 45° marking square and line up the beveled Masonite with the marks.

FOUR-FOOT GUIDE FOR CROSS-CUTS. The short, straight guide is used for intermediate rips and long crosscuts.

SWIFT, SQUARE CUTS. The 90° guide makes perfectly square cuts 2 ft. long.

THE MITER OPTION. To make mitered edges, assemble a guide with its base cut to 45°. Align the angled layout line with the mitered edge of the base.

WANEY EDGE, GO AWAY. You can use the long guide to put a straight edge on a waney board. Block up the guide so that the workpiece just fits under it. Then nudge the waney edge of the workpiece under the guide's base. Clamp both guide and workpiece, and rip off the edge.

Ripping Skinny Pieces Narrow pieces are typically best cut on a tablesaw. But on site or on an installation, there may be times when you want to cut a piece narrower than the cutting guide. In these cases it's difficult to clamp the two together without the clamps interfering with the saw. The solution is to clamp the workpiece to the table, with the clamps in the waste, and hold the guide down with different clamps. As with straight-lining, elevate the guide using scraps the same thickness as the workpiece, positioning them under the clamps. Slide the workpiece under the guide, line up the cut marks with the Masonite edge, and clamp the workpiece to the table. Then rip as usual. If you need to rip a number of skinny pieces to the same width, position the spacer blocks to serve also as stops, determining the width of the cut.

A cutting table and guides should make your life a little easier around the shop, especially if it's a small one. You may even find them helpful next time you go out in the cold to build a deck.

GARY WILLIAMS is a technical writer and woodworker in San Diego, California.

Jigsaws in the Woodshop

BY PAUL ANTHONY

The jigsaw, also called a sabersaw, is an indispensable job-site tool. Whether you're installing cabinets and countertops, fitting trim, or notching window sills, it's hard to imagine getting by without this versatile little saw. Lightweight enough even for overhead cutting, and accepting of a variety of wood and metal cutting blades, the tool can literally run circles around larger saws. It can cut curves and all sorts of odd shapes in a variety of materials, including solid wood, plywood, particleboard, and metal.

But this is one saw that doesn't stay packed away in my job-site toolbox. I keep it within reach for all sorts of shop tasks. With its narrow, reciprocating blade, it's great for cutting arched furniture aprons, shapely tabletops, corbels, and other curved pieces. And because the projecting blade is held at only one end, it can make interior cuts that a bandsaw can't. It's also the tool I reach for to make notches or other cuts in a large workpiece that is too cumbersome to hoist onto the bandsaw or tablesaw. You can use a jigsaw to break down full sheets of plywood for easier cutting on the tablesaw, and it's the ideal tool for separating curved pieces laid out closely together on a board to maximize wood usage.

In these pages, I'll show you what this cool little tool can do for you. I'll give you a few tips on picking one and share a few tricks for getting it to perform at its best.

Selecting a Saw

Woodworkers these days can select from a wide variety of jigsaws, ranging from about $30 to about $160*. (Cordless models can cost more.) As with most tools, you get what you pay for. In general, more money buys you more power, precision, and convenience.

If you work with thick stock or hard woods, power should be a primary concern. The more amps a saw produces, the easier it will glide through your work. Another important feature is adjustable orbital blade action, which allows you to choose between clean or fast sawing. Coupled with variable speed control, this can give you get great cutting performance. A good blower is also critical for clearing the cutline of dust. Make sure a saw has a truly flat base and that it can be adjusted relatively easily to make beveled cuts. Most saws these days feature quick, toolless blade changing, but some mechanisms are more convenient than other, so compare. Some packages include a zero-clearance insert and a plastic, non-marring auxiliary sole.

If possible, get your hands on a candidate saw to make sure it's comfortable and not too heavy for you. As for shape, you have two basic choices: top-handle and barrel grip. Top-handle advocates often prefer the control they get from grasping the saw directly above the blade. On the other hand, barrel-model proponents find that a hand closer to the workpiece gives them better control. You decide.

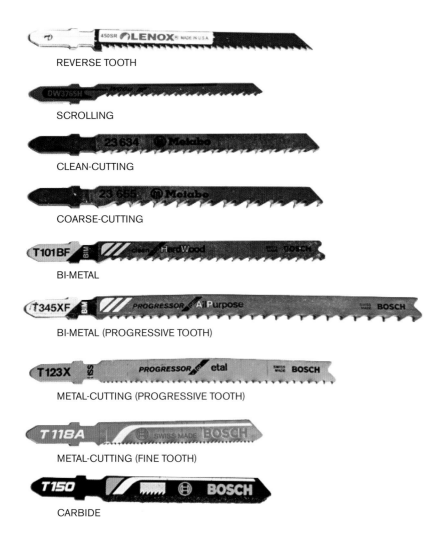

REVERSE TOOTH

SCROLLING

CLEAN-CUTTING

COARSE-CUTTING

BI-METAL

BI-METAL (PROGRESSIVE TOOTH)

METAL-CUTTING (PROGRESSIVE TOOTH)

METAL-CUTTING (FINE TOOTH)

CARBIDE

A BEVY OF BLADES AVAILABLE
for the jigsaw allows cutting wood, metal, and other materials.

A Bit about Blades

Of course, the versatility of a jigsaw also lies in the variety of blades you can use with it. There are a lot of different blades available for cutting wood and metal, as well as carbide blades for ceramics and other brittle materials.

Wood-cutting blades with coarse teeth will quickly rip through even thick, dense wood, but at the expense of a rough cut. A blade with fewer teeth will cut more cleanly but also more slowly. To make tight, scrolling turns, use a blade that's narrower from front to back. A reverse-tooth blade, with its downward-pointing teeth, produces a clean cut in thin veneers, MCP, and other tearout-prone face materials. Blades with

progressive teeth are designed for use in both thick and thin materials.

There are three different types of blade shanks: T-shanks (shown in the photos at left), hook shanks (used by Porter Cable® saws), and universal shanks. Only one kind of shank will fit a particular saw. T-shank and universal shank blades are widely available through home supply stores and woodworking catalogs. Hook shanks aren't as common, but some dealers that carry them can be easily found online by searching for "Porter Cable jigsaw blades."

What to Expect from a Jigsaw

For all the tricks it can perform, a jigsaw is primarily a curve-cutting tool. So is it a substitute for a bandsaw? Well, sort of, but not really. A jigsaw doesn't have the blade length or power to cut through very thick stock like a bandsaw can. Also, because a bandsaw blade is stretched between two wheels, it suffers little or no deflection in the cut, producing an edge that's square to the face of the workpiece. A jigsaw blade, which is restrained at only one end, can twist and deflect (typically when making a tight turn), causing a slightly beveled edge.

That said, the jigsaw has quite a few advantages over the bandsaw. For one thing, equipped with a clean-cutting blade, a jigsaw can produce a cut that needs only the slightest sanding. Also, a jigsaw will make interior cuts, which a bandsaw simply can't do. Likewise, a jigsaw can be used to shape large panels or to break them down into manageable pieces—something a bandsaw's throat capacity doesn't allow.

All that is in addition to the regular chores that a jigsaw excels at, such as trimming the back edges of cabinet sides to fit snugly against an out-of-flat wall, sawing cutouts for electrical boxes, or notching furniture panels to fit between legs. It can't be beat when it comes to many home

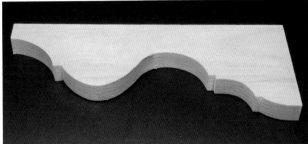

THIS CORBEL, FRESH OFF THE SAW, **displays edges that need only a bit of fine sanding to clean up.**

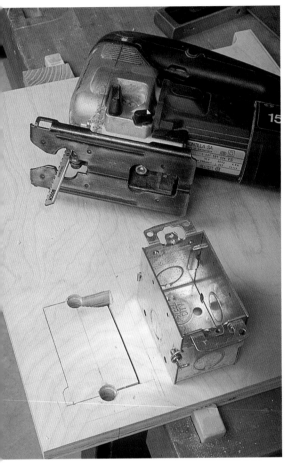

IT'S HARD TO BEAT A JIGSAW when it comes to making inside cuts for electrical boxes and other components.

Smart Jigsaw Practices

Always secure the workpiece in a vise, or clamp it to a sturdy bench so you can focus entirely on cutting to the line without worrying about the piece shifting.

Good light is crucial to good cuts. A work light on a portable post lets you position the light as needed. For accuracy, sight straight down the front of the saw to the juncture of the blade and cutline.

Before sawing to your cutlines, practice on a few representative lines drawn on a scrap area of the workpiece to get a feel for the proper blade speed, feed rate, orbital action, and potential cutting radius.

Whenever making critical cuts, use a fresh blade. If turning off the saw midcut to reposition a clamp or unsnag the cord, keep the saw in its exact stopped position to maintain a fair cut when starting again. Registration marks around the saw base can help.

improvement tasks, such as fitting trimwork, especially crown molding.

Just don't expect to be able to guide a jigsaw along a straightedge to make straight cuts. Sadly, I've never known a saw that would faithfully follow a straightedge. Jigsaws suffer from blade drift, just like bandsaws. If the blade isn't exactly parallel to the sides of the base, it's going to try to lead to one side or the other, causing the jigsaw blade to deflect in the cut.

Deflection can also result from varying grain density in a piece of wood. At best, this will create a beveled edge. At worst, you'll suffer pinching and burning. When I have to make a straight cut, I do it freehand, sawing a bit proud of the final dimension, then I straighten the cut afterward on the tablesaw or with a router guided by a straightedge.

Curve Cutting

When cutting curves of any sort, choose an appropriate blade. If you're cutting tight curves, use a scrolling blade. Its narrow front-to-back body allows more severe turns than a wider blade. When sawing curves with large arcs, such as those on arched furniture rails, a standard-width blade will help prevent wandering off the cutline.

When making multiples, I typically lay out the parts by tracing around a carefully made ¼-in.-thick plywood template. I lay out small parts on a long board that can be secured in a vise or clamped to a bench-top while sawing off the parts in sequence. Before turning on the saw, though, I plan the series of cuts so that I can saw downhill to the grain as much as possible to ensure smooth cuts.

The challenging part of scrolling is turning the saw without causing blade deflection. The trick here is to avoid push-ing the saw sideways. As you travel around a curve, focus your attention on the very front of the blade, which should represent your pivot point. Don't push the saw for-ward any faster than the teeth can cut. To help ensure fair curves, I spread a couple of fingers out along the edge of the base to prevent bumps caused by overcorrection when straying from the cutline. Don't apply sideways pressure with your fingers. They're only meant to serve as movement sensors. Just keep light pressure against the edge of the base with the same fingers pressed lightly against the workpiece.

Don't be discouraged if your cut ends up slightly beveled. It's not unusual. If you find that the blade is deflecting, you can cut a bit proud of the line, and then square

WHEN STARTING AT THE EDGE OF A BOARD, pinch the base to the workpiece to ensure a perpendicu-lar cut. Note the "guide line" leading in from the edge of the board to the workpiece cutline.

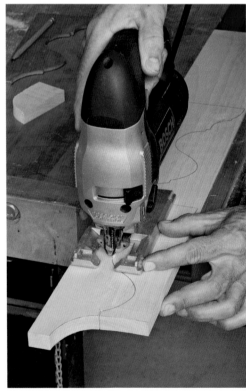

SPLAYED FINGERS PLACED LIGHTLY against the edge of the base and against the workpiece help ensure fair curves by detecting overcorrection. For tighter turns, place fingers closer together.

A Case Study in Cut Planning

A CLEAN-CUT SEQUENCE

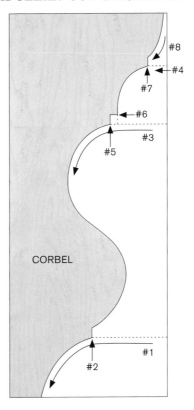

For the cleanest cuts, develop a cutting plan for sawing downhill to the grain whenever possible, and try to cut pieces free in sequence. To create fair edges, make a cut in one full sweep rather than coming in from opposite ends.

Cut #1: Sawing with the grain creates smooth cut.

Cut #2: Short, straight cut prepares piece to fall free after subsequent cut.

Cut #3: Entire cut made in one smooth pass to ensure a fair curve.

Cut #4: Same as cut #1.

Cuts #5 and 6: Create notch.

Cut #7: Same as cut #2.

Cut #8: Sawing with grain ensures smooth cut.

---

up the edge on a belt or spindle sander. But remember that a slightly beveled bottom edge on a low furniture rail or other part that's viewed from above may never be noticed.

Plunge Cutting

When making inside cuts, it's often more efficient to start the cut by plunging the blade into the work instead of setting up a drill to bore starter holes. Making a plunge cut involves standing the saw up on the front edge of the base, turning on the motor, then slowly tilting the saw downward as the blade enters the work. Performing this maneuver for the first time might be a bit nerve-wracking, but you'll quickly get comfortable with it.

WHEN PLUNGE CUTTING, align the blade with the cutline, turn on the saw, and slowly tilt it into the workpiece while holding the base to prevent shifting.

A Crowning Achievement

Fitting crown molding at inside corners necessitates coping and back beveling the end of one mating piece. This is a perfect job for a jigsaw fitted with a scrolling blade. (Note that the cutline is defined by the intersection of the molding face and a miter cut on a miter saw.)

TILTING THE SAW for a back-bevel cut, begin by making straight cuts inward along the flat sections at the center and ends. Intersect the two center cuts to create a V-notch.

BEGINNING WITH THE BLADE in the V-notch, and with the saw tilted, cut outward to one end...

VOILA! Neatly coped and back-beveled in about a minute... then the other.

For accuracy and efficiency, try this approach: With the saw off and tilted up on edge, sight down the base from above, aligning the blade to the cutline. To hold the base in position, pinch it by one edge, with the same hand planted solidly on the workpiece. Then turn on the saw and slowly pivot the blade downward, cutting along the layout line. (I usually drape the cord safely over my shoulder when plunge cutting.)

Scribe Cutting and Back Beveling

Scribe cutting and back beveling are crucial techniques for fitting cabinetry and trim-work against irregular walls and other surfaces. To accommodate this on-site fitting, cabinets are typically made with sides that extend slightly past the back. This overhang can be marked, or scribed, to conform to any irregularities on the host wall so that the cabinet sides meet the wall perfectly with no gaps. A jigsaw is the perfect tool for cutting these scribe lines.

Back beveling involves angling the cut to create a thin edge toward the face side that can be precisely and easily finessed with other tools for a perfect fit against an adjacent surface. I even like to back bevel my scribe cuts on cabinets so that I can easily fine-tune the fit with sandpaper or a block plane if necessary. Some trim, like crown molding, demands a severely back beveled edge for proper coped fitting, and a jigsaw makes quick work of the job. The cut can be further refined with chisels or files as needed.

When back beveling, I don't bother to adjust the angle of the jigsaw base, which is too time-consuming when constantly switching left to right for cuts. Instead, I just teeter the saw on the edge of the piece. To prevent any openings in the stock base from hanging up on an edge as the saw is twisting and turning to make a cut, I attach a solid auxiliary base. If your saw didn't

come with one, you can make one from a scrap of plastic laminate, attaching it to the stock base with double-faced tape.

Straight-cutting

Although a jigsaw isn't the ideal tool for making straight cuts, it can do a passable job. If necessary, the cut can be cleaned up afterward with a plane, tablesaw, or other tool. Sometimes a single cutline may include both curved and straight sections, in which case it makes sense to make the whole cut with the jigsaw, cleaning up the straight section afterward with a block plane or sandpaper wrapped around a wood block. Whenever making a straight cut, I minimize wandering by registering a finger and thumb splayed as far apart as possible against the side of the base.

*Note price estimates are from 2006.

PAUL ANTHONY is a woodworker, writer, and photographer living in Riegelsville, Pennsylvania.

WHEN CUTTING TO SCRIBE LINES on the rear edges of cabinet walls, the author tilts the saw to create a slight back bevel.

TO MINIMIZE MEANDERING when making straight cuts, splay fingers far apart against the side of the base and the work surface without applying sideways pressure.

Routers

If we had to honor just one power tool as having had the greatest effect on woodworking in the last half century or so, it would probably be the router. It's been said that the router can undertake 90 percent of all woodworking chores if it has to. It certainly shines when it comes to making clean, accurate joinery and performing many shaping operations. It is the tool of choice in many shops for cutting clean, straight-walled mortises quickly and accurately for those of us who don't have a mortising machine.

An enormous variety of bits is available to perform all sorts of operations. Coupled with commercial or shopmade jigs, there's almost no limit to the router tricks you can perform. When mounted upside down in a table, a router becomes sort of a mini-shaper, allowing you to safely and accurately rout molding profiles or create multiple exact shapes by template routing. Using a router table also enables easy joint cutting, grooving, and other maneuvers where it's easier and safer to bring the work to the tool instead of the other way around.

Mortising with a Router

BY GARY ROGOWSKI

I cut my first set of mortises by hand. It was a fabulous learning experience. I found that chopping through red oak was like digging postholes in dry clay. I had to resharpen my chisel after each mortise, but I learned. I also bought a router.

A router is the quickest and most accurate tool for cutting mortises. Its versatility and speed is unmatched, and it can be used in a variety of setups, both upright and upside down in a router table. In minutes, a router cuts mortises that would take hours by hand. And you can reproduce your results with a minimum of hassle or setup time. When I have mortises to cut these days, the router is my first choice. Either a fixed-base or a plunge router can produce excellent results.

Choosing the Right Bit

There are a variety of bit sizes and types that can be used for mortising. Two shank sizes are commonly available: ¼ in. and ½ in. Either will work, but bits with ½-in. shanks flex less under load, give a better cut, and are less likely to break.

I don't bother with high-speed steel (HSS) bits because they need to be sharpened too often. Carbide-tipped bits cost two to three times more but they last much longer. Solid-carbide bits are great, too, but they're even more expensive.

Straight bits come in two flavors: single flute for quick removal of material and double flute for a smooth finish. Because you'll find double-fluted bits in most tool catalogs, you'll get more size options.

The flutes of a spiral bit twist around the shank. This gives a shearing cut that is even smoother than one from a double-fluted straight bit. Spiral bits are available both in solid carbide and carbide-tipped steel. They spiral up or down.

An up-cut spiral bit cuts quickly while pulling most of the chips out of the mortise. However, it also will tend to pull the workpiece up if it's not securely fastened. The up-cut spiral also can leave a slightly ragged edge at the top of the mortise where wood fibers are unsupported. Because the edges of a mortise are usually covered by the shoulders of a tenon, this kind of tearout generally isn't a problem.

A down-cut spiral bit pushes the work and the chips down. The result is a cleaner mortise but one that can become clogged with debris.

TWO FENCES KEEP A ROUTER IN LINE. **When routing to full-depth with a fixed-base router, you want to make sure it doesn't veer out of the mortise.**

I have used mostly double-fluted straight bits and a carbide-tipped up-cut spiral bit. Recently, though, I bought a solid-carbide up-cut spiral, which cuts even better.

Using a Fixed-Base Router

If the only router you have is a fixed-base router, you're not out of luck. It will just take a little more attention to detail and skill to get good mortises than it would with a plunge router.

A straight fence attached to the router is essential for accurately guiding the cut. Adding a long wooden auxiliary fence to your router's stock fence will give the router more stability. A second fence, clamped to the router base and on the other side of the workpiece, is a good idea, too (see the photo on the facing page). This fixes the position of the router laterally, so it can't accidentally slip to one side or the other during the cut. Combined with end stops, a double fence will virtually ensure accurately located mortises. The only thing left to set is the depth, and here you have a choice of methods.

Multiple Depth Settings One way of mortising with a fixed-base router is to take just a little bite with each pass, gradually lowering the bit until you're at full-depth.

MORTISING WITH A FIXED-BASE ROUTER

You will get a cleaner mortise by setting the bit to full depth right from the start. Cut the mortise in several passes with the router tipped at an angle.

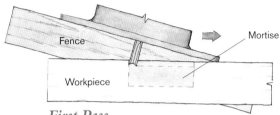

First Pass
The first pass, with the router held at an angle, should remove 1/8 in. to 1/4 in. of material.

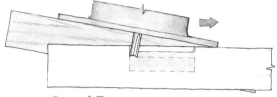

Second Pass
The angle of the router is lowered for the second pass, but bit depth remains the same. This and each successive pass removes from 1/8 in. to 1/4 in.

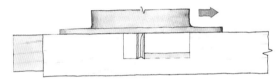

Third Pass
The last pass is made with the router flat against the workpiece and the bit straight up and down.

The biggest drawback with this approach is that it's hard to get a smooth-walled mortise. The reason is that the motor and, consequently, the bit may not stay centered in the base as you adjust the depth of cut.

With most routers, adjusting the bit height requires that you turn the motor in the base housing. When you do, the bit moves in relation to the fence, only slightly, but enough to give the walls of the mortise a stepped, rough surface (see the top photo on p. 44). Exceptions are DeWalt, Black & Decker®, and Elu® routers, which employ a rack-and-pinion adjustment system that keeps the collet and bit centered at a fixed distance from the fence.

One Depth Setting One way around this stepping problem is to set the bit at full depth right from the start. To mortise, you just move the router at an angle to the workpiece so you introduce a little more of the bit to the wood with each pass (see the drawings and photo on p. 43). The router is tilted, resting on one edge of its base, until the final pass is made. An extra-wide auxiliary fence is advisable, and a second fence clamped to the router base on the other side of the workpiece is essential.

MULTIPLE DEPTH SETTINGS CREATE STEPS. To adjust the bit height on most fixed-base routers, you have to twist the motor in its base. This often results in stepped, sloppy sidewalls.

WITH HARDBOARD SHIMS, YOU SET THE BIT JUST ONCE. By removing one shim after each pass, you can take safe, manageable bites without having to change the router's depth setting. Increments of either ¼ in. or ⅛ in. are possible.

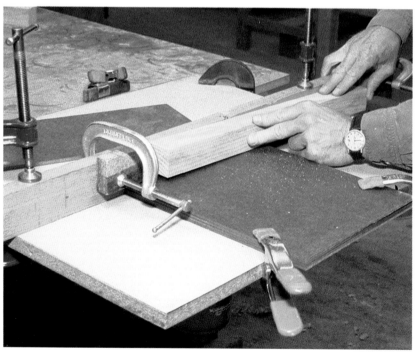

Router-Table Mortises

Why would anyone want to cut mortises on a router table? Well, for narrower stock, a router table provides plenty of support. When routing narrow pieces from above, a handheld router can become tippy and unstable. The edge of a door stile, for example, just doesn't offer very much support for a router base. With a router table, you have both the table and the fence against which to register the workpiece, and you have only the weight of the workpiece to control. For small table legs or cabinet doors, mortising on the router table is worth trying.

When mortising on a router table, use the fence to position the mortise from side to side and stops to establish the ends of the mortise. As you face the table, the work should move from right to left. This feed direction will help keep the work tight against the fence. Start with the workpiece against the right-hand stop, and lower the work into the bit. Because most bits don't cut in the center, it helps to lower and simultaneously move the work along just a little to avoid burning. Move the workpiece from right to left across the bit until it hits the other stop.

If you're using a plunge router, you can set the turret stops for incremental cuts, make three passes, and finish up at full-depth. But if you're using a fixed-base router, you'll have a problem getting a smooth-walled mortise if you adjust the bit height between passes—just as you would when using the router upright.

My solution to this problem is to use shims made from ¼-in. hardboard, like Masonite, notched around the bit, to elevate the workpiece above the table (see the bottom photo at left). In this way, I can set the bit at full height and just remove a shim after each cut, gradually working down until the workpiece is on the table and the last cut is made.

LAYOUT LINES ARE MUCH EASIER TO SEE WHEN THEY'RE NOT HIDDEN. The pencil marks show where the router base should stop, and the tick marks indicate that you're getting close.

STOPS ARE FOOLPROOF. Clamp or screw stops in place to limit the travel of the router, front and back. You won't have to worry about trying to see layout marks when the chips are flying.

Mortising with a Plunge Router

The best tool for mortising is the plunge router used on top of the work. This is the job it was designed for. There are many different kinds of fixtures that can be used with the plunge router. Two that I use frequently, a U-shaped box and a template with a fence, are discussed below.

There are several schools of thought as to how to plunge the bit into the work. One method is to plunge a full-depth hole at each end of the mortise and then make a series of cleanup passes between those two holes. The drawback to this method is that you may get some burning as you plunge to full depth because most bits don't have center-cutting capability.

Alternately, you can make a series of successively deeper, full-length passes, always moving left to right with the bit lowered and locked in place each time. For me, making full passes without locking

the plunge mechanism on each pass works best. I keep the router moving. Try each of these methods to see which one works best for you.

Using a Stock Router Fence The simplest method for mortising with a plunge router is to mark the mortise ends on the workpiece and to set the last turret stop for the full depth of the mortise.

To adjust the bit's position, place the router on a marked-out workpiece, and lower the bit so it's just touching the surface of the work. Rotate the bit so its cutting edges are in line with the width of the mortise. Adjust the fence so it's flush against the side of the workpiece and the edges of the bit are within the layout lines. Then clamp the workpiece firmly to the bench, and rout away. Keep in mind, though, that the router will be tippy on narrow stock.

You can try to bring the bit just up to the end marks of the mortise with each pass, but it can be difficult to see them with

**ONE FIXTURE CUTS MANY MOR-
TISES. This simple U-shaped box
is one of the most versatile mortising fixtures you can build.**

I've made a number of them dedicated to particular pieces of furniture.

But having one fixture that handles a variety of different-size parts is really useful, too. The one in the photo at left is made of ¾-in.-thick medium-density fiberboard (MDF). Its sides are rabbeted for the bottom (this helps align it during assembly). I also made the bottom longer than the side walls so I could clamp it down easily to any work surface.

The best way to deal with multiple identical mortises is to clamp an end stop to the side wall of the fixture (see the photo on the facing page). This way, each new piece will automatically be fixed in the right spot. Stops to index the mortise length also can be clamped onto the fixture. I prefer clamping these on rather than using an adjustable stop—I don't want to risk the stop being nudged out of place.

When placing the workpiece in the fixture, always make sure the piece is sitting flat on the fixture bottom and tight to the inside wall and end stop. Clamp the workpiece securely. Spacers can be used underneath pieces to bring them higher in the fixture or to push a piece away from the sidewall. Make sure the spacers are milled flat and support the workpiece well. Be sure that the clamps holding the work don't get in the way of the router.

To improve stability, attach a wooden auxiliary fence to the one that comes with the plunge router. Then position the bit in the right spot. Remember to hold the fence tightly to the wall, and be sure to move the router so the fence will be drawn up against the wall of the fixture by the rotation of the bit.

Dedicated mortising fixtures are extremely useful when you plan to reproduce a number of cuts on a regular basis. I made an angled fixture to cut the mortises for a stool I build at least once a year. The end stop locates each leg in the proper spot. A

all those chips flying around. Another way to accomplish this is to line up the edges of the bit at both ends of the mortise and make a pencil mark at the outside edge of the router base (see the left photo on p. 45). These marks are a lot easier to see than layout lines at the ends of the mortise.

If you're concerned about cutting beyond the layout lines, just clamp on stops to limit router travel. It takes only a second. Clamp the stops directly onto the workpiece once you've determined the length of the mortise (see the right photo on p. 45).

Mortising with the U-shaped box One of the most versatile router-mortising fixtures that I've come across is a simple U-shaped box (see the drawing on the facing page). I first saw one of these boxes in a magazine article by Tage Frid. Since then,

spacer block positioned against the stop locates the second set of mortises in the legs. Stops screwed to the outside of the fixture wall limit the length of travel of the fence and, therefore, produce mortises that are the correct length.

Templates and Template Guides

A template guide is a round metal plate with a thin-walled rub collar that extends out from its base (see the top photo on p. 48). The guide is screwed to the router base, and a router bit fits through it without touching the inside wall of the collar. The outer wall of the rub collar is guided by a straightedge or template as the router cuts (see the bottom photo on p. 48).

Templates that are made of hardboard, plywood, or MDF include a slot to guide

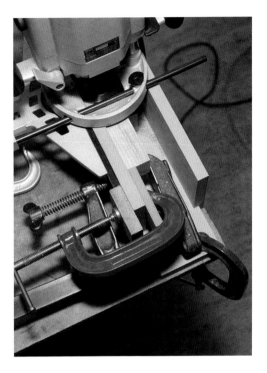

MEASURE ONCE, AND CLAMP A STOP IN PLACE. The less measuring you have to do, the fewer errors you're likely to make. The stop on the inside of the fixture positions the workpiece. The one on the outside is a fence stop, which establishes one end of the mortise.

U-SHAPED MORTISING FIXTURE

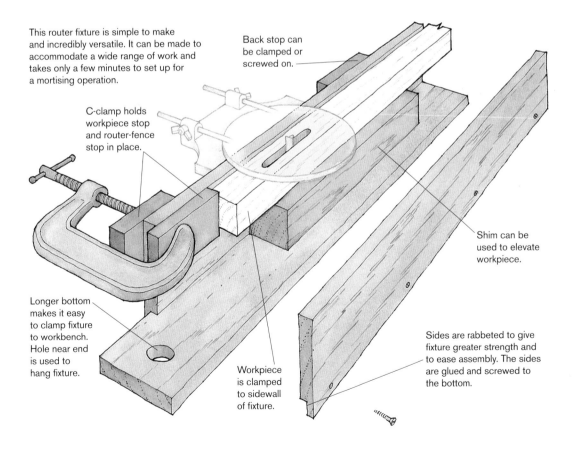

This router fixture is simple to make and incredibly versatile. It can be made to accommodate a wide range of work and takes only a few minutes to set up for a mortising operation.

Back stop can be clamped or screwed on.

C-clamp holds workpiece stop and router-fence stop in place.

Shim can be used to elevate workpiece.

Longer bottom makes it easy to clamp fixture to workbench. Hole near end is used to hang fixture.

Workpiece is clamped to sidewall of fixture.

Sides are rabbeted to give fixture greater strength and to ease assembly. The sides are glued and screwed to the bottom.

STOPS ARE BUILT IN. A template prevents side-to-side movement of the bit and automatically sets the length of the mortise.

the rub collar as it makes the cut. The template is clamped to a workpiece with its slot centered over the mortise. I make up a template for a mortise when I'm doing a job I expect to repeat. To make a template, nail a piece of ¼-in. hardboard about 5 in. wide and 10 in. long to a piece of wood approximately 2 in. sq. and a little longer than the hardboard (see the drawing on the facing page).

The wood block is the fence, and the hardboard gets a slot cut in it that is exactly the width of the rub collar. Cut the slot in the template on the router table. To be sure the slot is parallel with the fence—which ensures that the mortise is square to the stock you're routing—tack the hardboard back a little bit from the edge.

Set up the router table with a straight bit that matches the outside dimension of the rub collar. The template slot is pencil-marked on the hardboard. The diameter of the template guide is greater than that of the bit you'll use when mortising. So you'll need to add the distance from the outside of the rub collar to the edge of the router bit to each end of the slot in the template (see the drawing on the facing page). Typically, this offset is between ¹⁄₁₆ in. and ⅛ in.

Before cutting the slot in the hardboard template, take a minute to determine the setback from the edge of the workpiece to the edge of the mortise. Then set the router-table fence accordingly. I like to double-check that the fence is in the right spot. So I make a nibble cut at the end of the template, and then measure the distance from that point to the fence. This

USING A TEMPLATE AND GUIDE TO MORTISE

Routing mortises with a hardboard template and router-template guide is quick and virtually foolproof. The size of the slot in the hardboard determines the size of the mortise. The template is clamped to the workpiece, and the assembly is then clamped to the bench.

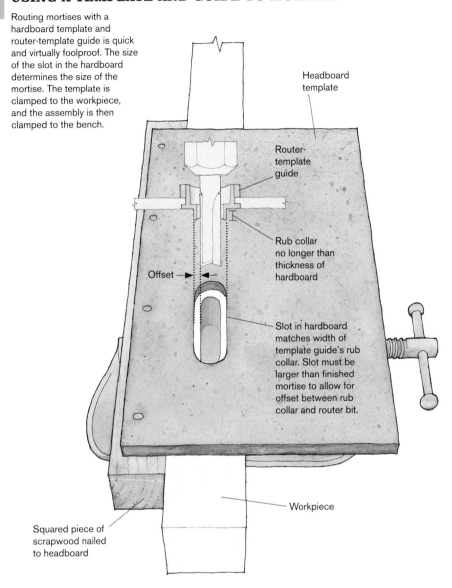

Headboard template

Router-template guide

Rub collar no longer than thickness of hardboard

Offset

Slot in hardboard matches width of template guide's rub collar. Slot must be larger than finished mortise to allow for offset between rub collar and router bit.

Workpiece

Squared piece of scrapwood nailed to headboard

method ensures that you get the correct distance. Once you have it, plunge the template down onto the bit as close to the center of the slot as possible, and then slide the template back and forth just up to the pencil marks at each end.

Templates like these are versatile. For example, a template made to cut a mortise ¾ in. from the edge of a table leg also could be used to cut the same size mortise ½ in. from the edge. How? Simply by inserting a ¼-in. shim between the template fence and the workpiece.

Once you have made the template and clamped it to the workpiece, position the plunge router with the template guide on the work. Set the bit depth, taking into account the thickness of the template. An up-cut spiral bit will pull most of the debris out of the mortise as the cut is made. Compressed air can help clear a mortise that's really packed with chips.

GARY ROGOWSKI designs and builds furniture in Portland, Oregon. He is a contributing editor to *Fine Woodworking*.

All about Router Bits

BY JEFF GREEF

For many woodworkers, a good-quality router may seem like an expensive tool. But few of us realize as we start to acquire tools that the cost of a router, or even several routers, pales in comparison to what we'll spend over time for bits. The growing selection of bits is what makes the router so versatile. They're capable of everything from molding edges to cutting raised panels. But with so much to choose from, it's harder than ever to buy wisely.

It's surprising that a tool with roots in metalworking should become such an indispensable tool for woodworking. The router has no hand-tool counterpart—it's a milling machine.

Router and bit technology was transplanted first to industrial woodworking operations and then to the small shop. And industry is still the source of advances we see in bit design. At one time, for instance, carbide was an exotic material for industrial use only. Now it's more common than steel.

Similarly, new materials, coatings, and bit styles are slowly working their way into the mainstream. It's easy to amass a wallet-flattening, little-used collection. You have to weigh the bit's intended use as well as its cost and overall quality. See pp. 54–55 for suggestions on bits for specific cutting operations.

Carbide Stays Sharp Longer Than Steel

High-speed steel and tungsten carbide are the two most widely used materials in router bits. Steel is inexpensive, and because of its uniform crystalline structure, steel can take a keen edge and can produce a very smooth finish. Steel bits may be the right choice for short runs or one-time operations. You easily can sharpen flat-fluted steel bits and, with a grinder, modify the profile. But steel wears quickly, especially in highly abrasive materials like plywood, medium density fiberboard (MDF), and particleboard.

Tungsten carbide is an alloy of carbide granules and powdered cobalt fused under high pressure and temperature. The hardness of carbide is directly related to the amount of cobalt used—the smaller the percentage of cobalt binder, the harder the alloy.

But an extremely hard metal is brittle, too fragile for a cutting edge. So manufacturers strive for the best compromise between hardness and shock resistance. Because of extreme hardness, carbide holds an edge 25 times longer than steel. And although more expensive than steel, carbide is generally a better value.

NO SHORTAGE OF CHOICES. Router bits come in a variety of profiles, materials and sizes. Storing them in a fitted box helps protect edges and makes bits easy to find.

BOTH BITS MAKE A CUT ½ IN. WIDE, but the ½-in. shank (left) reduces chatter and allows a more aggressive cut than the ¼-in. shank bit.

SPIRAL FLUTE CUTTERS SLICE WOOD FIBERS. The down-shear bit (left) leaves a crisp edge at the top surface. The up-shear bit efficiently ejects chips.

MACHINIST'S END MILLS LOOK JUST LIKE ROUTER BITS FOR WOOD. End mills make good, inexpensive alternatives to spiral bits.

SHEAR ANGLE REDUCES TEAROUT ON END GRAIN. The angled cutter on this rabbeting bit cuts cleanly in redwood.

STRAIGHT BITS CHOP THE WOOD. Bits without a shear angle cut cleanly with the grain but not as smoothly on end grain.

Most carbide bits have carbide-cutting tips brazed to a steel body, combining the hardness of carbide and the economy and shock resistance of steel. Manufacturers also offer solid carbide bits. These bits are much more expensive. But a solid carbide bit has two advantages: It will withstand high temperatures generated by high feed rates and continuous use, and it's more than three times stiffer than steel so that chatter and tip deflection are minimal. Sharpening carbide bits is more difficult than steel, but for minor edge touch-ups, a diamond honing stick can be used.

Polycrystalline diamond bits are now being advertised as the ultimate bit for highly abrasive man-made materials. A typical bit costs approximately $500★ (which is 40 times more expensive than carbide but lasts 150 times longer). Users are large commercial manufacturers, but if history serves, we may someday see these bits in small shops.

Matching the Bit to the Job

How well a bit performs depends on factors like shank diameter, number of flutes (or cutting edges), shear angle of the cutter and type of pilot.

Use Largest Shank Diameter Shank diameter should correspond to cutter size (see the bottom left photo on p. 51). Large bits need the stiffness of ½-in. shanks to minimize vibration and deflection. Many bits with small cutting profiles are available only with ¼-in. shanks. If you have a choice between a ¼-in. or a ½-in. shank, pick the larger one. The router's collet will grip better, and the extra mass minimizes chatter (the result of vibration and deflection) to produce a better cut. And select the shortest cutting edge that meets your needs because excessive length increases vibration.

More Flutes for a Smoother Cut The gap, or flute, in front of the cutting edge provides clearance for chip removal. Most bits have two flutes, but some have one, three, or four. More flutes (and, therefore, more cutting tips) produce a smoother cut, but they reduce the feed rate the bit will allow. Conversely, a single-flute, straight bit works great for making rough cutouts in stock quickly.

Choose a Shear Angle That's Right for the Job Bits cut better when the cutting edge is angled slightly in relation to the centerline of the bit. This is called the shear angle. The effect is similar to skew-cutting with a plane or a chisel. Bits with no shear angle chop their way through the stock. The shear angle causes more of a slice than a chop, producing a smoother cut. Most manufacturers I spoke with believe the difference is pronounced only on end-grain cuts (see the top photos on the facing page).

The shear direction can be either up or down. Up-shear bits (the most common) quickly clear chips from the cut and tend to pull the router base down on the work. Down-shear bits are used where an upward cut would leave a ragged edge at the top surface. Down-shear bits make exceptionally clean cuts in veneered and laminate-covered surfaces. However, they do not clear chips well when mortising and tend to push the router base off the work.

Spiral bits take shear angle to the extreme. The helical flutes (see the bottom middle photo on p. 51) provide a continuous slicing action and are excellent at ejecting chips from the cut. They are especially well suited to mortising. For a more economical alternative, you can use two-flute, machinist's end mills. These are cutting bits designed for machining metal, but they also cut wood. Like spiral bits, end mills have helical flutes (see the bottom right photo on p. 51) and cut wood very well. The range of sizes is more limited than router bits, but they are inexpensive and are easily available at industrial tool-supply stores.

A note of caution when using up-shear spiral bits and end mills: the force developed by the high shear angle tries to pull the bit out of the collet. Be sure the collet and bit are in good condition, free of rust and burrs. The bit should be well seated, not bottomed out, in the collet; and the collet nut must be securely tightened.

Ball-Bearing Pilots Work Best for Edge Profiling A pilot bearing, found on edge-trimming and edge-molding bits, guides the bit and limits the depth of cut (see the right photo on p. 56). One-piece steel bits generally have a solid pilot, which is simply a small knob at the end of the shank that rubs against the edge of the work. Solid pilots work, but two problems can arise. If you don't keep the bit moving, the spinning pilot generates enough heat to burn black marks in the edge of the stock. And because of their small diameter, solid pilots can dig into the surface on which they ride, particularly on softer woods. That causes the cut to go slightly deeper than intended. Ball-bearing pilots take care of these problems. The large-diameter pilot bearing is unlikely to dig into the wood, and burning is eliminated because the bearing doesn't spin against the wood.

Arbors with Removable Cutters Are Versatile

Bits come in two basic designs: those with cutters permanently attached to the shank body and those with separate cutters that attach to a threaded shank, or arbor, with a nut. When you want a different profile with an arbor and cutter set, all you do is change the cutter itself.

Bits with separate cutters are versatile and cost far less than buying a number of separate bits. I have one arbor on which I can fit one of two rabbeting cutters with any of three different diameter pilot bearings (see the left photo on p. 56). This gives me six different rabbet depths. Pilot bearings of different diameters often can be switched even on bits that do not have interchangeable cutters. The bearings change the depth of cut and expand the bit's usefulness. In fact, a slightly smaller diameter pilot bearing is the only difference between a beading and a roundover bit.

Bits with separate cutters are versatile and cost far less than buying a number of separate bits.

Bits for Specific Cuts

You'll get the best results by choosing a router bit specifically designed for the job. If the bit is to be used regularly, a bit with a ½-in. shank and high-quality carbide is a good choice.

 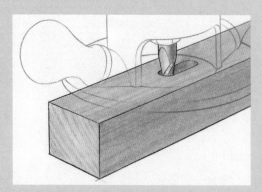

PLUNGE MORTISING AND DADOES
A spiral up-shear bit is unmatched in its chip-clearing ability. These bits cut fast and clean with minimum chatter. When cutting into laminate or splintery wood, use a down-cut spiral to eliminate chipping at the top edge of the cut. It will be slow going, though, because you will have to stop frequently and blow the chips out of the cut.

 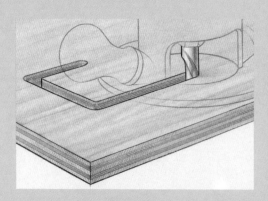

CUTTING THROUGH STOCK WITH TWO GOOD SIDES A compression bit (half of which is an up-shear and the other half a down-shear) is a specialty bit used when the edge of both upper and lower surfaces must be crisp. This bit design sacrifices feed rate and chip-clearing ability for unblemished edges.

 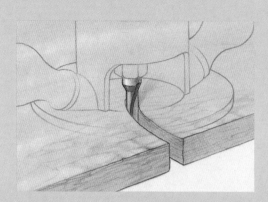

MAKING ROUGH CUTOUTS THROUGH STOCK A single-flute, stagger-tooth bit cuts aggressively and roughly. The tooth orientation minimizes chatter.

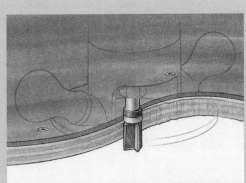

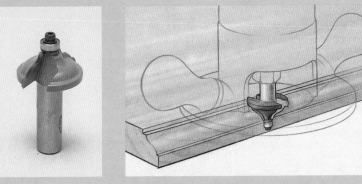

EDGE MOLDING AND RABBETING A bit that has a slight shear angle cuts more smoothly. For freehand routing and following curves, a ball-bearing pilot is the easiest to use. An edge-guide attachment or a fence lets you use a bit that doesn't have a pilot.

TEMPLATE AND PATTERN ROUTING Flush-trimming or pattern-routing bits have a pilot bearing mounted on the shank, either above or below the cutting tips, and are used with a template to guide the bit. The top-pilot location has one big advantage over a bottom-mounted bearing. The template can be mounted above the work and the bit plunged into the work.

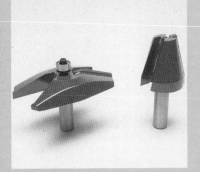
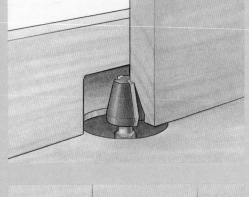

PANEL RAISERS Large-diameter bits let you lay the stock flat on a router table. These bits generally produce a smooth finish. With them, you can easily follow curves. But these bits should be run at about 12,000 rpm, which is slower than most fixed-speed routers. Face molding, or safety raisers, can run at higher speeds but the stock must be held on edge against a fence. Molding a curved piece of stock is not easy.

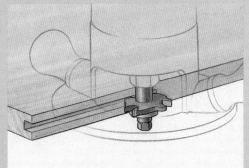

GROOVING FOR SPLINES AND BISCUIT A slot cutter is really a small saw with a precise kerf width. You can mount cutters from $\frac{1}{16}$ in. to $\frac{1}{4}$ in. on a standard arbor. Some new sets allow stacking cutters like a dado set to get widths up to $1\frac{1}{16}$ in. Changing the diameter of the pilot bearing controls the depth of cut.

INTERCHANGEABLE PARTS ARE VERSATILE. A variety of cutters and pilot bearings can be mounted on one arbor, saving the cost of buying a number of single-purpose bits.

PILOTS GUIDE BITS FOR UNIFORM CUT. The solid pilot on the end of the bit at left spins against the stock and leaves burn marks. The ball-bearing pilots on the center and right bits eliminate burning.

Replaceable Cutters and Special Coatings

Carbide insert tooling, long available in industry, lets you replace just the cutters when they get dull. A disposable cutting bit is fastened to the body with screws. Initially more expensive than fixed-cutter bits, insert tooling may be cheaper in the long run for heavy-use applications because the cutters are cheap to replace. Insert tooling offers a consistent cutting diameter or profile. The same can't be said for standard bits whose dimensions are altered by sharpening.

Brightly colored, Teflon® coatings are now widespread on several brands of bits. These coatings reduce pitch buildup and promote chip clearing. In my work, I have not found this to be a big advantage, but colored bits do enhance safety. A spinning red or yellow bit is easier to see than a dull gray one.

The coating used on industrial metalworking bits, such as titanium nitride and zirconium nitride, are beginning to push into woodworking. Because these coatings are slippery, they withstand tremendous heat and promote faster chip clearing on very abrasive materials. The result is cooler cutting and longer tool life.

Anti-Kickback Designs Are Widely Available

Most manufacturers now offer an anti-kickback design on their bits, which limits the amount of wood the bit can bite on each revolution (see the right photo on the facing page). This prevents overfeeding, which can cause kickback. Many manufacturers I spoke with believe this design is most useful on shaper cutters and on large router bits like panel raisers where kickback is a serious threat. The smaller bits, they said, don't present enough danger to warrant the design. I agree with them.

How to Spot a Quality Bit

Finish grinding is the most expensive process in bit manufacture and the most critical. A smooth cut requires a sharp edge, and a sharp edge requires a smooth face and edge. Technically, grinding faces smooth is easy; grinding edges is not, particularly on curved, pattern-shaping bits. I have seen wide variation in the smoothness of edge grinding on bits, and now it's the first thing I look for.

Take a pencil with you when buying a bit. Run the tip along the edge of the bit. If the tip scrapes along rather than slides smoothly, chances are the bit has been ground to a rough finish and will leave small nicks in the work (see the left photo at right). A rough grind also causes the bit to dull faster because the minutely serrated cutting edge loses relatively big chunks of carbide granules.

Carbide tips must be brazed securely to the steel body or the brittle carbide can break loose and fly like shrapnel. Always inspect bits for brazing voids. Don't use any that appear unsafe. In industry, a general rule is to reject any bit with a void larger than a pinhole. Many manufacturers I spoke with said that a visual inspection of a bit says a lot about its quality. If the brazing is splattered or a grinding wheel has touched a spot it shouldn't have, attention to detail was lacking. The presence or absence of any kind of warranty with a bit is probably a good measure of the manufacturer's confidence in its work.

Why are there such wide price differences in bits that look similar? Generally, it's because there are many manufacturing practices affecting quality that you can't see. There is no universal quality standard for rating carbide, and it all looks the same. The care taken by the manufacturer when brazing the carbide to the body and grinding the edge may not be obvious. Yet these factors can affect the longevity of the material because overheating reduces carbide's ability to hold an edge. Some bit shanks are hardened, others are not. The quality of grinding on the shank itself determines how accurately the bit spins and cuts. All of these factors are reflected in the cost.

Choosing Bits and Building Your Collection

The most important factor to consider when deciding how much to spend on a bit is cost per cut. Many expensive bits are made to be used in commercial situations where the bits will be used to destruction. In the long run, it is more cost effective for

A PENCIL SLIDES EASILY ALONG A SMOOTHLY GROUND EDGE. The lead is scraped away on a coarsely ground edge.

CHIP-LIMITING, ANTI-KICKBACK DESIGN reduces the bite that the bit can take and prevents overfeeding.

commercial shops to buy the most expensive bits.

But if you won't be using a bit very much, it doesn't make sense to buy the most expensive one. A less-expensive bit might not hold up as long, but you may not use it enough to have it resharpened even once.

Many bit manufacturers and retailers offer boxed bit sets at lower prices. Before you buy one of these sets, though, seriously consider whether you will use more than half of them. The price break you get on the set may be substantial, but if you use less than half the bits, you will have spent more money than if you had bought only the bits you'll need.

Choose bits as you go according to the design and profile you need and the quality you want for that bit.

Note price estimates are from 1996.

JEFF GREEF is a woodworker and writer in Santa Cruz, California.

Template-Routing Basics

BY PAT WARNER

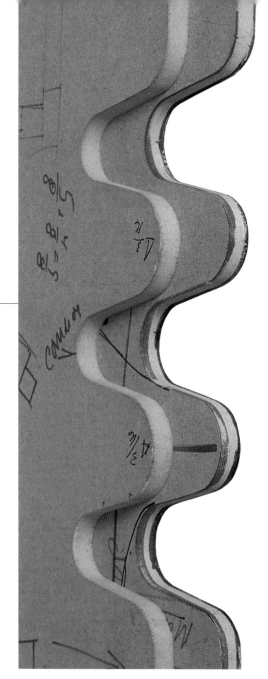

In 24 years of self-taught woodworking, I've made a lot of mistakes. Early in my career, though, I made a fortunate one. It started a learning process with the router that I'm still working on today.

I had discovered what looked like a devilishly simple technique for cutting dadoes. I used a board clamped across the workpiece to guide the router base. The first dado looked great, but the second wandered visibly off course. That day, I learned that a router base is never concentric with the bit. Turning the router as I cut the dado put a curve in it.

I began to look for better ways to guide routers. Some of the best, I have learned, are with templates. These are simply patterns of the shapes you want to cut. The router registers against a template, using it as a guide through the cut. The simplicity of templates, though, gives no hint of how powerful a tool they make the router.

The router's usefulness and versatility begin with the tremendous variety of bits that are available. With only a ball bearing on the end of the bit as a guide, you are really limited to detailing edges. When you use a template, however, you free the router from following the edge of the workpiece. The router becomes capable of two more fundamental woodworking tasks: milling repeatable patterns and all kinds of joinery.

You can easily make your own inexpensive, simple and accurate templates for a wide variety of joints and patterns. The initial investment of time to make a template for a precise task is well worth it. Your router will perform that task far faster and far more reliably than other tools can. And it's much harder to make mistakes when you are using templates.

Templates will allow you to repeat cuts and shapes perfectly, but only if you remember to use the same bit with the same

Three Bits for Routing with Templates

STRAIGHT BITS AND COLLAR GUIDES ARE THE MOST VERSATILE

Collars are not as accurate as bearings, but they have the decided advantage of allowing you to cut at any depth in both side and bottom cuts. Fitted to the router's base and used with straight bits, they work much like pattern bits. Collar guides also act as a shield for the bit. You'll find that you will inflict a lot less injury to the template and the work by using them.

Collar guides do have disadvantages. Because the collar must be larger in diameter than the cutter, the line of cut is displaced from the template. This offset means the finished work will never be exactly the same shape as the template. And collar guides are never exactly concentric with the bit: 1/16 in. eccentricity is typical. A way to compensate for this is to keep the same part of the collar in contact with the template throughout the cut.

PATTERN BITS ARE THE MOST ACCURATE

I choose pattern bits when I need the most accuracy. The bearings are typically concentric to the bit within .002 in. or better. Bearings do not leave as smooth a cut as collar guides, though the difference is generally minute. This is due to the way bearings can bounce against the template ever so slightly and very rapidly. Over time, this bouncing tends to wear the template edge unevenly.

The biggest disadvantage to bearing bits is that they're restricted to a small range of depth settings. The bearing must always engage the edge of the template. I've also found that bits of this design often have diameters slightly larger than their bearings. If you run this kind of bit with some of the cutter in contact with the template, you'll rout away some of the template. Measure your bits with calipers or test them to make sure this doesn't happen.

FLUSH-TRIMMING BITS ARE THE MOST COMMON

The main advantage to using flush-trimming bits for template work is that they are easier to find and slightly cheaper than pattern bits. They also come in smaller diameters than pattern bits, allowing cuts into tighter inside curves.

Otherwise, they have many disadvantages. Bottom cuts such as mortises are impossible. In other applications, the workpiece can hide the template from view, and the router must ride on the work. If it's a small or thin piece, the router will not be stable.

---

collar at the same depth. The best place to record this information is directly on the template itself.

Make Precise Templates

The best way to learn the basics of template routing is to make and use some simple templates. But before looking at the practical applications for templates illustrated on these pages, it's a good idea to start with some general advice about how to make them, what materials to use, and the best ways to use them.

The most difficult part of template routing is making the template itself. All the important information about the final shape you want to rout is encoded in the design of the template. The more accurately you make your templates, the more time you'll save in the long run. You'll do less sanding, fitting, and fudging afterward.

Sawing, rasping, and filing are time-consuming and tedious ways to make templates. It's also very hard to make a perfect curve with hand tools. I never make a template by hand unless there is no other way. I've found that accurate templates are most

Cutting Multiples

A straight bit and collar guide make a good combination for cutting a stack of profiled pieces, like decorative shelf supports. The bits can cut stock of any thickness and will produce a smoother edge than a bearing-guided bit.

One thing to keep in mind: The template and the finished piece will not be identical because the collar guide keeps the bit away from the edge of the template.

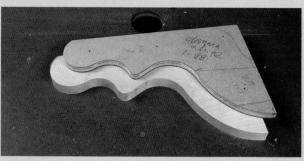

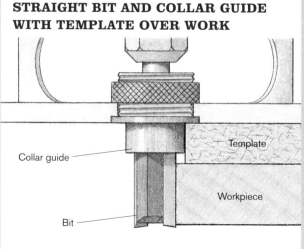

STRAIGHT BIT AND COLLAR GUIDE WITH TEMPLATE OVER WORK

Collar guide

Template

Workpiece

Bit

easily made with sanders and, yes, routers, templates, and other guides.

Templates should be dimensionally stable, durable and capable of taking fine details. Solid wood is a poor choice because it's not dimensionally stable. Steel is stable and durable, but to a fault. If you accidentally touch a spinning bit to one, you'll probably wreck both the bit and the template. Acrylic and Lexan are transparent and allow you to see the work beneath. They also won't kill bits. But be aware that

a slow bearing will generate enough heat from friction to melt them. Medium-density fiberboard (MDF) is the best all around choice. Mind you, it isn't perfect. It's toxic and unpleasant to work with.

Four Everyday Templates

You can use any one of the three kinds of router bits designed for template work. Each has its own strengths and weaknesses. Some bits are especially well-suited to certain

A Template for Butt-Hinge Mortises

A pattern bit is a good choice for cutting shallow mortises precisely and quickly. To make the template, align the hinge on a piece of template stock, and then mark the outline with a pencil. Bandsaw out most of the waste, and reposition the hinge on the template stock. Clamp straight-edged scrap around the hinge to define the edges of the mortise (1). A paper shim will prevent the mortise from being too tight. Then remove the hinge, and rout to the line with the scrap as a guide (2). Remove the scrap, and you have a finished template that cuts an accurate mortise (3).

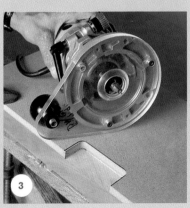

MAKING THE TEMPLATE

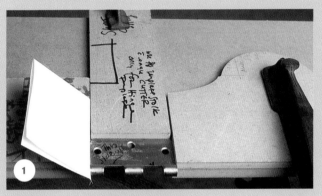

Pattern bit

Scrap

Template stock

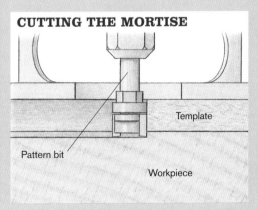

CUTTING THE MORTISE

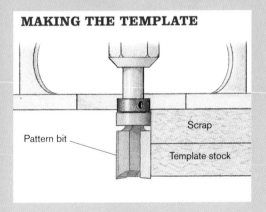

Template

Pattern bit

Workpiece

Template for Routing Small Pieces

Templates can be made so they hold small pieces as well as guide the router. Coupled with a pattern bit, this template makes short work of cutting tapered coffee-table legs. The workpiece is held on the template with toggle clamps. To keep toggle clamps out of the way while routing, the author flips the template upside down on the workbench (right). Blocks between template and bench provide room for the toggle clamps.

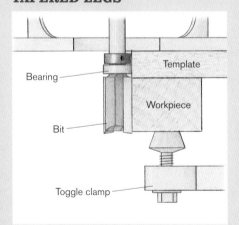

USE A BIT FOR TAPERED LEGS

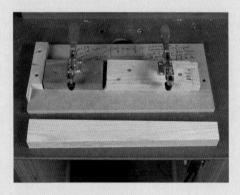

Bearing

Template

Workpiece

Bit

Toggle clamp

kinds of templates, but all of them can bring speed and reliability to repetitive work.

Template for Repeatable Shapes

Using a scrollsaw and an oscillating sander to make a single curved shape, like a decorative shelf support, might be just as fast as template routing it. But only the first time. If you make any more, template routing will be faster and easier. A router bit leaves a much smoother edge than a scrollsaw, and the edge will need far less sanding. Make the template much the way you would make the support if you had no templates. Smooth, gradual curves on MDF are best obtained by sanding to layout lines on a stationary belt sander.

For this kind of work, it's easiest to use a straight bit with a collar guide because you can adjust the cutting depth to match the thickness of the shelf-support stock (see the photos and drawing on p. 60). Collar guides, however, will displace the cut from the exact edge of the template. With straight lines, this merely entails positioning the template the offset distance from the layout line. The lines will be just as straight.

It's a different story with curves. A collar will make the bit cut slightly larger radii on outside curves and smaller radii on inside curves. The result will be a finished piece slightly different from the template. In complementary template work, this is a crucial consideration. But with something like the profile of a shelf support, the difference is not consequential. To tell where the bit will actually cut, run a pen in a loose bearing with the same offset as the collar along the template to draw the layout line.

Cutting Shallow Mortises
Cutting shallow mortises that are clean and evenly deep—like those that you would want for butt hinges—is a difficult task with traditional tools. Except for the very smallest hinges, a router guided by a template will give you more accurate cuts faster and with less variation between them. The photos

and drawings on p. 61 show you how to make one.

Once you've made this template well, it's hard to go wrong using it as long as you are careful. Router stability on the template is essential to an accurate and safe cut. A 6-in. round base router with a $\frac{1}{2}$-in.-diameter bit will have no more than 45 percent of its footprint on the template in an edge cut. If you make a turn around a 90° corner, that percentage is reduced to less than 20 percent. A router that wobbles with a lot of cutter engaged can break the cutter, tear the stock and template, or even cause a kickback that sends the router to the floor. The machine has to stay flat and stable at all times.

This butt hinge has rounded corners the same diameter as the bit. If it had square corners, you'd have to do some handwork to make the hinge fit. A bit with a larger diameter than the corners would also require handwork. Just never use a bit with a smaller diameter, or you'll have gaps to patch.

Cutting Tapers on Small Pieces
Some workpieces are far too small to rout safely if they are sandwiched between a workbench and a template. To taper legs for a coffee table, for instance, I built a template (or a jig, if you like) that holds the workpiece firmly in place with toggle clamps, as shown in the photos and drawing on the facing page. Guide blocks position the side and end of the leg but leave enough room behind them to clamp the template upside down to a workbench edge. In use, neither the toggle clamps nor the clamps holding the template to the bench get in the way.

To get a good, smooth taper, you need only secure the guide blocks at the desired angle in relation to the edge of the template. As the router follows the edge, it cuts the taper angle of the blocks in the leg. Compared with tablesaw techniques that require more complex jigs, put fingers at risk, and leave a coarse cut, this one is far superior.

Once you've made this template well, it's hard to go wrong using it as long as you are careful.

Routing a through Mortise

Deep mortises can be cut accurately by starting with a template and straight bit with a collar and finishing up with a flush-trimming bit. First rout the mortise as deeply as you can with the template as a guide (1). Then drill through to the other side. Remove as much waste as you can, and then flip the workpiece over (2). A flush-trimming bit that follows the upper part of the previously cut mortise will finish the job.

FIRST PASS WITH PATTERN BIT

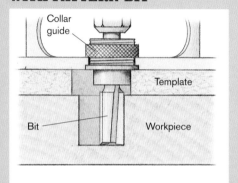

Collar guide

Template

Bit

Workpiece

FINISH WITH FLUSH-TRIMMING BIT

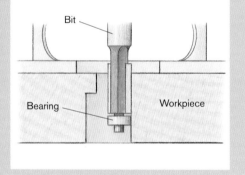

Bit

Bearing

Workpiece

Template for through Mortises The plunge router is the best tool for inside template cuts, such as mortises, but it needs a lot of support to make it safe and accurate. Plunge routers are top heavy and have comparatively small bases. This makes them excellent candidates for router teeter–totter problems. A template for mortising must be large enough so that the plunge router's base is completely supported by the tem-

plate at all times during the cut. The photos and drawings above show a very simple technique to make a through mortise deeper than any bit you own.

PAT WARNER is something of a jack-of-all-trades. A woodworker, college instructor, and tool-industry consultant, he also manufactures the Warner Offset Routerbase. His book *Getting the Very Best from Your Router* was released last fall by Betterway Books. He lives in Escondido, California.

No-Frills Router Table

BY GARY ROGOWSKI

Remember the commercial about the knife that sliced, diced and performed myriad other tasks, even gliding through a tomato after cutting a metal pipe? Well, that's what a router table is like. You can cut stopped and through grooves, dadoes, rabbets, and dovetailed slots. You can raise panels and cut sliding dovetails, tenons, and mortises. It's no wonder that many woodworkers can't imagine working wood without one.

But router tables can be expensive. In one woodworking catalog, I saw a number of packages selling for between $250★ and $300. I'd rather spend my money on wood. That same money would buy some really spectacular fiddleback Oregon walnut.

I've been building furniture for years, and my bare-bones router table has given me excellent, accurate results. The router table in the photo on p. 66 is a variation that is inexpensive, simple to construct, and extremely versatile. It's a simple, three-sided box made from a half-sheet of ¾-in.-thick melamine with the front left open for easy access to the router. I made mine with a top that's 24 in. deep by 32 in. wide, which keeps it light enough to move around yet big enough to handle about anything I'd use a router table for. It's 16 in. high, which

is a good height for placing it on boards on sawhorses or on a low assembly bench.

Biscuits and Dadoes Join Parts

When you buy the melamine, make sure the sheet is flat. And buy it in a color other than blinding white, which is tough on the eyes.

The melamine I used had a particleboard core. Biscuits are stronger than screws in particleboard, so I joined the two sides to the top with #20 biscuits. To make the cuts in the underside of the top, I took a spacer block 5 in. wide, aligned it with the end of the top, and set my plate joiner against it for the cuts. The width of the block determined the overhang of the top. Marks on the spacer block gave me my centers.

The biscuit joints probably would have been plenty strong by themselves, but I wanted to add a little extra strength to the joint. So I decided to dado the underside of the top for the sides. I couldn't dado very deeply, though, or the biscuits would have bottomed out. I settled on a ¹⁄₁₆-in.-deep pass centered over the biscuit slots (see the top photo on p. 67). Before cutting the dado, however, I dry-fitted the sides and top with biscuits in place to check alignment.

Then I scored heavily around the edges of the side pieces with a marking knife and routed the shallow dadoes.

Before gluing the sides to the top, I rabbeted the back edge of the two sides for a ¼-in. panel to strengthen the table and prevent it from racking. Then I glued the sides to the top one at a time, using battens to distribute the clamping pressure. I made sure each side was square to the top and waited for the glue to set up.

I used a router and rabbeting bit to cut a stopped rabbet in the back edge of the top.

Then I glued and screwed down the ¼-in. medium-density fiberboard (MDF) back panel (see the bottom photo on the facing page). Hardboard or plywood would have worked as well.

I use a fixed-base router in my router table because it's lighter than most plunge routers and won't cause the table to sag over time. Also, it's much easier to change bits. I just drop the router motor out of the base, change bits, reinstall the router and I'm back to work.

SHALLOW DADO INCREASES GLUE SURFACE. To strengthen the joints between the sides and top, the author routs a dado 1/16 in. deep in the underside of the top directly over biscuit slots.

FIBERBOARD BACK PREVENTS RACKING. Although it's only 1/4 in. thick, the fiberboard back greatly strengthens the table. The fiberboard is glued and screwed into a rabbet all around the back of the table.

I attached the router base to the underside of the tabletop with machine screws that go down through the top into the tapped holes in the router base. To mark the location of the screw holes, I removed the router subbase and made pencil marks on the top. Then I drilled and countersunk holes into the tabletop.

With the base attached to the table, I marked out where the bit hole should go and drilled a 3/4-in. hole into the table. I put a 2 1/8-in.-diameter chamfer bit in my router—the largest bit I have. I started the

tool and gradually moved the bit up and through the tabletop (see the left photo on p. 68).

To prevent workpieces from diving into this hole when using small bits, I made a set of inserts that fit in a shallow recess around the bit hole. Holes in the inserts accommodate bits of different sizes with minimal clearance. I routed out the rabbeted recesses for the inserts first, using a plunge router guided by a straightedge. I squared the corners with a chisel.

CUT THE HOLE WITH A ROUTER BIT. With the router base screwed to the underside of the top, the author advances his largest bit through the table. Go slowly.

A RECESS FOR INTERCHANGEABLE INSERTS
A plunge router and chisel make short work of a recess in the tabletop that accepts inserts for different-sized bits.

I made the inserts of ¼-in. tempered hardboard. Their square shape keeps them from spinning during use and makes them easy to fit. I cut a bunch of them on the tablesaw and then sanded each to a perfect fit on a belt sander.

L-Shaped Fence Provides Dust Collection

The fence I've always used might be called low-tech, but there's really no tech to it at all. It's simply a straight, wide, flat piece of wood jointed so that one edge is square to a face. I clamp it to the router table wherever I need it. The fence doesn't have to be parallel to a table edge to work. When a bit needs to be partially hidden for a cut, I use another board with a recess cut into its face.

The only thing my primitive fence lacks is dust collection. Hooking up a vacuum or a dust collector just won't work in some situations, such as when I plow a groove. But with other operations—raising a panel,

rabbeting a drawer or box bottom, or cutting an edge profile—having a fence with a dust port can really help clear the air.

The fence I built for this router table is made of two pieces of ¾-in.-thick MDF about 4½ in. wide and 49 in. long rabbeted together to form an L-shape (see the photo on the facing page). I cut a semi-circular hole at the center of each for dust collection. This allows for better pickup. I also routed slots in the vertical part of the fence so I could attach auxiliary fences for specific operations, such as raising panels or rabbeting. Once these slots are routed, the two pieces of the fence can be glued together. Make sure the fence clamps up square because virtually everything you use the table for depends on it.

To create sidewalls for the dust-collection hook-up, I added two triangular-shaped pieces of ¾-in.-thick MDF to frame the dust-collection port (see the left photo on p. 70). I glued these triangles in place on either side of the dust holes, just rubbing them in place and letting them set up without clamping. After the glue had cured, I filed the triangles flush with the fence, top, and bottom.

To complete the dust-collection hook-up, I measured the diameter of the nozzle on my shop vacuum and cut a hole to accommodate it in a piece of ¼-in. hardboard. I left the hardboard oversize, clamped it to the drill-press table, and used a circle cutter on my drill press. Then I cut the hardboard to size and glued and screwed it to the two triangular walls.

Auxiliary Fences Solve Specific Problems

A two-piece auxiliary fence can be used to close up the area around the bit when routing profiles, rabbeting, or performing similar operations. This way, there's no chance of a small piece diving into the gap between bit and fence. And with a smaller opening around the bit, the dust collector or vacuum will work more efficiently. When the fence is situated back from the bit, such as when mortising, another set of auxiliary pieces can be used, so there's no gap between the two halves (see the right photo on p. 70).

I made the auxiliary fence from two more pieces of MDF. The auxiliary fence is drilled and countersunk for machine screws that ride in slots cut in the main fence. I use nuts and washers to tighten the two pieces in position.

When using the auxiliary fence, I close the two halves around the moving bit to provide a custom fence. When I'm done with it, I can set the fence aside for future use or just cut it off square and use it again. Closing the fence into a bit with a diameter that's less than the thickness of the fence will not open up the back of the fence to the dust-collection port. In this situation,

CLAMP THE FENCE SQUARE. **Adjust the clamps (left) to get the two pieces square over the entire length of the fence.**

SCREW DUST-COLLECTION PORT TO FENCE. Smear a bead of glue along the two triangular sidewalls. Drill holes and screw the hard-board back to them.

USING A CLOSED AUXILIARY FENCE Routing away from the fence calls for auxiliary pieces butted tightly together to form a smooth, continuous surface.

I pivot the fence through the spinning bit before setting the fence for depth of cut.

Make sure that the outfeed side of the fence doesn't stick out any farther than the infeed side. If it does, it will prevent you from feeding your work smoothly past the bit. If your work catches on the outfeed side of the fence, easing its leading edge with a file or a chisel may help. If it doesn't, you can always shim the infeed side with slips of paper.

Another router table problem I've found is what to do with large upright pieces,

such as panels cut with a vertical panel-raising bit. The solution is to screw a taller auxiliary fence to the main fence. The fence can be pivoted right into the bit, so there's no gap on either the infeed or outfeed side of the bit, yet there's dust collection behind the bit.

*Note price estimates are from 1997.

GARY ROGOWSKI has been building furniture in Portland, Oregon, since 1974 and teaching wood-working since 1980. He is a contributing editor to *Fine Woodworking*.

The Ultimate Router Table

BY JOHN WHITE

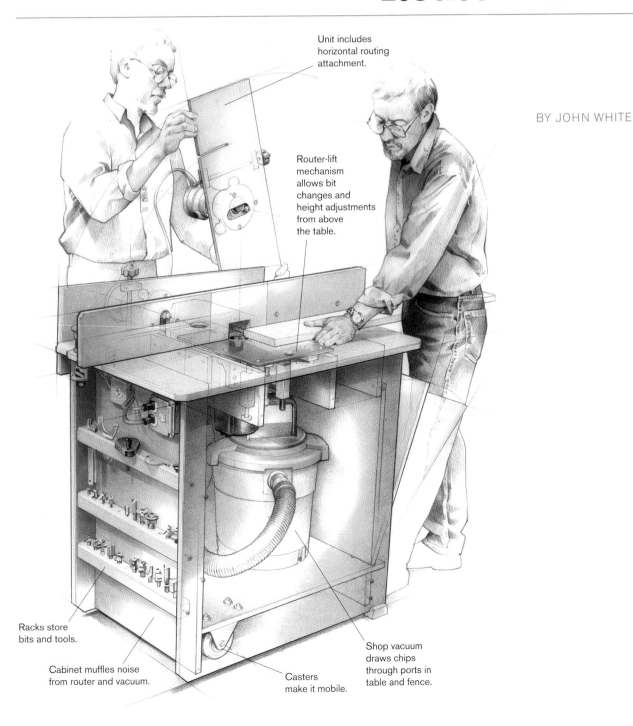

Unit includes horizontal routing attachment.

Router-lift mechanism allows bit changes and height adjustments from above the table.

Racks store bits and tools.

Cabinet muffles noise from router and vacuum.

Casters make it mobile.

Shop vacuum draws chips through ports in table and fence.

The ultimate
router table would
be as convenient
as a shaper or
tablesaw.

I have always been dissatisfied with the popular designs for router tables and the versions available on the market. In some way or another, they are all less convenient than standard woodworking machines. For one thing, you have to reach under the table a lot to adjust bit height, change bits or hit the power switch. The ultimate router table would be as convenient as a shaper or tablesaw—all of the common tasks and adjustments are done from above or outside the unit. It would also have the dust-collecting ability and vibration-dampening mass of a cabinet-mounted tool.

I came up with a router cabinet that meets all of the above criteria and is super-quiet to boot. The design relies on the JessEm Rout-R-Lift®, a screw-driven mechanism that allows you to raise and lower the router and bit by cranking a handle inserted from above. The JessEm unit is also sold by Jet® as the Xacta® Lift, for the same price—around $200★ in many catalogs. By adding a shopmade mounting block to the lift, I was able to raise the router high enough to allow bit changes from above the table as well.

Eliminating the need to reach underneath the top let me mount the table on a cabinet, which could enclose a shop vacuum and muffle its sound and the roar of the router itself. A dust-collection manifold fits under the tabletop and behind the lift unit. A fence system with a dust port ties into the system below.

I mounted a switched outlet for the router and vacuum unit outside the cabinet. Just for fun, I threw in racks for bit and tool storage. Casters under one end of the cabinet make it mobile—like a wheelbarrow—but still stable on the floor.

Materials cost just over $300, including the shop vacuum and the router lift but not a fixed-base router (the more powerful, the better for use in a table). The investment in

time and money was significant but reasonable, considering the performance and convenience I gained.

MDF and Knockdown Fasteners Make a Strong Cabinet

The entire unit—cabinet, table, and fence—is made of ¾-in.-thick medium-density fiberboard (MDF), with two coats of Watco® oil for added durability. I used MDF because it offers flatness, mass and stability at a very low cost. To make sure the cabinet would remain sturdy, I opted for cross-dowel knockdown fasteners over glue and screws. Casters and wood blocks keep the MDF edges off the floor, where they might soak up moisture and then fracture.

Cutting out the MDF parts should be straightforward, but be sure to wear a dust mask, and don't count on the factory edges of the panels being square. Squareness and accuracy are very important with such a large cabinet, especially with interior parts that must fit tightly. Chamfer the edges of the tabletop to prevent chipping. This isn't a bad idea for the other MDF parts, as well. I used a laminate trimmer with a 45° router bit to zip quickly along the many edges.

I have a few tricks for drilling accurate holes for knockdown fasteners (see the facing page). On the back side and tabletop, counterbore the heads of the fasteners to maintain a flat surface.

To support the casters, install backing blocks inside the cabinet. Assembled, this unit weighs more than 100 lb.

Installing the Access Panel One end panel is removable so that you can open the cabinet and empty the shop vacuum. Size this panel to fit the cabinet walls snugly, but overlap the support strip at the top of the opening. Drill two ¼-in.-diameter holes in the bottom edge of the panel for the pins or cutoff bolts that will keep the panel in

Knockdown Fasteners Make Strong Joints

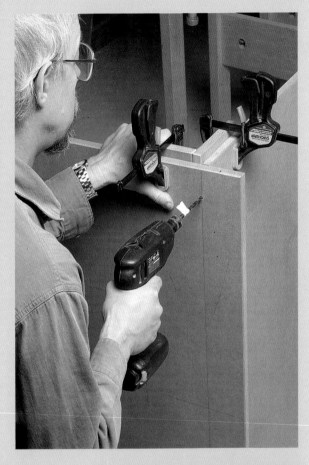

CROSS-DOWEL FASTENERS REQUIRE ACCURATE HOLES. To hold the pieces at right angles for drilling the long holes, make a right-angle jig and clamp it to the workpieces at the top and bottom of the joint.

ALUMINUM FLASHING MAKES A LAYOUT JIG FOR THE CROSS-DOWEL HOLES. With a drill bit in the bolt hole, use the jig to locate the centerpoint of the cross-dowel hole.

THE CROSS DOWELS WILL BE INVISIBLE IF YOU DON'T BREAK THROUGH THE OUTSIDE. Use a stop collar to control the depth.

SIMPLE PARTS, SMART FUNCTION

The cabinet is made entirely from ¾-in.-thick MDF joined with knockdown fasteners. The front-to-back braces below the table-top support the router plate and double as the sides of the dust manifold. Two filler blocks close the gap around the lift mechanism, which makes for efficient dust collection.

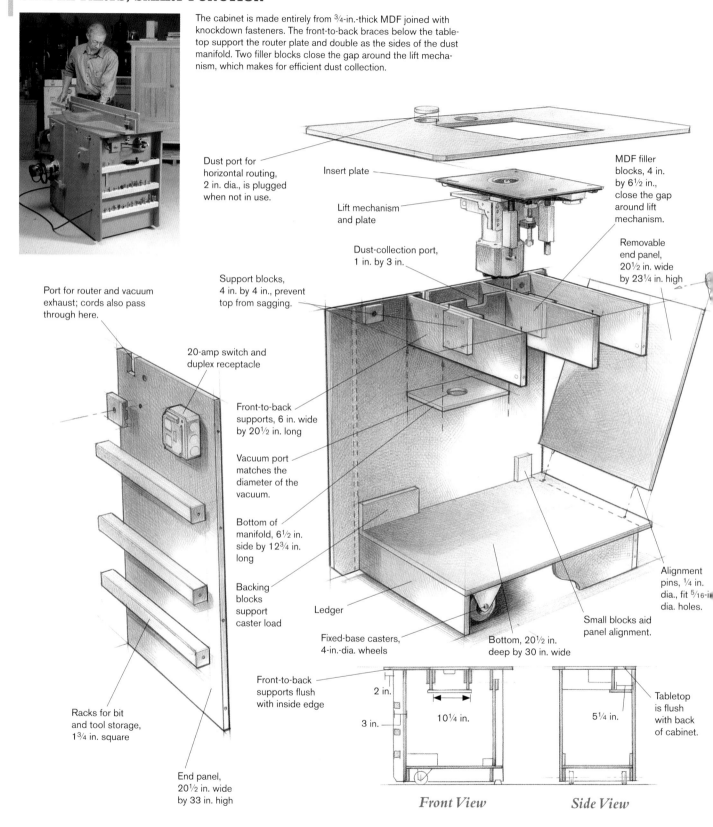

Dust port for horizontal routing, 2 in. dia., is plugged when not in use.

Insert plate

Lift mechanism and plate

MDF filler blocks, 4 in. by 6½ in., close the gap around lift mechanism.

Removable end panel, 20½ in. wide by 23¼ in. high

Dust-collection port, 1 in. by 3 in.

Port for router and vacuum exhaust; cords also pass through here.

Support blocks, 4 in. by 4 in., prevent top from sagging.

20-amp switch and duplex receptacle

Front-to-back supports, 6 in. wide by 20½ in. long

Vacuum port matches the diameter of the vacuum.

Bottom of manifold, 6½ in. side by 12¾ in. long

Backing blocks support caster load

Ledger

Fixed-base casters, 4-in.-dia. wheels

Front-to-back supports flush with inside edge

Racks for bit and tool storage, 1¾ in. square

End panel, 20½ in. wide by 33 in. high

Alignment pins, ¼ in. dia., fit ⁵⁄₁₆-in. dia. holes.

Small blocks aid panel alignment.

Bottom, 20½ in. deep by 30 in. wide

Tabletop is flush with back of cabinet.

2 in.

3 in.

10¼ in.

5¼ in.

Front View

Side View

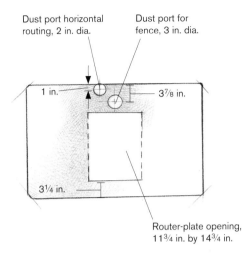

Dust port horizontal routing, 2 in. dia.

Dust port for fence, 3 in. dia.

1 in.

3⅞ in.

3¼ in.

Router-plate opening, 11¾ in. by 14¾ in.

Latch assembly, made of MDF, bolt, nut, waser and rubber O-ring

Cabinet front and back, 34 in. wide by 33 in. high

Hardwood support blocks levela and protect base.

position. Press the pins into the panel, then drill 5/16-in.-diameter holes in the base of the cabinet to receive the pins. Glue the two stop blocks to the walls of the cabinet, which will make it easier to put the panel quickly back in position.

Add the latch assembly. I recommend placing a rubber O-ring under the rear washer to regulate the action of the latch.

Router Lift Requires an Exact Cutout

The only tricky procedure on the tabletop is making a precise cutout to fit the router-lift insert plate. Start by flipping over the top. Lay out the front edge of the cutout 3 in. from the front edge of the tabletop. Then lay the lift-plate assembly on the tabletop, locating its front edge along the layout line. Next, screw MDF strips around the edges of the insert plate, being careful not to punch through on the top side. Additionally, to avoid too snug a fit (MDF swells in high humidity), add a layer of masking tape along the edges of the guide strips before attaching them to the underside. These strips will guide your jigsaw and router cuts.

Keep the jigsaw cut about ¼ in. away from the strips; the router will handle the rest. Then remove the masking tape, and rout the finished opening. A ¾-in.-diameter pattern-cutting bit will leave the correct ⅜-in. radius at the corners to match the lift plate.

Drilling Vacuum-Port Holes There are a number of large holes in this unit. I use an adjustable-wing circle cutter (or fly cutter) for all of these. A wing cutter must be used in a drill press. Proceed slowly and with caution, keeping your hands and clothing well clear of this whirling dervish of a bit.

The large hole in the tabletop connects the fence's dust port with the dust-collection system below. Another one is necessary if you opt for the horizontal

Router Lift Is the Heart of the Table

It all started with the JessEm Rout-R-Lift, which allowed White to design a cabinet-based unit that encloses dust-collection and muffles noise yet puts all controls and adjustments on the outside.

LEVELING SCREWS OFFER PRECISE ADJUSTMENT. The weight of the router lift is carried by the two front-to-back braces, instead of the tabletop as is the case with most router tables.

NO REACHING BELOW TO ADJUST HEIGHT. The adjustment crank is inserted from above.

A CUSTOM ROUTER MOUNT FOR EASY BIT CHANGES

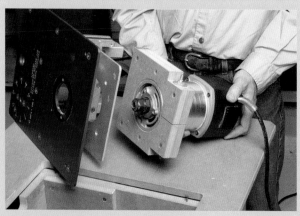

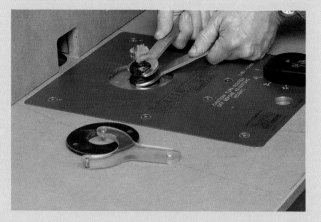

REPLACING THE ROUTER'S BASE WITH A SHOPMADE MOUNTING BRACKET allows the nose of the router to be raised high enough for wrenches to reach it.

Make an Accurate Cutout for the Insert Plate

MDF GUIDE STRIPS ENSURE ACCURACY. Lay the insert plate on the underside of the tabletop and screw on the strips. A layer of tape leaves room for seasonal movement of the MDF.

THE STRIPS GUIDE THE JIGSAW. Make the rough cutout about ¼ in. from the MDF strips.

THEN THEY GUIDE THE ROUTER BIT. Remove the tape, and use a bearing-guided bit to cut the opening flush with the strips. A ¾-in.-diameter bit will leave a ⅜-in. radius at the corners.

router attachment. In that case, one of these holes should always be plugged when the other is in use. Attach fender washers on the underside of the table around each hole to support the plugs.

Support Structure Aids Dust Collection

With the top completed, you are ready to assemble the support structure below. The two main braces for the router-lift insert plate also serve as the sides of the dust-collection manifold at the back of the cabinet. Locate and attach these pieces first.

Secure these front-to-back braces so that their outside faces are just even with the edges of the insert-plate cutout. Then attach the notched crosspiece, positioning it to miss the lift mechanism by ¹⁄₁₆ in. or less. The smaller the gap here, the less suction lost around the lift plate. The notch in the crosspiece is a dust port that draws air

through the bit opening into what will be the dust manifold. Now cut out the piece for the bottom of the manifold and use the wing cutter to drill a hole for the vacuum hose. Only a cutoff section of the vacuum hose will fit into the cabinet, so size the hole in the box for the hose diameter, not an end coupling. Lock the hose in place with two fender washers positioned to catch the spiral grooves in the hose. Screw the bottom piece to the manifold.

A few steps remain to create good air suction through the bit opening. Attach another layer of ¾-in.-thick MDF to each support brace, along its inner face, to create a close fit around the sides of the insert plate. Then, using double-sided tape and/or screws, attach a thin metal flap (I made mine from aluminum flashing, about 0.020 in. thick) to the insert plate as shown in the drawing on p. 78, to deflect the exhaust blast from the router motor and to

FOLLOW THE AIRFLOW

The vacuum draws air and chips through the bit openings in the table and fence, into the dust manifold and down the hose into the vacuum, where the dust and chips are filtered out. An angled flap of sheet metal deflects the router's exhaust blast away from the bit opening and into the cabinet.

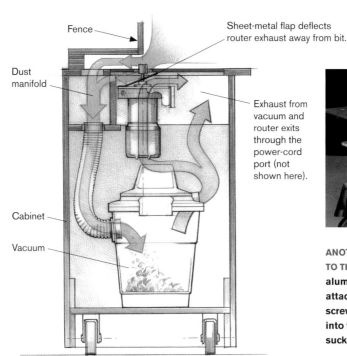

Fence

Sheet-metal flap deflects router exhaust away from bit.

Dust manifold

Exhaust from vacuum and router exits through the power-cord port (not shown here).

Cabinet

Vacuum

ANOTHER IMPORTANT MODIFICATION TO THE ROUTER LIFT. **A square of aluminum flashing–bent slightly and attached with double-stick tape or screws–deflects the router's exhaust into the cabinet, allowing chips to be sucked past the bit.**

allow air and chips to be drawn into the dust manifold.

Last, screw two blocks to the outside of the large front-to-back braces to prevent the tabletop from sagging near the opening in the middle of the plate.

Mount the Router in a Shopmade Base

Fine-threaded drywall screws in the support braces act as levelers for the four corners of the insert plate. MDF loves to split at its edges, so drill pilot holes for any screws, making them slightly larger than usual. I typically go with drywall screws that are at least 2 in. long. Normally, coarse-threaded screws are better for MDF, but these levelers are for fine adjustment.

You'll have to mount the router body in a shopmade base to position it high enough in the table to allow bit changes to be made from above. (The router's original base can

be mounted and left on the horizontal routing attachment on the back of the table.) But you can skip this step if you don't mind removing the router-lift mechanism from the table to change bits.

Use a wing cutter to drill a large hole, exactly the size of your router body, through a block made of two thicknesses of MDF. Then cut a thin kerf through the edge of the block to allow for tightening, and drill the long hole for the tightening bolt. Attach the mounting block to the lift plate with coarse-threaded drywall screws.

Install the Switch Box and Fence

I mounted a 20-amp switch and outlet box on the end of the cabinet to connect the vacuum and router to one easily accessible on/off switch. I also mounted a small block next to the box to act as a cord manager.

Simple but Effective Fence

The fence features a removable insert, a dust manifold that ties into the one below the table and modified pipe clamps that grab the table edges.

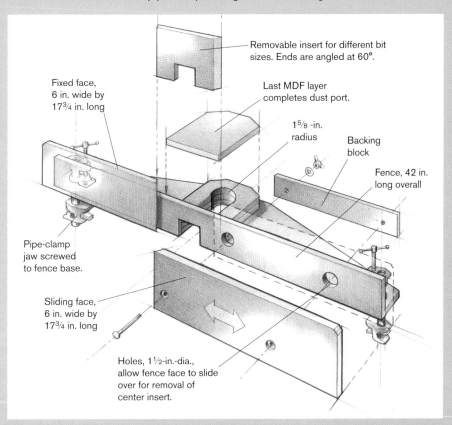

Removable insert for different bit sizes. Ends are angled at 60°.

Fixed face, 6 in. wide by 17¾ in. long

Last MDF layer completes dust port.

1⅝-in. radius

Backing block

Fence, 42 in. long overall

Pipe-clamp jaw screwed to fence base.

Sliding face, 6 in. wide by 17¾ in. long

Holes, 1½-in.-dia., allow fence face to slide over for removal of center insert.

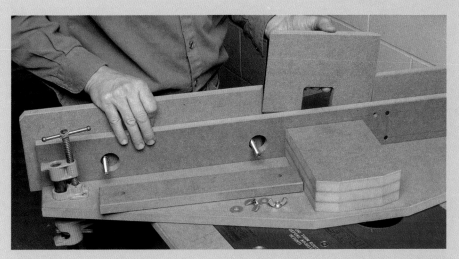

A REMOVABLE FENCE INSERT. One half of the fence slides sideways, allowing for interchangeable inserts that fit various bit sizes. The edges of the fence faces and insert are angled to hold the insert in place, but a few brads with the heads clipped off also help.

Horizontal Routing Attachment

The back of the table is flush with the cabinet so that White could include a horizontal routing attachment—useful for making tenons, raised panels, and sliding dovetails, among other operations.

ADJUST THE BIT HEIGHT. The fine-adjustment screw moves the router up and down, and the clamping bolt locks everything in place. A coil spring keeps tension on the screw, preventing it from drifting as a result of vibration.

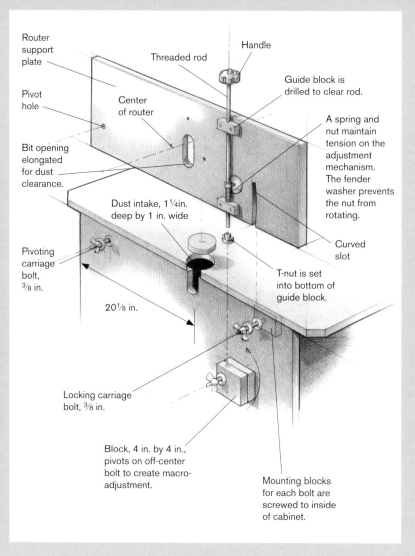

Router support plate

Handle

Threaded rod

Guide block is drilled to clear rod.

Pivot hole

Center of router

A spring and nut maintain tension on the adjustment mechanism. The fender washer prevents the nut from rotating.

Bit opening elongated for dust clearance.

Dust intake, 1¼in. deep by 1 in. wide

Curved slot

Pivoting carriage bolt, ⅜ in.

20⅛ in.

T-nut is set into bottom of guide block.

Locking carriage bolt, ⅜ in.

Block, 4 in. by 4 in., pivots on off-center bolt to create macro-adjustment.

Mounting blocks for each bolt are screwed to inside of cabinet.

The fence is joined with long drywall screws but incorporates a dust box that ties into the dust-collection manifold through a hole in the tabletop. Also, a sliding face allows the fence to have an interchangeable center insert. Carriage bolts and wing nuts lock the sliding face in position.

Pipe clamps make a simple clamping system, gripping the edges of the table but also sliding freely. Drill small holes through the adjustable jaws of the pipe clamps, and screw them permanently into place.

Creating this "ultimate router table" takes some time and money, but the added precision and ease of use will reward you many times over.

*Please note price estimates are from 2001.

JOHN WHITE is a contributing editor and the shop manager for *Fine Woodworking*.

Five Smart Router Jigs

BY YEUNG CHAN

Few woodworkers enjoy the luxury of a spacious shop, and I'm no exception. Lacking the space for many large machines, I rely on my router when building furniture. However, used on its own, the router is limited in its abilities. More often than not, I use it in conjunction with various shopmade jigs that increase its ability to quickly and accurately cut circles, make edge profiles, cut dadoes, trim edge-banding, and even substitute for a lathe.

The five jigs illustrated here are all made from cheap and stable plywood or medium-density fiberboard (MDF) and require only a few pieces of hardware, available through Lee Valley℠ or Rockler® (see Sources). These router jigs are as easy to use as they are to make.

YEUNG CHAN builds custom furniture in Millbrae, California.

ADJUSTABLE CIRCLE-CUTTING JIG

All pieces of the jig are made of ½-in.-thick plywood.

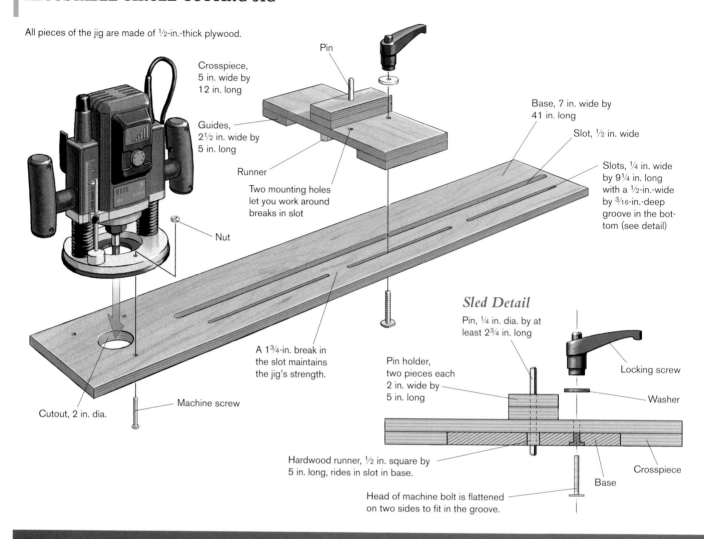

Pin

Crosspiece,
5 in. wide by
12 in. long

Guides,
2½ in. wide by
5 in. long

Runner

Two mounting holes
let you work around
breaks in slot

Nut

Base, 7 in. wide by
41 in. long

Slot, ½ in. wide

Slots, ¼ in. wide
by 9¼ in. long
with a ½-in.-wide
by ³⁄₁₆-in.-deep
groove in the bot-
tom (see detail)

A 1¾-in. break in
the slot maintains
the jig's strength.

Cutout, 2 in. dia.

Machine screw

Sled Detail

Pin, ¼ in. dia. by at
least 2¾ in. long

Pin holder,
two pieces each
2 in. wide by
5 in. long

Hardwood runner, ½ in. square by
5 in. long, rides in slot in base.

Head of machine bolt is flattened
on two sides to fit in the groove.

Locking screw

Washer

Crosspiece

Base

Cut Perfect Circles

This jig can be used to rout a circle with a maximum diameter of 72 in., but the design can be modified for other diameters. First, drill a ¼-in.-diameter hole, ¼ in. deep, in the middle of the workpiece. If you don't want the hole to show, work on the underside. Next, mark a point on the desired edge of the circle, place the sled over the base, and fit the jig's pin in the center hole. Move the base in or out until the bit is on the mark, then lock the sled.

Turn on the router and plunge down to start the initial cut, which should be less than ⅛ in. deep, just enough to define the circle. Use a jigsaw to cut away the outside pieces, leaving about ⅛ in. outside the final size of the

circle. This method enables you to support the corners as they are cut off so that they won't damage the finished workpiece. Once the bulk of the waste has been removed, the router has to make only a light final cut. If you're working with solid wood, pay attention to the grain's orientation and the bit's rotation. Climb-cut when necessary to avoid tearout.

MAKE A SHALLOW CUT TO DEFINE THE CIRCLE.
**The initial cut made with the router should be only
about ⅛ in. deep.**

Trim or Cut Large Panels

It is a difficult job to cut a large panel on a tablesaw that's not equipped with a sliding table. So I made a simple jig that can be used to cut out a section from a full sheet of plywood or medium-density fiberboard (MDF) or to clean up a rough cut made by a jigsaw or a circular saw.

Once you've assembled the jig, run the router along the straight edge of the fence to create a matching straight edge on the base. To use the jig, clamp it at both ends of the workpiece with the edge of the jig aligned with the desired cut. As the router rides along the jig, it leaves a perfectly straight, clean cut.

STRAIGHTEDGE JIG

Always use the same-diameter router bit with this jig. A smaller bit will cut wide of the jig's edge, while a larger bit will eat into the jig.

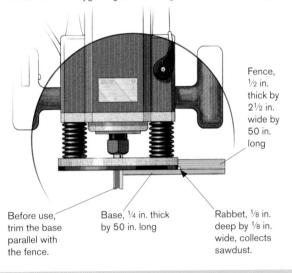

Fence, ½ in. thick by 2½ in. wide by 50 in. long

Before use, trim the base parallel with the fence.

Base, ¼ in. thick by 50 in. long

Rabbet, ⅛ in. deep by ⅛ in. wide, collects sawdust.

STRAIGHTEN EDGES. Rough-cut the panel, then clean up the cut with this straightedge jig.

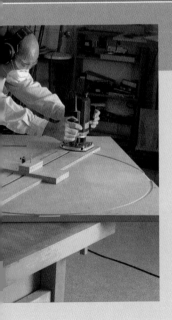

REMOVE THE WASTE. Following the track left by the router, saw away the waste.

THE FINAL CUT. The router now has to remove only a small amount of material, creating less dust and leaving a clean cut.

Cut Dadoes at Any Angle

I reach for this jig when I have to cut multiple parallel dadoes on a panel. Most of the time these grooves are perpendicular to the short fence of the jig, but they can be cut at different angles. Like the straightedge jig on p. 83, this one needs to be clamped at both ends during use. As long as you use the same size bit each time, and the same angle, the entry cut on the jig's short fence will show the location of the dado. Use an up-cut spiral bit, which will prevent chips from jamming in the dado. For deep dadoes, make several passes.

VARIABLE-ANGLE JIG. Although dadoes usually are perpendicular to the long edges of a panel, this jig can make cuts at other angles.

CUT CLEAN AND ACCURATE DADOES. Clamp the dado jig at both ends and make the cut in two or three passes.

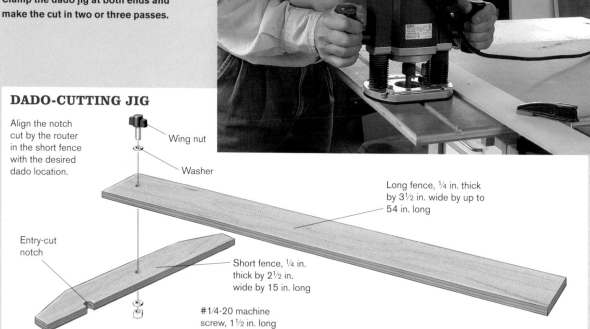

DADO-CUTTING JIG

Align the notch cut by the router in the short fence with the desired dado location.

Wing nut

Washer

Long fence, ¼ in. thick by 3½ in. wide by up to 54 in. long

Entry-cut notch

Short fence, ¼ in. thick by 2½ in. wide by 15 in. long

#1/4-20 machine screw, 1½ in. long

Trim Edge-Banding Quickly and Cleanly

One of the hardest parts of using solid wood to edge plywood or laminate panels is trimming the edge-banding flush with the plywood. If you use a plane, you risk cutting through the thin plywood veneer, and sanding can leave cross-grain scratches on the plywood. This router jig enables you to trim the banding flush, quickly and flawlessly.

Mount the router on the jig, and set the depth of the bit so that it just clears the plywood surface. A router with micro-adjustment comes in handy. Adjust the guide block to align the bit so that the carbide tips extend just a hair over the plywood. Clamp the guide block tight, and you're ready to go.

Pay attention to the router bit's rotation and the direction you move the router. To avoid tearout, you want the leading edge of the bit to enter the wood first. Known as climb cutting, this method can be dangerous if the bit pulls the router forward uncontrollably. Because the amount of wood being removed is so small, you should be able to control the router easily.

FLUSH-CUT EDGE-BANDING. This jig allows you to cleanly cut solid-wood edge-banding flush with the plywood panel.

EDGE-BAND TRIMMING JIG

The router bit should be positioned a hair above the plywood surface. The spacer/guide block is clamped to the jig to steer the router along the edging.

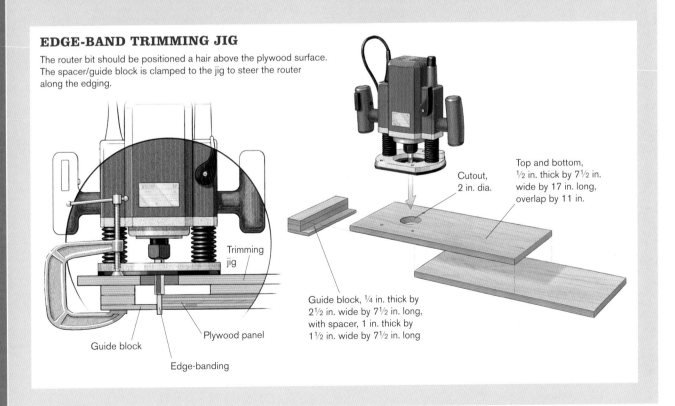

Trimming jig

Guide block

Edge-banding

Plywood panel

Cutout, 2 in. dia.

Top and bottom, ½ in. thick by 7½ in. wide by 17 in. long, overlap by 11 in.

Guide block, ¼ in. thick by 2½ in. wide by 7½ in. long, with spacer, 1 in. thick by 1½ in. wide by 7½ in. long

Make Turnings with a Router

This jig allows you to "turn" round columns and posts using a router. To use the jig, first drill a $^5/_{16}$-in.-diameter hole, 1½ in. deep, in each end of the workpiece, then insert a steel rod to hold the workpiece inside the jig. Lock a drill stop on each end of the rod where it enters the jig to prevent the workpiece from shifting during the turning. Clamp two wood guide pieces to the edges of the router subbase to restrict the router's side-to-side movement.

Turn on the router, slowly plunge down, and move the router halfway up and down the jig as you slowly rotate the workpiece. As you increase the depth of cut, you'll create a cylinder. Then repeat the process on the other half of the workpiece. Throughout the process, make small cuts for a better finish and a safer operation.

You can adapt this jig to create different turnings. Offset the hole at one end of the jig to make tapered turnings, or clamp blocks to the long sides of the jig to produce stopped turnings. If you design the jig with gently curving sides, the workpiece will become football shaped as it is turned.

ROUTER-CUT TURNINGS.
By guiding the router back and forth while turning the workpiece, a square blank gradually becomes a cylinder.

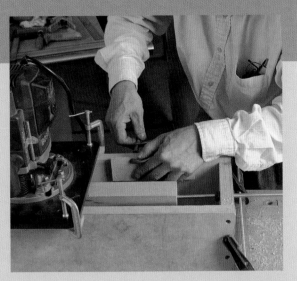

...ED TURNINGS. Lower the hole at one end of the ...per the turned workpiece.

STOPPED TURNINGS. Clamp blocks to the side of the jig to leave a square section on the turning.

Sources   87

Lee Valley
800-871-8158
www.leevalley.com

Rockler
800-279-4441
www.rockler.com

TURNING JIG

The dimensions of this jig will vary based on the size of the blank to be turned. The four sides of the jig can be screwed together or clamped for greater flexibility. Steel rods passing through each end of the jig hold the blank.

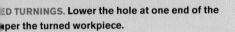

Guide pieces, clamped to subbase

Router subbase

Workpiece

Workpiece

Steel rod, 5/16 in. dia.

Drill stop is tightened with hex key.

The dimensions of the ends and sides will vary according to the diameter and length of the turning.

Tablesaws

At the heart of most woodshops, you'll find a tablesaw. Outfitted with the right accessories and jigs, this workhorse of a machine will saw everything from small sticks to full-size plywood panels. It can rip and crosscut, saw tapers, grooves, dadoes, and almost any kind of joint. It can even shape coves to create moldings.

Unfortunately, the tablesaw is a bit misunderstood. Although we often just shove work through it, it's actually capable of some pretty delicate operations. But for a tablesaw to really work well and safely, it must be tuned up properly. Clean, accurate cuts depend on a fence that's properly aligned to the blade, miter gauge slots that sit perfectly parallel to the blade, and correctly adjusted blade stops. Safety depends on proper cutting approach as well as a decent guard and splitter that are in place and properly set up.

In this section you'll learn how to tune up your saw for accuracy and safety and how to perform common operations with confidence. Just as important, you'll discover how to make jigs that are absolutely critical for getting the most from your tablesaw.

A Tablesaw Primer: Ripping and Crosscutting

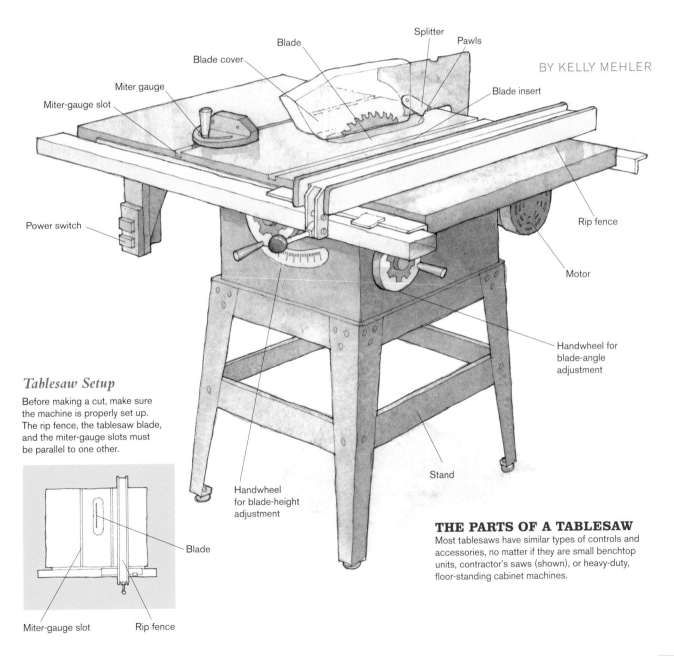

BY KELLY MEHLER

Blade cover

Blade

Splitter

Pawls

Miter gauge

Blade insert

Miter-gauge slot

Power switch

Rip fence

Motor

Handwheel for blade-angle adjustment

Tablesaw Setup

Before making a cut, make sure the machine is properly set up. The rip fence, the tablesaw blade, and the miter-gauge slots must be parallel to one other.

Blade

Handwheel for blade-height adjustment

Miter-gauge slot

Rip fence

Stand

THE PARTS OF A TABLESAW

Most tablesaws have similar types of controls and accessories, no matter if they are small benchtop units, contractor's saws (shown), or heavy-duty, floor-standing cabinet machines.

With its flat, circular spinning blade doing the hard work, the tablesaw can make all sorts of cuts, among them grooves, dadoes, rabbets, and a variety of other woodworking joints. However, the tablesaw most commonly is called on to do just two basic tasks: make wide boards narrower, a process called ripping, and make long boards shorter, a process called crosscutting. When ripping, the rip fence is used to guide the stock. Crosscutting is done with the aid of the miter gauge.

Because so much tablesaw run time is spent ripping and crosscutting, it's especially important to have good work habits while making these two fundamental cuts. After all, when used properly, a good tablesaw can produce remarkably smooth and accurate cuts safely and with little effort.

The Saw Must Be Set Up Properly for Best Results

A tablesaw won't cut easily, accurately, or safely if it's improperly set up. So before making any rip or crosscut, make sure the saw is in good working order and properly adjusted (see "Tablesaw Tune-Up" on p. 98). Also, the table of the saw should be flat, with any deviation limited to no more than 0.010 in. The same goes for any extension tables. And when assembled, those tables all should be flush.

Then, too, the sawblade should be sharp. A sharp combination blade can produce good cuts when ripping and crosscutting.

Use the Blade Cover, Splitter, and Pawls

The saw must have a blade guard that includes a cover, splitter, and pawls. Granted, such a guard system isn't a foolproof device, but it does improve safety. The cover itself acts as a barrier, helping to block any misdirected hand or finger from contacting the spinning blade. That's a big plus. Also, the splitter and pawls minimize the chance of kickback or ejection.

Kickback occurs most often during a ripcut, usually when the workpiece twists away from the rip fence just enough to contact the rising teeth at the back portion of the blade. When that happens, those back teeth can grab the workpiece, lifting it and instantly launching it, usually right back at the operator. But a properly adjusted splitter helps prevent the workpiece from contacting the back teeth, so kickback is less likely to happen.

Ejection occurs most often when ripping a relatively narrow piece, just after the sawblade cuts the piece free. At that point, if the piece should tip, twist, or bend, it can become pinched between the blade and the rip fence. And if the piece is not restrained by a push block or pawls, the force of the spinning blade can send the piece straight back at warp speed. Indeed, I've seen photos of a ¾-in.-square by 4-ft.-long piece that shot back 6 ft. and fully penetrated a sheet of ¾-in.-thick plywood.

Flat, Square Stock Is a Must

A warped board or one with uneven edges can be difficult to control when ripping or crosscutting. Such boards are likely to rock during a cut, binding against the side of the blade. At best, you end up with a rough edge that isn't square. At worst, you get kickback or ejection (see the drawings on p. 94).

Before you make any tablesaw cuts, check that the face surfaces of the board are flat. Also, any edge that will meet the rip fence or the miter gauge must be straight. If necessary, first joint an edge straight or plane a flat face.

How to Avoid Kickback or Ejection while Ripping

Smooth ripcuts can become routine if you follow a few basic cutting techniques. Not only will you get smooth ripcuts but you'll also be able to make them more safely. That's important, especially when you consider that most tablesaw accidents occur during ripcuts. A safety point: Don't rip a board that is wider than it is long. With the shortest edge of the board bearing against the rip fence, the board easily can twist away from the fence and into the side of the blade, an invitation to kickback.

When you're faced with making a narrow ripcut, typically one that's between 1¼ in. wide and 3 in. wide, the blade cover usually ends up interfering with your right hand as you use the push block to feed the board through the blade. To avoid that problem, use a tall push block, which puts your hand well above the cover as the stock is pushed along.

For the narrowest ripcuts, between ⅛ in. wide and 1¼ in. wide, use a notched sled when the stock is less than about 24 in. long (see the top left drawings on p. 93). A handle on top helps you push the sled while keeping its edge against the rip fence. To set the width of the cut, simply measure the distance from the sled's inside edge to the sawblade's inside edge. For longer parts that require a narrow ripcut, clamp a short auxiliary fence to the rip fence. Allow the stock to slide under the blade cover. However, when the front of the push block reaches the cover, you'll have to stop pushing and go to the back of the saw. The pawls will keep the stock in place. Once at the back, you can complete the final few inches of the cut by pulling the narrow piece through the blade.

Essential Accessories

Tablesaws come from the factory with everything needed to start making ripcuts and crosscuts. But a few important accessories improve both the safety and the accuracy of the saw.

OUTFEED SUPPORT

There's not much distance between the back of the blade and the back of the saw table. As a result, boards can end up falling off the back of the saw at the end of a cut. Also, when ripping a long board, you must bear down hard to prevent it from tipping off the back at the end of the cut. That's not something you want to do with your hand passing near the blade. So it's important to have some sort of auxiliary support at the back of the saw. A sturdy table is best, but even a support stand will help.

PUSH BLOCKS

When making a ripcut less than about 8 in. wide, a push block or push stick is a must to keep your fingers a reasonably safe distance from the blade. A typical push stick holds down little more than the trailing end. Instead, I prefer a push block (right) because it provides downward pressure along its full length. That way, the board is less likely to flutter and, more important, is less susceptible to kickback. It takes just a few minutes to make a push block. Use any ¾-in.- or 1-in.-thick stock and cut it to shape with a bandsaw or sabersaw.

ZERO-CLEARANCE INSERT

A stock blade insert typically has a wide opening, which is fine for bevel cuts or wide ripcuts. However, narrow rippings can drop down through the opening in the insert, endangering your pushing hand as it drops toward a spinning sawblade. To avoid this, I use a zero-clearance insert for almost all of my cuts. Most woodworking mail-order catalogs sell inserts made from phenolic plastic and precut to fit most any make and model of saw. Or you can cut your own from plywood.

Ripping

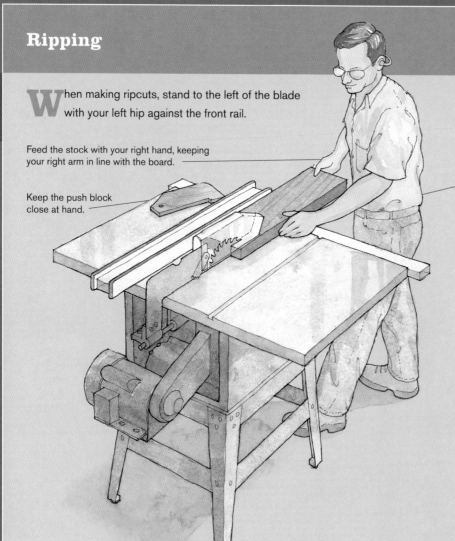

When making ripcuts, stand to the left of the blade with your left hip against the front rail.

Feed the stock with your right hand, keeping your right arm in line with the board.

Keep the push block close at hand.

Apply enough downward pressure on your left hand to keep your palm anchored to the table. Then push with your middle finger and forefinger to keep the board against the fence. Once the end of the board has moved past your left hand, it is a good habit to remove that hand from the saw table.

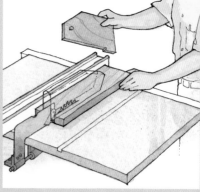

2. Once the trailing end of the board reaches the front of the table, use the push block to feed the board.

A SIMPLE RIPCUT

Most tablesaw accidents occur during ripping. By following a few basic techniques, you'll not only get good-quality cuts but you'll also get them with a better degree of safety.

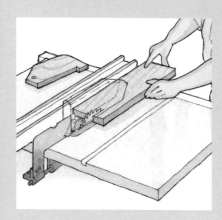

1. Place the front end of the board on the saw. Then, with the edge of the board against the rip fence, feed the board into the blade at a steady rate. If the motor slows down, slow the feed rate.

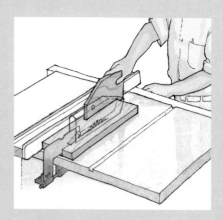

3. Continue pushing the trailing end of the board with the push block until the board is an inch or two past the sawblade.

RIPPING NARROW BOARDS

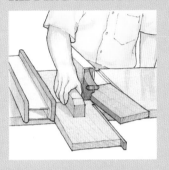

When ripping parts less than about 1¼ in. wide, use a notched sled, guided by the rip fence, to push the stock through the blade. A handle makes for easier pushing.

A shopmade L-shaped fence mounted to the rip fence creates extra space between the blade cover and the rip fence, making it easier to feed the stock, especially when a tall push block is used.

RIPPING LARGE PANELS

Full-size (4 ft. by 8 ft.) sheets of plywood and other sheet goods are heavy and awkward to handle, which make them a chore to cut. But with a little forethought and practice, the procedure can be reasonably straightforward.

1. Place the leading edge of the sheet on the front of the saw with the back end resting on the floor.

2. Stand at the left corner of the sheet with your body more alongside the left edge than the end. From that position it's easier to hold the edge of the sheet against the rip fence. When making the cut, both arms should be comfortably outstretched with your left arm along the left edge and your right arm on the end.

3. As you feed the sheet and begin to approach the front of the saw, shift your body more to the end of the sheet. Once at the front of the table, assume your normal starting stance to complete the cut. Have a helper support the other end of the sheet.

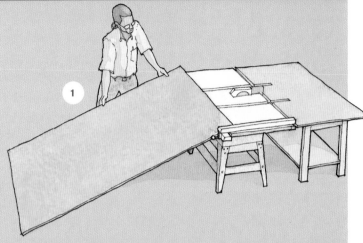

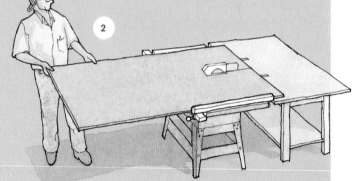

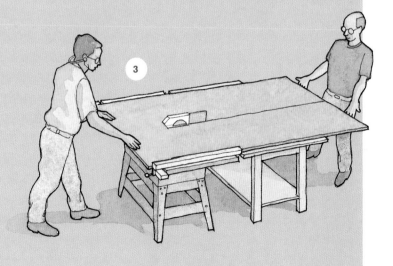

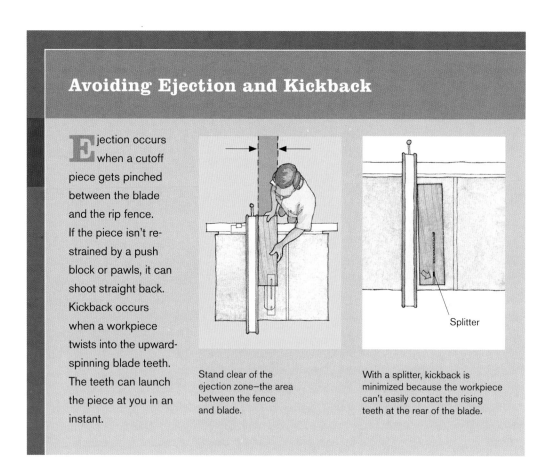

Avoiding Ejection and Kickback

Ejection occurs when a cutoff piece gets pinched between the blade and the rip fence. If the piece isn't restrained by a push block or pawls, it can shoot straight back. Kickback occurs when a workpiece twists into the upward-spinning blade teeth. The teeth can launch the piece at you in an instant.

Stand clear of the ejection zone—the area between the fence and blade.

Splitter

With a splitter, kickback is minimized because the workpiece can't easily contact the rising teeth at the rear of the blade.

Use a Firm Grip While Crosscutting

The most common crosscut is made with the miter gauge set at 90° to the miter-gauge slot, resulting in a square cut. However, consistently smooth, square crosscuts don't happen automatically. You need to follow a few basic procedures.

Position the Board on the Miter Gauge

Place the board on the saw table. Use your left hand to hold the board against the miter-gauge fence and slide the gauge forward with your right hand until the leading edge of the board almost touches the blade. At this point, use one or two hands as needed to align the sawblade with the cut line on the board.

Push the Board through the Blade

When everything is aligned, use your left hand to hold the board firmly against the miter-gauge fence until the cut is completed. The holding force you apply should

be straight back, and your fingers should be at least 6 in. from the blade cover. Slide the board an inch or two away from the blade before starting the saw. Use your right hand to push the gauge toward the back of the saw, and feed the board at a steady speed. Stop pushing once the cut is finished, but continue to hold the board firmly against the miter-gauge fence.

Pull Back the Board Once the board has been cut, continue to hold the board firmly against the fence, and pull both the board and the gauge back to the starting position. Once back to the starting point, you can relax your hold on the board and shut off the saw.

Oftentimes, as the board and miter gauge are pulled back, the spinning blade will slightly touch the cut edge of the board and cause a little extra splintering. To avoid the problem—and if the board is small and light enough—I'll use my left hand to shift

Crosscutting

The starting position for a square crosscut is about the same as the one used for ripping. Stand in front of the miter gauge with your left hip against the front rail.

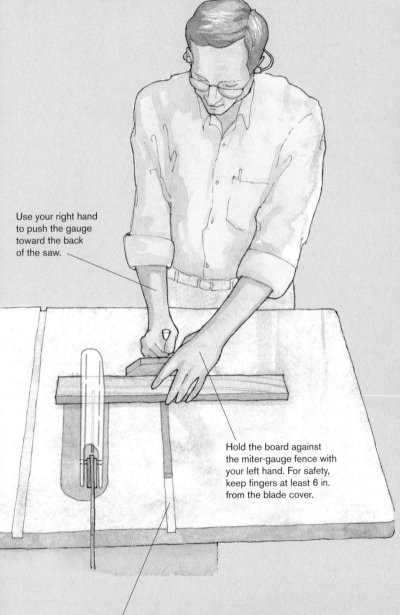

Use your right hand to push the gauge toward the back of the saw.

Hold the board against the miter-gauge fence with your left hand. For safety, keep fingers at least 6 in. from the blade cover.

The miter gauge works just as well in either of the two miter slots. But because most people are right-handed, the majority of tablesaw users push the miter gauge with their right hand, so the gauge has to go into the left slot.

A SIMPLE CROSSCUT

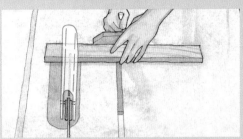

1. Keep the board away from the blade (an inch or two) before starting the saw. Push the miter gauge with your right hand, feeding the board at a steady speed. Stop pushing after the cut, but continue to hold the board against the fence.

2. To avoid having the spinning blade touch the cut edge of the board when the miter gauge is pulled back to the starting position, possibly causing a little extra splintering, it's best to shift the board away from the blade slightly.

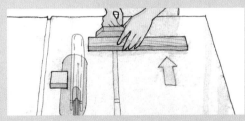

3. While holding the board against the fence, pull both the board and the gauge back to the starting position. Then shut off the saw.

REPEAT CUTS FOR LONG PARTS

When you're cutting several boards to the same length, a stop block clamped to the auxiliary miter-gauge fence will ensure uniformity. First, cut one end square on each piece. After that, clamp the stop block to the fence, making sure the distance from the block to the blade matches the length you want. Then, one piece at a time, butt the square end of the board against the block and make the cut.

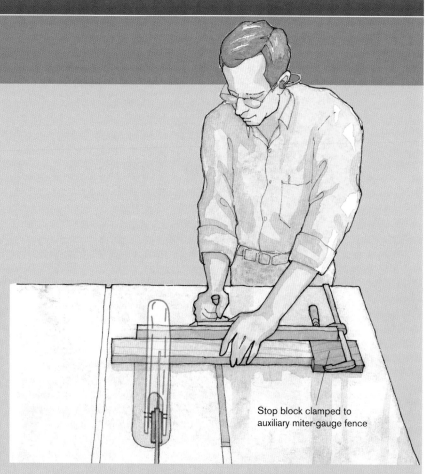

Stop block clamped to auxiliary miter-gauge fence

REPEAT CUTS FOR SHORT PARTS

To save time, clamp a stop block to the rip fence when you need to cut several short pieces of wood to the same length. Position the fence so that the distance from the block to the blade equals the needed length measurement. To avoid binding the cutoff piece between the blade and the stop block, which could cause kickback, the block must be far enough in front of the blade so that the board isn't touching the block during the cut.

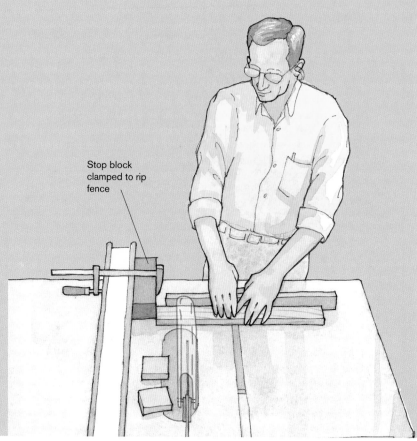

Stop block clamped to rip fence

Use an Auxiliary Fence to Crosscut Long Boards

A typical miter-gauge fence is relatively short, so it doesn't offer a lot of support to long boards. An easy solution is to screw a long auxiliary wood fence to the miter-gauge fence. You can make the wood fence to any length, but just be sure it's flat and straight.

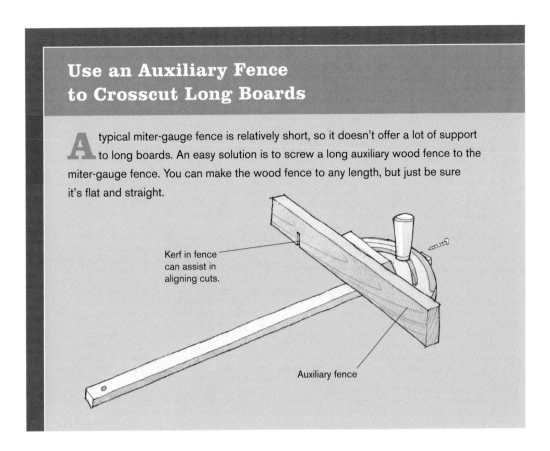

Kerf in fence can assist in aligning cuts.

Auxiliary fence

the board ⅛ in. to ¼ in. away from the blade before pulling it back. Bigger and heavier boards, however, won't move as easily. So if I'm cutting a big board while in splinter-phobic mode, I simply shut off the saw before removing the board and pulling back the gauge.

Add a Stop Block to the Rip Fence When Cutting Several Short Pieces to the Same Length
It's not uncommon to need several short pieces of the same length. In that case, clamp a stop block to the rip fence with the fence positioned so that the distance from the block to the blade equals the desired workpiece length. To avoid kickback, the block must be far enough from the blade so that the board isn't touching the block when the piece is cut free.

Add a Stop Block to the Auxiliary Miter-Gauge Fence When Cutting Longer Boards to the Same Length
Make sure the distance from the block to the blade matches the length you want. First, though, using only the auxiliary fence, cut one end of each board square. Then butt the square end of each board against the block and cut one piece at a time.

Another versatile jig that gets a lot of use in my shop is the crosscut sled. The sled makes crosscutting even more accurate and safe.

Once you've mastered the basic techniques of ripping and crosscutting, you'll be ready to tackle the other various tasks suitable for the tablesaw, such as cutting miters, tenons, and tapers.

KELLY MEHLER is also the author of *The Table Saw Book* (The Taunton Press, 2002).

Tablesaw
Tune-Up

BY ROLAND JOHNSON

COMMON TABLESAW PROBLEMS

Tablesaws are so sturdy and powerful that they seem not to need any special attention. But like any complex tool, they can develop a variety of problems that erode performance. Keeping your saw clean, lubricated, and properly adjusted will make the machine safer, more accurate, and easier to use.

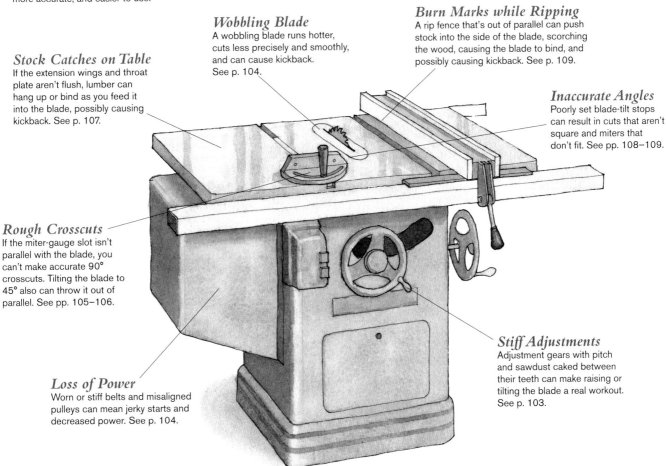

Wobbling Blade
A wobbling blade runs hotter, cuts less precisely and smoothly, and can cause kickback. See p. 104.

Burn Marks while Ripping
A rip fence that's out of parallel can push stock into the side of the blade, scorching the wood, causing the blade to bind, and possibly causing kickback. See p. 109.

Stock Catches on Table
If the extension wings and throat plate aren't flush, lumber can hang up or bind as you feed it into the blade, possibly causing kickback. See p. 107.

Inaccurate Angles
Poorly set blade-tilt stops can result in cuts that aren't square and miters that don't fit. See pp. 108–109.

Rough Crosscuts
If the miter-gauge slot isn't parallel with the blade, you can't make accurate 90° crosscuts. Tilting the blade to 45° also can throw it out of parallel. See pp. 105–106.

Loss of Power
Worn or stiff belts and misaligned pulleys can mean jerky starts and decreased power. See p. 104.

Stiff Adjustments
Adjustment gears with pitch and sawdust caked between their teeth can make raising or tilting the blade a real workout. See p. 103.

Ask woodworkers to name the busiest tool in their shop, and it's a safe bet many will point to the tablesaw. A machine that can rip sheet goods down to size, cut boards to length, and create a variety of joints is bound to carry part of the workload in almost any project.

Yet in many woodshops, tablesaw maintenance consists of little more than changing blades, cleaning the tabletop, and squaring fences. Only when the blade-tilt or -raise mechanism starts to screech in protest does anything beneath the table get attention.

Our shop workhorse deserves better. A yearly inspection and tune-up should be a basic requirement; saws kept in damp or unheated conditions should be cleaned and lubricated more often. The comprehensive tune-up presented here is basically the same for all tablesaws. Check your owner's manual for any details that might differ.

Clean and Lubricate the Inner Workings

On most cabinet saws, removing the tabletop exposes the inner workings and makes a tune-up much easier.

First, unplug the saw, then remove the throat plate and the blade to avoid damaging the blade or yourself. Measure and record the distance from the left-hand miter

TO GET INSIDE, remove the motor and—with a friend's help—turn the unit upside down on a low bench or short sawhorses. You also might need to remove a bottom panel, as on this saw.

Remember, when using volatile solvents, make sure you have an adequate fresh-air supply and wear a vapor mask.

Finish the cleaning process with a compressed-air blowdown to speed drying and remove crud softened by the solvent. The overall goal in all of these steps is to clear away as much dust and pitch as possible, leaving clean, dry surfaces for an effective lube job. Be sure the solvent is completely cleaned out or dry before applying new lube to the contact surfaces.

Before moving on, give some attention to the motor. Blow compressed air through the housing until the exhaust air is clean.

LUBRICATION CHART

Orange indicates high-wear areas that require heavy-duty lubricant and yellow indicates hard-to-reach areas that require a penetrating lubricant.

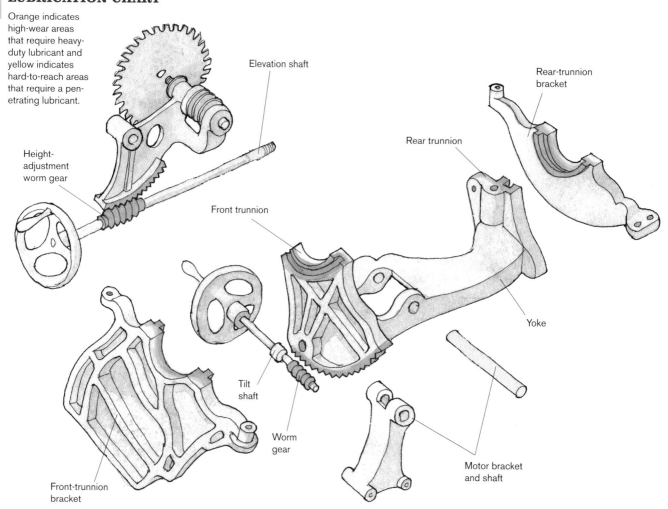

Elevation shaft

Rear-trunnion bracket

Rear trunnion

Height-adjustment worm gear

Front trunnion

Yoke

Tilt shaft

Worm gear

Motor bracket and shaft

Front-trunnion bracket

Lubrication Tips

CLEAN BEFORE LUBRICATING

TO HELP REMOVE MINOR PITCH BUILDUP and rid the gears of old grease, use a quick-drying aerosol degreaser and scrub with a wire brush. Surfaces need to be clean and dry before lubricants can adhere well and do their work.

TYPES OF LUBRICANTS

ON THE WORM GEARS AND RACKS, use a molybdenum-based drying lube. The spray, which withstands heavy pressure, is dense enough to stay in place without running.

USE A PENETRATING LUBRICANT ON HARD-TO-REACH AREAS. For the worm-gear shafts on the arbor-pivot and -raising assemblies, Johnson uses a penetrating spray that dries quickly.

Check the Arbor and Bearings

If you are experiencing a wobbling blade or excessive vibration, use a dial gauge with a magnetic base to check the arbor for runout —imperfections in the straightness of the shaft or the flatness of the blade-mounting flange connected to it. An arbor with excessive runout will cause the blade to wobble. This robs power, heats up the blade, and can increase the chance of kickback.

This check can be done before or after the top is removed, as long as there is a stable surface on which to mount the dial

CHECK FOR RUNOUT. Set the pointer of the dial indicator perpendicular to the rim of the arbor flange. Rotate the flange to check for variations in flatness.

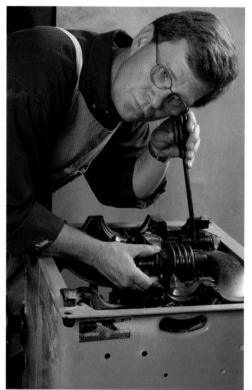

AN OLD HOT-RODDER'S TRICK. A long screwdriver, with the tip held firmly on the bearing housing, makes a good listening device for checking the condition of the bearings.

ALIGN THE PULLEYS. Use a length of drill rod or other straightedge to determine whether the motor and arbor pulleys are aligned with one another.

gauge. Start by tilting the arbor to 45°, which makes it easier to reach.

Take and compare several measurements from both the inner face of the arbor flange and from the nonthreaded portion of the arbor shaft. Turn the arbor to get readings from different points. There should be no variation at all in measurements taken from the shaft itself. Acceptable runout on the arbor flange is a maximum of 0.0015 in.

If the arbor shows runout, replacing it is the best option, but check the bearings first to make sure they're not causing the problem. It's a good idea to check them anyway.

With the belts removed, turn the arbor shaft by hand and listen to the bearings. The sound should be smooth and rolling, and the shaft should turn freely. If there is a dry or scraping sound, or even slight roughness in their operation, replace the bearings. Doing so is inexpensive and easy, and will greatly increase the life and performance of your saw.

You can order replacement bearings from the tablesaw manufacturer or check a local automotive-supply house or machine shop. Once you've removed the arbor assembly, all that's needed to remove the old bearings and install the new ones is an arbor press. Machine shops, electric-motor repair shops, and even most automotive-repair shops will have an arbor press and the expertise to use it.

To replace the arbor, check with the manufacturer for a new part. If the saw is out of production, search old-tool Web sites for a used or old-stock arbor. As an expensive last resort for a saw that's really worth saving, a machine shop could make a replacement arbor.

Loss of Power

Start by checking belts and pulley alignment. Use a length of drill rod or other straightedge to determine whether the motor and arbor pulleys are aligned with one another.

THE PULLEYS ON A CONTRACTOR'S SAW ARE MUCH FARTHER APART, **increasing the chance of unwanted vibration. On many older saws, performance can be improved by installing a high-quality segmented belt and a good pair of machined and balanced pulleys.**

On most cabinet saws, three short belts transfer power from the motor to the arbor. Misalignment can make the belts drag on the pulley, robbing power, building up heat, and wearing out the belts. Replace worn or stiff belts as a matched set to ensure that all three share the load.

To check pulley alignment, I lay a straightedge across the side of one pulley and check how squarely—if at all—it meets the surface of the other wheel. Make adjustments by first loosening the setscrews that hold the motor pulley to its shaft. Carefully pry the pulley away from the motor or use a deadblow hammer to tap it farther onto the shaft.

Use care: Excessive force could damage the motor's armature bearings. Once alignment is accurate, tighten the setscrews.

Poor Quality Crosscuts?

One common tablesaw problem happens when the blade is not running parallel to the miter slots. In such a situation, if the miter gauge is set to 0° for a 90° crosscut, the actual cut won't be accurate.

To check for parallel, I use a dial micrometer mounted on a modified miter gauge or hardwood runner in the left-hand miter slot. This is the time to retrieve that baseline measurement of the miter-slot distance that you made before removing the top. Adjust the table position to set the miter slot to that original measurement.

With the blade at full height, mark a tooth at the front. Measure from this tooth to the miter slot, then rotate the tooth to the back of the throat opening and measure again. Adjust the tabletop (or the trunnions on a contractor's saw) to bring the measurements in line. Repeat the parallel-checking

ADJUSTING THE TABLETOP.
A sandwich of plastic (plywood may be substituted) and steel, screwed to a wooden runner, creates a sliding platform for the micrometer's magnetic base (1). Use the micrometer to measure the distance from the miter slot to the front and rear of the blade (2). Measurements should differ by 0.005 in. or less. Snug the tabletop bolts, then use a deadblow hammer to make minute adjustments to the top (3).

CHECK AGAIN FOR PARALLEL. After bringing the miter-gauge slot parallel with the blade, tilt the blade to 45° and repeat the process.

LEVEL THE TOP. On a cabinet saw, place shims between the top and the flange on the base.

process with the blade set at 45°, shimming the top or trunnions if needed. Then recheck for parallel at 90°. Sometimes this will take a few cycles before both positions are parallel. When you reach nirvana, tighten the bolts and recheck once more.

Level the Tabletop

Experiencing poor-quality miters? If the blade is parallel to the miter slot at 90° but not at 45°, it means the table is out of level from front to back. Shim the top (or the trunnions on a contractor's saw) to compensate. I use automotive alignment shims and brass sheet stock. I buy ¹⁄₆₄-in.

LEVEL THE THROAT PLATE. Adjust the riser screws in the throat plate to align it with the saw top.

and 1/32-in. alignment shims and sheets of 0.005-in., 0.010-in., and 0.015-in. brass for a combination that results in very accurate adjustments.

Level the Wings and Throat Plate

Feeding lumber over the saw is easier and safer when the throat plate and extension wings (and extension table) are flush to the saw table. Lifting a hung-up board to clear the tabletop can cause a jam, possibly resulting in a ruined cut or dangerous kickback.

Some throat plates can be raised or lowered with setscrews, so a straightedge and Allen wrench are all you need to align the surfaces. A homemade plate can be shimmed with masking tape or trimmed flush with a block plane, if needed.

To adjust an extension wing or table, very slightly loosen the mounting bolts and tap the surfaces flush with a deadblow hammer. Check with a straightedge, tighten the bolts, and check again to make sure everything stayed put.

Adjust the 45° and 90° Stops

Virtually all tablesaws have adjustable devices that stop the arbor assembly when

LEVEL THE WINGS. Use a straightedge to check whether the extension wings are flush and parallel with the top (above). If necessary, shim the wing with brass sheet stock (left) until it is parallel with the tabletop.

LEVELING THE WINGS

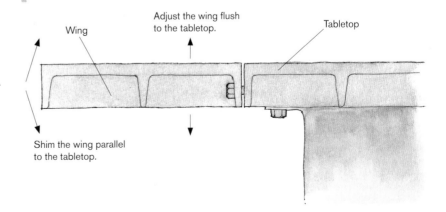

Wing

Adjust the wing flush to the tabletop.

Tabletop

Shim the wing parallel to the tabletop.

Clean and Coat the Tabletop

After all the mechanical components are operating in harmony, it's a good idea to dress the tabletop. Start with a thorough cleaning, using a spray solvent. Then polish with a fine-grit Scotch-Brite™ nylon pad or 600-grit sandpaper mounted on a wood block. Finish with a coat of nonsilicone wax or one of the topcoatings designed specifically for this purpose. I use Bostik® TopCote®, applying a couple of coats. I apply another coat whenever I notice the wood starting to drag as I feed it over the table.

SETTING THE BLADE UPRIGHT. The 90° stop is usually easy to reach. Simply loosen the stop bolt and use a square to set the blade to exactly 90°. Then turn the stop bolt snug to the stop, and tighten the locknut on the stop bolt.

the blade is perpendicular to the table and when it's tilted at 45°. Most often these devices consist of a bolt and locknut mounted on the arbor-carriage assembly.

On the saw table we tuned up, the stop bolts are mounted on the front-trunnion assembly. The 45° tilt can be accessed through the slot on the front of the cabinet that is for the blade-lift crank handle. The 90° stop can be reached through the motor opening in the side of the cabinet.

To adjust the stops, set the blade to the desired angle, loosen the locknut, and then retighten it after repositioning the stop bolt. I use a plastic 45° drafting triangle to set the tilt angle and a 6-in. sliding square to set the 90° stop. Always recheck after tightening the locknut to make sure the adjustment stayed accurate.

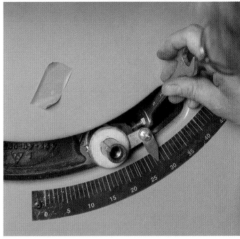

Adjust the Rip Fence Parallel to the Blade

If you find you're getting burn marks while ripping, one of the last adjustments you should perform is to set the rip fence parallel with the miter slot and thus parallel with the blade. Some woodworkers angle the fence a few degrees away from the back of the blade to help avoid binding. I like to keep things parallel and rely on a well-tuned saw and stable, well-dried lumber to keep me out of trouble.

The sides of the fence also should be checked with a reliable square for an accurate 90° to the tabletop. Some fences don't have an easy means of adjustment. One solution is to attach a supplemental wood fence that is beveled or shimmed square to the saw table.

ROLAND JOHNSON is a contributing editor to *Fine Woodworking.*

SOME CONTRACTOR'S SAWS ALLOW ADJUSTMENT via setscrews on the saw's top. Most saws, however, require you to reach in from underneath (left) to access the stops.

Tablesaw
Kickback

BY GARRETT HACK

On the first day of class I ask my woodworking students if they've had a kickback on the tablesaw. I always get a fair number of hands in the air, but few of the students can tell me what happened. And often those who have had the unsettling experience of carving a nice, deep furrow in a piece of wood and having it fly across the shop don't usually know what caused it. It all happens so fast that it's over by the time they realize it's occurred.

Before I let my students get near a tablesaw, I do a little dog-and-pony show to demonstrate the dangers of kickback. Using Styrofoam® to represent a piece of plywood, I show how the cut should be made and then what occurs if the piece drifts away from the rip fence. Crouching out of the flight path, I simply let go of the piece for a second, and off it goes.

A kickback occurs when the leading corner of a piece being cut rotates away from the rip fence. The piece then gets caught up between the back of the blade and the fence. As the back of the blade—the part that cuts upward—begins to gnaw into the freshly cut edge of the piece, the piece quickly rotates, getting caught diagonally between the fence and the blade. The corner of the piece closest to the operator and against the rip fence is the pivot point

In a Blink of an Eye, You Have Trouble

1. The author stands in a normal position to begin the cut, but for demonstration purposes, he moves out of the way before allowing the workpiece to kick back. Do not try this yourself.

2. As the piece veers slightly away from the fence, it binds up between the fence and the blade. Though the gap between the fence and the piece is too small for the camera to pick up, it is enough to cause plenty of trouble. The back of the blade lifts the piece off the table, with the back corner of the piece (against the fence and closest to the operator) acting as a pivot point.

3. The piece rides across the spinning blade and is catapulted into the air.

4. With a few horsepower of force behind it, the piece bullets across the room until it crashes into something. The author would have risked being hit had he stood where an operator normally stands.

5. The crescent shape on a piece that kicks back is the result of the piece riding across the top of the spinning blade. Using a splitter almost eliminates the chance of this happening.

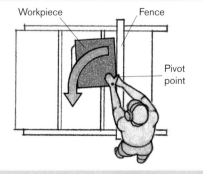

Workpiece   Fence

Pivot point

A Shopmade Splitter

KELLY MEHLER

Most woodworkers understand the importance of a zero-clearance insert and either buy blanks or make their own. To add a splitter to one of these inserts, I just glue a piece of wood into the slot behind the blade. The splitter stock should be the same thickness as the blade and should fit in the mating slot the raised blade cuts in the throat plate. The splitter is most effective when it is placed closest to the back of the blade. Because the blade progresses toward the back of the insert as it is raised for thicker cuts, I suggest at least two inserts—one for cutting thin stock, up to about 1 in., and another for thick stock.

To make an insert for thick stock, you must elongate the slot by flipping the insert end for end and then raising the blade. This allows you to place the splitter farther back on the insert. I always drill a finger hole in the insert for easy removal. A short adjustment screw can be embedded into the side and/or end of the insert to take up any play in the fit, and the splitter can be sanded.

The important thing is to align the right edge of the splitter with the right side of the blade (the side closest to the fence). This keeps the workpiece against the fence for a smoother cut. Also, it virtually eliminates the chance of kickback.

I make the splitter by slicing a piece of hardwood and trimming it until I get a tight fit in the slot. Then I glue it in place. I make my splitters out of hardwood, but there is no reason why they could not be made of aluminum, plastic or any other durable material.

KELLY MEHLER is a woodworker in Berea, Kentucky, and the author of *The Table Saw Book* (The Taunton Press, 1993).

---

around which a radius cut is made. The piece then acts like a pole-vaulter. Rotating further and moving faster now, the piece rides up and over the blade and is hurtled into the air to the left side of the blade. If you're lucky, it will fly over your left shoulder. If you're not lucky, a board with a few horsepower of force behind it will hit you. This is also why it is such a bad idea to stand to the left of the operator and watch him or her work.

Afterward, you'll usually spot a crescent-shaped cut on the bottom of the piece. This crescent cut is the result of the piece rotating as it crosses over the top of the blade. It's as if you had drawn a circle with a compass, putting the center point at the corner closest to the operator and against the fence.

Certain types of cuts are more prone to kickback than others. A square piece being trimmed is the most likely to cause trouble, because any drift away from the fence will cause the piece to bind. Any piece cut against the rip fence that is either square or rectangular (with a width approaching at least half or more of its length) is a very hazardous cut. Typically troublesome pieces are drawer bottoms and small parts.

But if the piece is kept solidly against the rip fence and pushed all the way through the cut and beyond the blade, it's unlikely that a kickback will occur. Keep

SIMPLE BUT SAFE. A splitter is essential to any safe shop, but it doesn't have to cost a thing. Flip a zero-clearance insert end for end and raise the blade to elongate the slot. Fit a piece of hardwood tightly into the slot and then glue it in place.

your eyes on the rip fence just past the blade to make sure the piece is firmly in contact with the fence throughout the cut. The critical time is often just after the front of the blade has cut all the way through the piece. The waste lies on the table rattling against the blade, distracting you from the very real task of keeping the piece firmly against the rip fence until it is well past the blade. A moment's inattention and…

After the class understands the danger of kickback, I repeat the operation with the splitter and blade guard in place. When I let go this time, nothing happens. Then I use a push stick to force the piece away from the rip fence and into the blade.

Again, nothing happens. This is because the splitter prevents the rotation of the piece away from the fence.

Kickbacks can be prevented. They are virtually impossible with an antikickback splitter in place. The splitter keeps the stock solidly against the rip fence and prevents any rotation toward the blade. Without this rotation, kickback is virtually unheard of. Use the splitter that came with your saw, buy an after-market splitter, or make one (see the story at above); but don't make cuts on the tablesaw without one.

GARRETT HACK, a contributing editor to *Fine Woodworking*, makes furniture on his Vermont farm.

Tablesaw Splitters and Blade Covers

BY KELLY MEHLER

Standard tablesaw guard systems in the United States are no good. There, somebody has said it. Nearly every woodworker knows this, but we all have to listen to the experts remind us in books, magazines, and on television to use our guards. They have removed the guards on their tablesaws, they tell us, so we can better see the operations they are demonstrating. Nonsense. The reason why they and so many woodworkers discard standard guards is because they are inconvenient.

Underwriters Laboratory® recommends that a splitter, antikickback fingers, and a blade cover be included on every tablesaw sold in the United States. American manufacturers combine these components into a three-in-one system that bolts to the saw's carriage assembly. This combination system severely limits the flexibility of the machine. So it usually is cast aside in a dark corner of the shop, collecting dust.

Among the problems with the three-in-one system is that the user is limited to making through-cuts. Because the splitter sits higher than the blade, any partial cut such as a groove or a joint can't be done without removing the entire system. Use of crosscut sleds and other jigs is also impossible with the system in place. So it

comes off. But taking off these systems and putting them back on in perfect alignment with the blade is neither quick nor easy.

Making matters worse is the fact that if anything gets in the way—the cover, the splitter, or the antikickback fingers—the entire system must be removed. Today you can buy splitters and blade covers that attach separately, and one can remain in place doing its job when the other must be removed.

Because most three-in-one systems won't stay up when lifted, common tasks around the blade are difficult to perform (such as measuring to the rip fence, checking the blade height and changing the blade). And ripping narrow work is difficult if not impossible with a standard blade cover in place.

European saws provide the best solution for tablesaw safety: a splitter that sits just below the level of the top of the blade and never has to be removed. Mounted to the arbor assembly, it moves up and down and also tilts with the blade. The blade cover is usually narrow and unobtrusive, can be removed easily and provides for efficient dust collection. However, for an American tablesaw, the best option is to purchase these safety devices as accessories.

Why You Need a Splitter and Blade Cover

In my opinion, using a tablesaw without appropriate guarding at the blade is not an option. You may be very clever in how you avoid danger on the saw, but without the two most important safety devices—a splitter and a blade cover—you are relying on your wits alone to prevent catastrophe. One thoughtless moment when you are tired, daydreaming, or in a hurry, and disaster could strike. According to an esti-mate by the U.S. Consumer Product Safety Commission, there were more than 30,000 emergency-room admittances for tablesaw-related injuries in 1999. Many such incidents can be avoided by using a splitter and blade cover.

Add-on splitters and blade covers are much more convenient than standard equipment and are, therefore, more likely to be used. Getting comfortable with them on my machine was no more trouble than getting used to putting on a seat belt.

HOW A SPLITTER WORKS

As the workpiece encounters cutting forces at the front of the blade, it tends to rotate toward the rising teeth at the back. A splitter impedes this motion, virtually eliminating kickback.

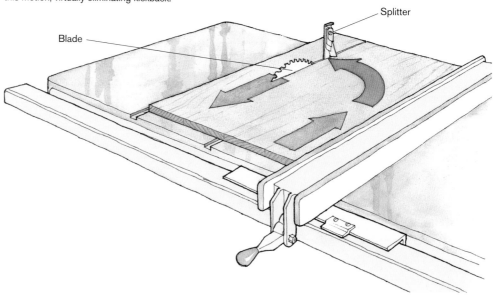

Splitter

Blade

A Splitter Should Be Your Priority A splitter is the most important piece of safety equipment because it virtually eliminates the potential for kickback—both the most common and the most vicious tablesaw accident.

Workpieces tend to rotate onto the back of the tablesaw blade, where they can be lifted and thrown toward the user at up to 120 mph. Most woodworkers have a story of a near-miss, and horrific accidents are not uncommon.

The splitter forms a barrier to this rotation (see the drawing above). Without the specter of kickback always looming in the background, the user can work faster and with greater peace of mind (and a brighter future).

The splitter would be more aptly called an antikickback plate. On the other hand, the antikickback fingers, or pawls, included on most splitters are misnamed and are unnecessary equipment, in my opinion. They don't prevent kickback but occasionally prevent what I call "pushback," in which

the blade pushes the workpiece straight back. And they can't even serve that minor function consistently.

Three Splitters

Most American tablesaws are able to support a splitter retrofit, with the exception of benchtop portables. There currently are four splitters available. However, because of differences among machines, not every splitter fits every saw. For instance, Delta makes two of the three choices, and Delta splitters are made to fit Delta tablesaws. On the other hand, Biesemeyer™ produces models that fit a wider range of saws. Excalibur® makes a splitter that fits many, but not all, saws.

Biesemeyer Splitter Is Solid and Adaptable Biesemeyer's Anti-Kickback Snap-In Spreader fits many tablesaws, both American and imported. The Biesemeyer has a cast-iron holder that attaches to the cradle assembly of a tablesaw. It has a solid feel resulting from its hefty holder and thick splitter. However, the almost ⅛-in.-thick splitter will not work with thin-kerf blades.

Delta's Disappearing Splitter is Easy To Use

The Disappearing Splitter was designed to fit the right-tilting Delta Unisaw® as part of its Uniguard® Blade Guard. The Uniguard has been discontinued in favor of the Deluxe Blade Guard, but the Disappearing Splitter is still available.

What I have always liked about the Disappearing Splitter is its ease of use. It never has to be removed from the saw. The splitter simply is pushed down and out of the way.

Thin-kerf blades can be used with the Disappearing Splitter, but the splitter's thin and narrow body also allow it to be easily bent. This calls for caution when handling large or heavy workpieces. Another drawback of this splitter is that it fits only Delta Unisaws, and only right-tilting models.

Delta's Latest Fits More Models

The newer Delta Removable Splitter fits all Delta cabinet and contractor tablesaws and Jet® Cabinet Saws. Delta designed this removable splitter to go with its Deluxe Blade Guard, but the splitter is available separately.

This splitter is removed from its holder by loosening the large, round knob that clamps it in place. While not as convenient to remove as the other two, this splitter still is easy to use. Like the Delta Disappearing Splitter, the Removable Splitter can be used with thin-kerf blades. It is slightly wider than the Disappearing Splitter and not as prone to bending.

Merlin Splitter Fits Widest Range of Saws

The Merlin Splitter is a large, thin metal fin that somewhat resembles a typical stock splitter. Because of its size, it's more intrusive than other splitters for some operations. One of its biggest advantages is that it fits a lot of saws, including some models by Craftsman, General®, and Powermatic®.

Although the initial installation took some time, it's easy to remove and reinstall during use.

Splitter Recommendations

It's critical that you select the splitter that is the most convenient for you and your machine.

The Delta Disappearing Splitter and the Biesemeyer Anti-Kickback Snap-In Spreader are similar in price, but they both have limitations. The Disappearing Splitter is the most convenient but fits only the right-tilting Unisaw. The heavy-duty Biesemeyer comes closer to the blade than the Disappearing Splitter, reducing the likelihood of kickback, but it must be removed from time to time. The newer Delta Removable Splitter isn't as easy to remove and replace as the others, but it is by far the least expensive. The Merlin Splitter fits a lot of saws, but it's somewhat large, and it's not cheap. The bottom line is that I would use any one of these splitters on my tablesaw, as long as it fit my machine and blade thickness.

Six Blade Covers

The blade cover does not protect against kickback; however, it does present a barrier between the user's hands and the spinning blade, preventing accidental contact.

All six blade covers available have many advantages over stock covers. First, each of these covers is separate from the splitter, allowing it to be moved out of the way without affecting kickback protection. Also, each interferes minimally with everyday cutting tasks because it easily can be moved out of the way and quickly dropped back into place.

Each of these covers allows for small horizontal adjustments; the blade can be tilted, and the cover can be offset to rip narrow pieces and let push sticks pass by. The covers also can be pushed to the far right of the table to make room for tall workpieces or jigs. And each cover can be removed for oversize work that requires an

It's critical that you select the splitter that is the most convenient for you and your machine.

Tablesaw Splitters

BIESEMEYER ANTI-KICKBACK SNAP-IN SPREADER

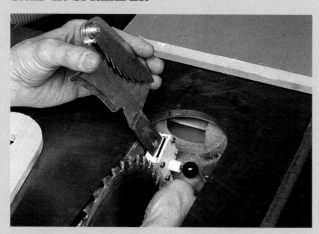

THE BIESEMEYER SPLITTER IS STURDY AND CONVENIENT.
A spring-loaded rod releases it and locks it precisely in position.

DELTA DISAPPEARING SPLITTER

THE DISAPPEARING SPLITTER NEVER HAS TO BE REMOVED,
making it the most convenient of the three. The splitter is simply pushed down below the table surface when not needed. However, it fits only right-tilting Delta Unisaws.

Model	Price*	Source
Biesemeyer Anti-Kickback Snap-In Spreader	$120	Biesemeyer 800-782-1831 www.biesemeyer.com
Delta Disappearing Splitter	$160 (part no. 34-868)	Delta 800-223-PART www.deltamachinery.com
Delta Removable Splitter	$29 (part no. 1349941)	Delta 800-223-PART www.deltamachinery.com
Merlin	$100	Excalibur 800-357-4118 www.excalibur-tools.com

DELTA REMOVABLE SPLITTER

KICKBACK PROTECTION FOR LESS MONEY. The Removable Splitter is separated from its holder by loosening a knob, making it slightly less convenient than the other units. It is included with the Delta Deluxe Blade Guard or can be purchased separately.

EXCALIBUR MERLIN

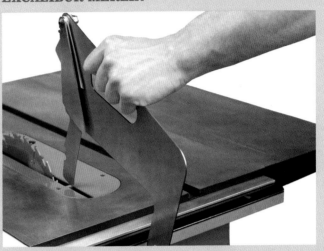

THE MERLIN SPLITTER hooks over an assembly at the rear, while the front clicks into a mount on the blade cartridge inside the saw.

Applications	Convenience	Durability	Comments
Delta and Jet cabinet and contractor's saws; Powermatic 72, 66, 64; General 350	Good	Excellent	Heavy duty but doesn't work with thin-kerf blades
Delta right-tilting Unisaws	Excellent	Adequate	Easiest to use but fits only right-titling Unisaws
All Delta cabinet and contractor saws	Adequate	Good	Included with Delta Deluxe Blade Guard
Certain Delta, Jet, General, Powermatic, and Craftsman saws	Good	Good	Fits widest range of saws, but intrusively large

Tablesaw Blade Covers

DELTA DELUXE BLADE GUARD WITH SPLITTER

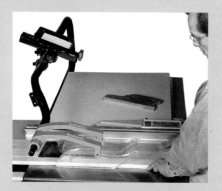

BIESEMEYER T-SQUARE BLADE GUARD SYSTEM

EXCALIBUR OVERARM BLADE COVER

THE SYSTEM INCLUDES THE DELTA REMOVABLE SPLITTER and features an innovative two-part blade cover. This complete system is a good value, though it doesn't offer dust collection.

THE BIESEMEYER BLADE COVER IS LIGHT, EASY TO USE AND OFFERS EXCELLENT VISIBILITY. But it's more expensive than most of the others, especially when dust collection is included.

THE EXCALIBUR IS A SOLID SYSTEM WITH EXCELLENT DUST COLLECTION. The cover can be locked in place anywhere up to 8 in. above the table.

Model	Price*	Source
Delta Deluxe Blade Guard with splitter	$250	Catalogs Delta 800-223-PART www.deltamachinery.com
Biesemeyer T-Square Blade Guard System	$400 (for 50-in. model)	Catalogs Biesemeyer 800-782-1831 www.biesemeyer.com
Excalibur Overarm Blade Cover	$380	Catalogs Sommerville Design & Mfg. 800-357-4118 www.excalibur-tools.com
Exaktor Industrial Overarm Blade Cover	$290	Exaktor 800-387-9789 www.exaktortools.com
Brett Guard, cantilever mount	$490	HTC Products 800-624-2027
Brett Guard, original mount	$280	HTC Products® 800-624-2027

EXAKTOR INDUSTRIAL OVERARM BLADE COVER

THE EXAKTOR BLADE COVER IS SIMILAR TO THE EXCALIBUR. However, the flat front on the cover doesn't ride up and over workpieces, and the extension arm is difficult to adjust.

BRETT GUARD, CANTILEVER MOUNT

THE BRETT GUARD IS HEAVY DUTY AND EASY TO USE. But using a splitter with it is problematic.

BRETT GUARD, ORIGINAL MOUNT

THE ORIGINAL BRETT GUARD MOUNTS ON THE SAW'S LEFT EDGE. It can be added to any saw, but its position limits cutting capacity on the left side of the saw table.

Applications	Convenience	Dust Collection	Comments
Works with Delta, Biesemeyer-style fences that don't utilize rear rail	Good	No	Comes with Delta Removable Splitter, accessory tray
Works with Delta, Biesemeyer-style fences that don't utilize rear rail, but ceiling and floor mounts are available	Excellent (after modification)	Yes ($95 extra)	Blade cover locks in upper position with one hand
All tablesaws with extension tables	Good	Yes	Mounting system puts stress on extension table; best dust collection
All tablesaws with extension tables	Fair	Yes	Similar to Excalibur with drawbacks, but better mounting system
All tablesaws with extension tables; accommodates only Delta Disappearing Splitter	Good	Yes (model with dust port is $39 extra)	Very heavy duty; comes with poor splitter
All tablesaws but accommodates only Disappearing Splitter	Good	No	Limits capacity on left side of saw table; comes with poor splitter

unusual amount of space. Four of the six covers offer dust collection.

Deluxe Blade Guard Is a Good Value for Delta Owners

The Delta Deluxe Blade Guard is designed for Delta tablesaws and fence systems. It will not work with fence systems that ride on a rear rail. According to Delta, you can cut off up to 12 in. on both the main support tube and the extension arm for mounting the assembly on a tablesaw that doesn't have a long extension table.

The extension arm doesn't move very far to the right of the blade, but it can be removed easily to make room for tall jigs or workpieces. For cutting very long and wide boards, the entire assembly can be rotated below the work surface after loosening a few mounting bolts.

Like the other blade covers, the cover for the Deluxe Blade Guard is a transparent, "basket" type. However, it is split into two, which allows one side of the cover to remain on the table, doing its job, while the other side may swivel up to allow a cutoff to pass underneath. There is no provision for dust collection, but this may not be a big consideration for those who collect dust from underneath the saw and haven't been using the blade cover anyway.

The Deluxe Blade Guard includes the Delta Removable Splitter and a plastic tray that mounts on the main support member and is designed to hold a note pad, tape measure, push stick, and the splitter when not in use. A light and a holder for the tablesaw's on/off switch are available as accessories.

Biesemeyer Is Well Designed, with One Exception

I tested one of the 50-in. models of the Biesemeyer T-Square® Blade Guard System, but larger and smaller sizes are also available. The support frame bolts to a Biesemeyer back fence rail (a back rail is available for those who don't have a Biesemeyer-style fence).

Four of the six covers offer dust collection.

I had only one problem with this system: the extension arm that allows the cover to be moved horizontally. To make lateral adjustments you must walk around the extension table to the end of the main support member to crank a long internal screw. While the latest models have a quick-release lever that frees the extension arm for a large, rapid move, I still found it inconvenient to go to the far end of the saw to release the screw. I solved the problem by removing the threaded rod altogether, which allows the cover to slide back and forth easily and then be locked in place, all without leaving the operating position.

The counterbalanced assembly lets the cover ride up and down easily over the workpiece while staying parallel to the surface. Also, it takes only one hand to lift the cover away from the blade (for measurements, for example), where it locks into place. A dust-collection kit is available for $95★ and consists of a 2-in. dust port and 10 ft. of heavy-duty 2-in. hose.

Excalibur's Blade Cover Fits All Saws with Extension Tables

The Excalibur Overarm Blade Cover is bolted directly to the side of the extension table, close to the back corner. Side attachment means that the Excalibur can be used with any fence system, because it won't interfere with rear fence rails. A lower support column extends to floor level, but there is no provision for attaching it to the floor. To stabilize the heavy boom and hold the main support arm parallel to the saw table, two metal braces triangulate from the lower column to points under the extension-table frame. The system puts a lot of torque on the end of the extension table, which can cause it to twist.

The blade cover attaches to steel support tubes that are also used for dust collection. The tube assembly is sealed for excellent efficiency. The blade cover is basically a metal frame with clear plastic panels. The rear panel can be removed to accommodate the tablesaw's original splitter or any retrofit splitter.

Exaktor Shares Features with Excalibur

The Exaktor Industrial Overarm Blade Cover is very similar to the Excalibur cover, with some exceptions. First, the front of the blade cover is not angled backward to allow the cover to ride easily over a workpiece. The user must either lift the blade cover onto the workpiece or lock it somewhere above the workpiece's thickness. Second, it takes two hands to both lift and push the inner support tube for side-to-side adjustments because the fit is a bit rough. Also, there is no channel in the main support boom to keep the smaller boom, which holds the hood, from rotating down when the locking knobs are loosened. And when the smaller tube rotates, the hood doesn't operate parallel to the table surface or workpiece.

Two slots at the rear of the blade cover accommodate a splitter. The trouble with having the splitter sit in a slot is that the cover cannot be slid to the left or right when pushing narrow pieces through the blade or when crosscutting using the miter gauge.

On the other hand, the Exaktor is less expensive than the Excalibur, and its mounting system is sturdier, so it places less stress on the extension table. The blade-cover assembly can be purchased separately for ceiling or other custom installations.

Brett Guards Are in Their Own Category

The Brett Guards differ from the other systems in the blade cover itself. Instead of a basket-type cover, a Brett Guard has a thick but shallow plastic box connected to a control housing that is adjusted manually. Unlike gravity-type covers, it presents a fixed barrier that does not ride up and over the workpiece on its own. While this thick, sturdy cover can hold down a workpiece,

providing some kickback protection, it also leaves the blade somewhat exposed after the workpiece has passed.

There are two types of Brett Guards, both manufactured by HTC. The original Brett Guard attaches to the left edge of the saw table, significantly limiting the working area on that side but providing a blade-cover option for shops with limited space. The cantilever-mounted Brett Guard is supported by an overarm frame like the other blade covers reviewed here.

The Brett Guards are easy to use, but the small splitter plate attaches like a standard splitter and is just as inconvenient. And the only splitter accessory that fits behind the large cover of a Brett Guard is the Delta Disappearing Splitter, which fits only right-tilting Unisaws.

Blade Cover Recommendations
All of the covers are preferable to the standard three-in-one system. However, I favor the Biesemeyer system because of its overall ease of use. The only disadvantage of the Biesemeyer cover is that it won't work with fence systems that use the back rail. For woodworkers who have a Delta tablesaw or Biesemeyer-style fence, especially if budget is a consideration, I also recommend the Delta Deluxe Blade Guard. There is no provision for dust collection, but this factor may be outweighed by the cost savings. Finally, the Excalibur Overarm Blade Cover offers good value with superior dust collection.

*Note price estimates are from 2001.

KELLY MEHLER is a woodworker and teacher in Berea, Kentucky, and the author of *The Table Saw Book* (The Taunton Press, 1993).

> *All of the covers are preferable to the standard three-in-one system.*

A Tablesaw Sled for Precision Crosscutting

BY LON SCHEINING

MITERS

CROSSCUTS

TENONS

Crosscutting with a standard table-saw miter gauge can be frustrating, inaccurate, even hazardous. Adding an extended fence helps, but the miter gauge still will be limited and imprecise. Don't bother with it. Instead, take the time to make a super-accurate, super-versatile and far safer crosscut sled.

A crosscut sled is a sliding table with runners that guide it over the saw in the miter-gauge slots. It has a rear fence set perpendicular to the line of cut to hold the workpiece. Because it uses both miter slots, the sled is remarkably and reliably accurate. It also easily accepts any number of stop blocks, auxiliary fences and templates, allowing miters, tenons and many other specialty cuts. Nearly every small commercial shop I know uses some variation of this sled. I use mine primarily to square the ends of 12-in.-wide stair treads.

Your sled should fit your work. There's no sense in making a huge, unwieldy sled if you'll use it mostly to cut 3-in. tenons. The one I use is 30 in. wide and 21 in. deep. It's capable of crosscutting a board up to 2 in. thick and 18 in. wide (see the main photo on the facing page). With a miter template (see the box on p. 128), the sled can cut a 45° miter on the end of a 3-in.-wide board. The rear fence is 5 in. high in the middle, 2½ in. high on the ends. Though I rarely crosscut a board thicker than 2 in., the fence needs to be at least 4 in. high to accommodate the height of the sawblade. The extra fence height also supports workpieces on end when I cut tenons.

Start with a Solid Platform of Baltic Birch Plywood

I build jigs like this from what I call not-yet-used materials (some call it scrap). I used void-free ½-in. Baltic birch plywood for the platform. Baltic birch is often mistaken for Finnish birch—its waterproof and much more costly cousin. Baltic birch is

Tailor the size of the sled to fit the work you do. The crucial features are a rear fence perpendicular to the line of cut and runners that slide easily without slop.

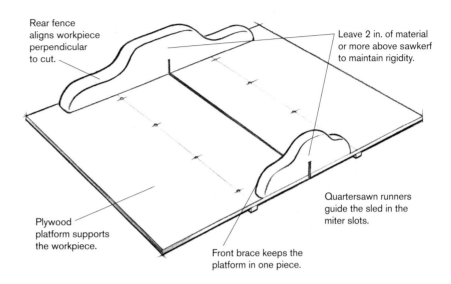

Rear fence aligns workpiece perpendicular to cut.

Leave 2 in. of material or more above sawkerf to maintain rigidity.

Plywood platform supports the workpiece.

Quartersawn runners guide the sled in the miter slots.

Front brace keeps the platform in one piece.

not as high quality, but for the price (about a dollar per square foot), it's perfect for making stable, durable jigs. But any plywood you have around the shop will probably work fine as long as it's flat.

The first step is to cut the platform to size. Make the platform as square as you can get it. You can check for square by measuring diagonally across the corners: The measurements should be the same across both corners. But before you make the sled, it's a good idea to make sure your tablesaw is tuned up.

For the sled to perform well, your saw's blade must be precisely parallel with the miter-gauge slots, and the table must be flat (for more on tuning up your tablesaw, see "Tablesaw Tune-Up", on p. 98).

Quartersawn Hardwood Runners for Smooth Sliding

I prefer to make runners from oak, instead of buying steel ones, because I can control their fit in the miter slots. Wood runners pose a few problems, however, that should

Making the Runners

A PERFECT FIT. Runner stock should slide freely in the miter slots (right). Finished runners should be just below the level of the table (above).

be taken into consideration. Expansion from seasonal humidity can cause them to bind in the miter slots, so I choose the material and its grain orientation carefully. They also need to be milled precisely.

Start with a close-grained flatsawn maple or oak board. Mill the thickness of the board to the width of the slot using a planer. Test the fit as you go, planing off a little material at a time. It should slide easily in the slot, but without slop (see the photos above). Next rip two runners from the board to a thickness slightly less than the depth of the miter slots, then cut them to length. By ripping strips off a flat-grained board, you have made quartersawn runners, which will be very stable. The idea is to make runners that don't rub against

the bottom of the slots and raise the sled off the table, but that still engage as much of the miter slot as possible.

The first construction step is to fasten the runners to the platform. To make sure they are right where they should be, attach them while they're in the miter slots. Lower the blade out of the way, and center the platform on the table, using the rip fence to keep the platform square on the runners (see the top photo on the facing page). Lay out the holes for the screws so they're centered on the runners, and drill them in the platform only. The screws should pass freely through the holes in the plywood.

The size of the drill bit you choose for the pilot holes in the runners is very important. Thin runners will bulge or split if the pilot hole is too small. Even a small bulge will make the runner bind in the miter slot. The holes should be slightly larger than the shank diameter of the screw. I use a dial caliper to measure the shank, and then I select the correct drill bit. On this sled, I used $\frac{5}{8}$-in.-long #8 screws that have a shank diameter of 0.122 in., so a $\frac{1}{8}$-in. drill bit (0.125 in.) was perfect.

First drill just one pilot hole in each runner, and insert a screw in each. These screws keep the runners firmly in place while you drill the other pilot holes. Remove the two screws, deburr all the holes, apply a small bead of glue to the runners and screw the platform to the runners. Clean off any glue that might have squeezed out.

Now take your incomplete sled for a test drive: move it back and forth in the miter slots to see if it runs smoothly. It's easy to tell just where the oak runners are binding because they'll be shiny and gray from rubbing against the sides of the steel slots. While the glue is still soft, it is possible to move the runners slightly. You should only be concerned at this point with how smoothly the platform slides.

Make Front Race and Rear Fence

The front brace's only job is to keep the platform in one piece. It doesn't much matter what size or shape it is (I add some gentle curves to mine) as long as it is a few inches higher than the sawblade's maximum cut—about 2 in. above the platform. I made this brace from 1¼-in.-thick red oak, 3¾ in. high, and about as long as the width between the miter slots. Shape it, smooth it, and glue and screw it to the front of the table from the underside of the platform.

This is also the time to make the rear fence. I used some 2-in.-thick white oak 5 in. wide and 23 in. long. The rear fence should be pretty stout to hold the sled table together. If you don't have 8/4 lumber, laminate two 4/4 pieces together. Make sure the board is perfectly straight on the inside face and square with the edge that will be attached to the platform.

Keeping things square becomes critical when you attach the rear fence. The most important thing to remember when making a sled is that, for the cut to be square, the rear fence must be square to the line of cut. If it's not, you have a useless sled.

Before you attach the rear fence, put the sled on the saw, raise the blade slightly above the thickness of the platform and cut through the platform about two-thirds of the way from back to front, being very careful not to cut all the way through the platform (see the photos on p. 129). Drill and countersink the holes in the platform, then securely clamp the fence to the platform so that it is square to the cut you just made. Use an accurate framing square to align it, checking from both sides of the fence. Now drill two center pilot holes (of four total) into the fence, and install the screws from the bottom side.

Before you can attach the rear fence once and for all, make some trial crosscuts and check the results. The position of the fence will almost certainly need fine-tuning. It's easy to rotate the rear fence back and forth a little with hammer taps or a bar clamp, even with the two screws snug. This is where patience is important. Keep making test cuts and adjusting as necessary until the cut is perfectly square. Don't, however, cut all the way through the platform at this time. Leave just enough plywood at the rear of the platform to hold the sled together; if you cut all the way through, the rear fence will be harder to align.

Attach the Platform to the Runners

USE MITER SLOTS TO ALIGN RUNNERS UNDER PLATFORM. The rip fence keeps the platform square and centered while you lay out (left) and drill the pilot holes (below). To avoid splitting the runners, the holes should be slightly larger than the shank diameter of the screw.

From 90° to 45° Cuts with a Simple Template

With this template, you'll be able to make accurate miter cuts on your tablesaw. The template is nothing more than a piece of Baltic birch plywood with two sides at 90° to each other and a back side that registers against the rear fence of the sled. This template sits far enough forward so that long workpieces clear the ends of the rear fence.

There are any number of ways to make such a shape. I used the opportunity to test the accuracy of my sled. First I laid out and rough cut the template from a corner of a sheet of plywood and got one of the sides straight on a jointer. This can also be done on the sled by aligning the edge over the sawkerf and nailing the template to the sled (don't let the nails go all the way through). I then cut the opposite side at 90° to the first using the rear fence.

To cut the base at 45° to the two sides, I cut to the layout line on the base by aligning it over the kerf and nailing the template to the sled. I've rarely gotten a base perfect the first time.

To find out which way it's out, I center the point of the template on the sawkerf and align the base against the rear fence. Then I scribe its outline on the sled. I flip it over and check it against the scribe marks. If it sits perfectly between the lines, I'm on the money. If not, I recut the back of the template as required. Finally, I attach it to the sled with a few screws, make some trial miters and adjust accordingly.

Attach the Rear Fence, and Make More Trial Cuts

When the sled makes true 90° crosscuts, it's time to attach the rear fence permanently. Clamp a long 4-in. by 4-in. block to the sled platform so that it fits tight against the rear fence. It will keep the fence's place. Remove the two screws that are temporarily holding the fence. Apply glue and reinstall the fence with the rest of the screws. Carefully check its position against the block. Remove the clamps and the block, and immediately make a trial cut, still without cutting all the way through the platform.

Adjust the fence if necessary with hammer taps or clamps. Even though the sled is screwed and glued together at this point, it's still possible to make fine adjustments, but only for a few minutes after glue-up.

Before you spend too much time admiring your handy work, sand all the sharp edges and coat the bottom with a lubricant such as spray silicone or TopCote. Even then, you're not done. You still have guide blocks and templates to make. They will let your sled cut perfect tenons and miters.

GARRETT HACK , a contributing editor to *Fine Woodworking*, makes furniture on his Vermont farm.

Use the Kerf to Square the Fence

DON'T CUT THAT SLED IN HALF. After you attach the front brace (left), cut only two-thirds of the way through the platform (right). The kerf is a reference to set the rear fence.

SQUARE THE FENCE TO THE SAWKERF. Check the fence's alignment from both sides of the kerf. Attach the fence with only two screws before you make trial cuts.

Safe Procedures at the Tablesaw

BY HOWARD LEWIN

A tablesaw doesn't have a conscience. It couldn't care less whether or not it cuts off your finger. And it will. If you know this going in, then you can guard against it. What I try to do is arm myself with knowledge of what the machine is likely to do and then stop it before it happens.

Kickback, the main cause of most tablesaw injuries, occurs when the board drifts away from the fence and pushes against the back of the spinning blade. As the teeth come out of the back side of the saw, they will actually lift the board off the table and launch it over the top of the blade. When that happens, the board is propelled with a few horsepower of force behind it.

Splitters are designed to prevent kickback, and they do. Yet they cause a great deal of anxiety to me and most of the woodworkers I know. This is probably because the splitters that are readily available in the United States aren't quite up to par. For a splitter to do its job, it has to be the exact width of the blade. If the splitter is narrower than the blade, then it allows room for the board to slide away from the fence. If it is thicker than the blade, it forces the stock into the front of the blade and jams the board.

European splitters, like those on Inca tablesaws, attach directly behind the blade and are curved to follow the blade's arc. The splitter adjusts and travels with the blade, allowing dado and bevel cuts. It is useful, and it works. The splitters on most American saws have to be removed to make these cuts. Often they are not replaced.

As for blade guards, they work fine, except when you really need them. When you are cutting plywood or long boards with wide dimensions, your hand is nowhere near the blade; therefore, it's pretty safe. It's when you have to do detail work close to the blade that you need a blade guard but can't use one.

Though splitters and blade guards should work better and should be more widely used, I see little use in pretending that they are.

What is imperative is that you take the necessary measures to ensure safety at the tablesaw. I always use zero-clearance tablesaw inserts, featherboards and push sticks. I keep a well-tuned saw, and I let a few rules guide my work.

- Never stand directly behind the sawblade.
- Make sure the blade is never more than ⅛ in. above the board being cut.
- Be aware of what the wood is doing at all times. And be ready to react.
- Never back a board out of a cut.
- At the slightest hint that a board is bowing away from the fence, lift it out of the cut and above the blade. Then begin to make the cut again.

To drive a car you have to pass a test. The same is true for flying an airplane or sailing a boat. Most people even take the time to get some kind of computer training these days. But the same people just take a tablesaw out of the box and cut away. It doesn't make much sense. If you make a mistake at the computer, what's the worst scenario—you lose a page, some bookkeeping? But make a mistake at the tablesaw and the consequences are much greater. Digits don't grow back. The photos and drawings on the following pages show the basic setups for safe cutting. With these things in mind, you can foresee problems and prevent them before they happen.

Shopmade Tablesaw Accessories

Push Sticks, Push Paddles, and Push Shoes
Push sticks lend leverage when guiding stock through a cut. The notch allows you to hold the push stick at about a 45° angle and keeps your hand about 10 in. above the blade. Wider push sticks give a more solid connection. Just make sure the grain runs lengthwise, so it won't break when the notched end passes through the blade. Cut them in bulk, so there's always one nearby. On narrow stock, push shoes hold the stock flush to the tabletop and afford even more leverage. Push paddles offer the most control. If the lumber is heavy or wide, use push paddles to help ease the way past the blade.

Throw No Sparks When you build a push paddle with dowels, you don't have to worry about the blade catching an errant screw. A layer of sandpaper over the paddle's face will help it grip the stock.

Zero-Clearance Inserts These inserts prevent the loss of thin strips in the wide

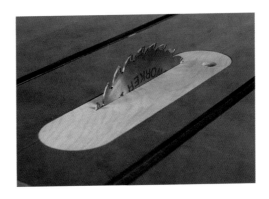

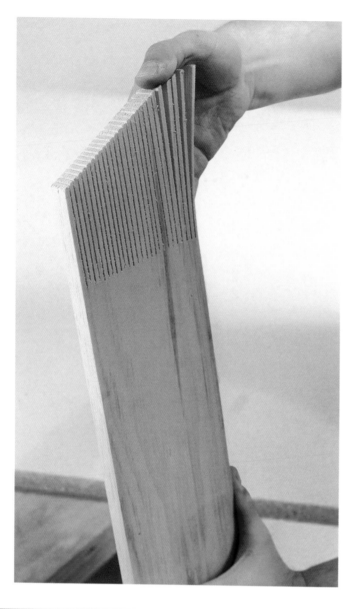

clearance allowed by most factory inserts. They also prevent tearout by supporting the stock all the way up to the blade. First make a pattern from the factory-cut insert, usually ½ in. thick, and then shape it to a press-fit from the pattern. Drill a ¾-in. hole in the insert to serve as an easy finger pull. Change inserts when you have to switch blades or make beveled cuts.

Featherboards When clamped to the tablesaw, featherboards help the board ride the fence throughout the cut. Even if a board does wander from the fence, the feathered end helps prevent it from kicking back. They are easily made with scrap stock and a bandsaw. The angled end should be cut at 30° to 40° and the feathered kerfs bandsawn at about ¼ in. intervals. For larger stock, use wider and thicker featherboards. It's good to make them in various sizes so an appropriate one is always nearby.

Crosscutting

The safest and easiest way to crosscut is to use a sled. It enables you to keep your fingers at a safe distance from the blade. A smooth feed rate and a sharp, pitch-free blade with at least 30 to 40 teeth should allow you to crosscut without a glitch. A crosscut sled can also be set up to cut angles and compound miters.

Ripping

Before ripping a board to size, make sure you have a perfectly flat side against the fence. Do not stop the cut or reduce pressure until you have pushed the material past the blade. If the board begins to drift from the blade or if the board moves in any way that makes you uncomfortable, lift it out of the cut and begin again. A sharp, clean blade goes a long way toward keeping procedures safe. For general ripping, 30 to 40 teeth are adequate. For thicker stock—2 in. or more—use wider kerf blades with fewer teeth.

Warning

Fine *Woodworking* does not recommend the removal of splitters, blade guards or other safety devices from tablesaws. The author of this article believes that many woodworkers choose to operate tablesaws without such devices. Our observations as editors confirm this. We also recognize that many woodworkers own older machines or used tablesaws that came without these safety mechanisms. In all these cases, it is essential that the safety steps outlined in the following article be taken to minimize the risk of injury.

STOP BLOCKS AND MITER GAUGES

Crosscutting with a Miter Gauge

You can also crosscut using a miter gauge with an extension fence screwed or clamped to it. The extension fence will support the board all the way up to the blade.

Using the Rip Fence as a Stop

Clamp an extra piece of wood to the fence to act as a stop block. This prevents wood from getting trapped between the fence and the blade, which can cause it to bind and kick back. Never use the fence alone to crosscut boards.

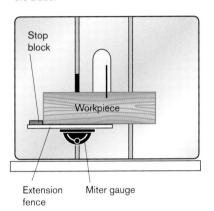

Stop block

Workpiece

Extension fence

Miter gauge

To cut a number of pieces to the same length, attach a stop block directly onto the extension fence.

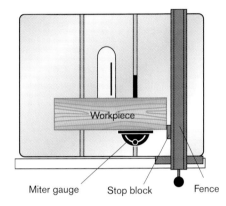

Workpiece

Miter gauge   Stop block   Fence

When possible, use the miter gauge between the fence and the blade.

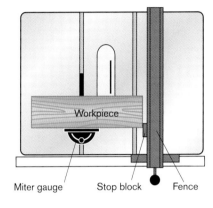

Workpiece

Miter gauge   Stop block   Fence

For trimming smaller pieces to length, move the miter gauge to the left of the blade.

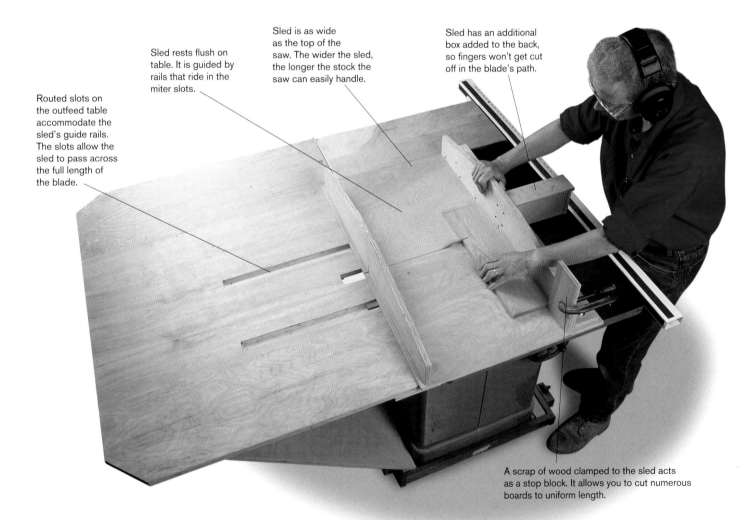

Routed slots on the outfeed table accommodate the sled's guide rails. The slots allow the sled to pass across the full length of the blade.

Sled rests flush on table. It is guided by rails that ride in the miter slots.

Sled is as wide as the top of the saw. The wider the sled, the longer the stock the saw can easily handle.

Sled has an additional box added to the back, so fingers won't get cut off in the blade's path.

A scrap of wood clamped to the sled acts as a stop block. It allows you to cut numerous boards to uniform length.

Always stand to the left of the blade, never directly behind the board you are cutting. This is the only way that you can exert the pressure necessary to keep the board against the fence. It also puts you in the best spot if the board does kick back.

Always use featherboards placed just in front of the blade to prevent kickback.

Extension tables help keep the boards flat on the table and lessen the chance that a board will wander as it moves past the blade.

KEEP TO THE FENCE

When pushing a board through a cut, always apply pressure on the side closest to the blade.

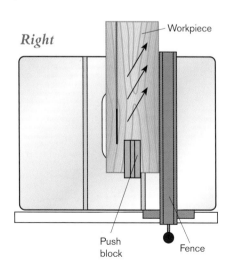

Right

Workpiece

Push block

Fence

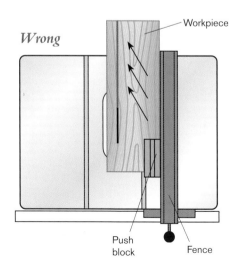

Wrong

Workpiece

Push block

Fence

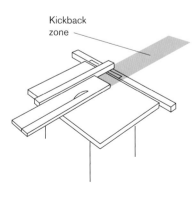

Kickback zone

MANAGING BOWED STOCK

If you must rip or crosscut a board that is bowed or cupped,
even slightly, place the board with the concave side facing down.

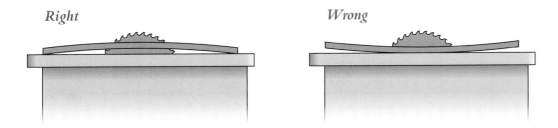

Right

Wrong

RIPPING BEVELS

With the fence to the left
of the blade, always stand to
the right. Though awkward
to right-handers at first, it's
the safest alternative.

When cutting narrow stock,
use a push paddle with a
slight twisting motion to keep
the board against the fence.

With the fence to the left of the
blade, the bevel cuts away from
the fence, not toward it.

Featherboard

Beveling

On right-tilting saws, cutting bevels traps the board between fence and blade, which should cause you great anxiety. You can avoid this problem by moving the fence to the left of the blade. Using zero-clearance inserts is the only way to ensure small cut-offs don't get sucked into the saw.

Beveling with a Left-Tilting Saw When you use a left-tilting saw, there is no need to move the fence to the less familiar left side of the saw. For beveled cuts, the blade is automatically angled away from the fence. For most, the result is a safer and much more comfortable procedure.

Needing a left-tilting arbor is probably not reason enough to buy a new saw, but if you're in the market, and right-handed, it's an option worth looking for.

Powermatic and Craftsman have been making left-tilting saws for a number of years, and a few other manufacturers, Delta and Jet among them, have recently introduced these machines.

Ripping at an Angle When you move the fence to the left of the blade, the pointy edge of the stock can register off the face of the fence, making for a much safer cut.

With the fence in its normal position, there is a good chance the point of the

BEVELING WITH A LEFT-TILTING SAW

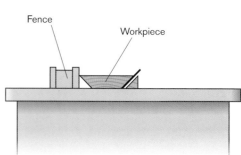

RIPPING AT AN ANGLE

Right

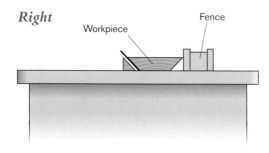

When you move the fence to the left of the blade, the pointy edge of the stock can register off the face of the fence, making for a much safer cut.

Wrong

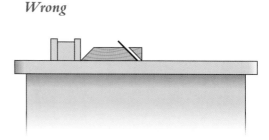

With the fence in its normal position, there is a good chance the point of the bevel will slip down below the fence and twist the board in midcut. This can cause sever kickback.

RAISING A PANEL

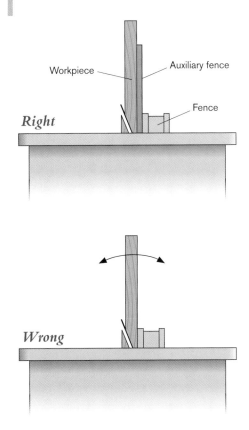

Without a tall auxiliary fence, a panel held vertically can sway from side to side, causing kickback.

bevel will slip down below the fence and twist the board in midcut. This can cause severe kickback.

Raising a Panel To make raised-panel cuts on a right-tilting tablesaw, you must move the fence to the left of the blade. This way, the blade is angled away from the fence. And you must use an auxiliary fence tall enough to allow a firm handhold on the piece being beveled. Because of the small offcuts you're creating, zero-clearance inserts are absolutely necessary.

HOWARD LEWIN is a woodworker and woodworking teacher in Hawthorne, California.

Rabbets, Grooves, and Dadoes

RABBETS

When cutting rabbets, an auxiliary fence clamped or screwed in place keeps the blade from digging into the primary fence. On wider stock, where there is more than 6 in. against the fence, a miter gauge is not required—simply run the edge of the board along the fence. You can also use a crosscut sled or a miter gauge to cut rabbets. And remember, never go backward across a blade.

GROOVES

To cut a groove on the edge of a board, an auxiliary fence and zero-clearance inserts are essential. Use a featherboard in front of the blade to hold the stock against the fence. On narrower boards, be sure to use a push stick, and apply downward pressure through and past the blade. Cut the groove as close to the fence as possible.

DADOES

Always dado as close to the fence as possible. Narrow stock requires a miter gauge and a stop block. On wider stock, where there is more than 6 in. against the fence and less than a 4-in. gap between the blade and the fence, a miter gauge is not required. Never dado far from the fence even with a miter gauge. You can also use a crosscut sled dedicated to making dado cuts.

Taming Tearout on the Tablesaw

BY STEVE LATTA

One major factor that separates a good piece of furniture from a mediocre one is how cleanly it is constructed. Nothing will kill the look of a finished piece more than tearout. Those rough edges are inexcusable and can be avoided if you pay attention to how wood fibers react to different types of tooling.

Most tearout on the tablesaw occurs when the blade exits the stock and breaks the wood fibers rather than cutting them.

As a result, splinters may show up on the underside, back corner, and back edge of a workpiece. This is especially relevant to crosscutting on the tablesaw. But tearout is not hard to eliminate or manage. The first item to look at is the sawblade.

The Correct Blade Is the First Line of Defense

It is important that the blade is designated for the type of cut being performed and that it's sharp and clean; a dull blade, or one covered with pitch, will produce a poor-quality cut. Crosscutting blades and many general-purpose blades have teeth with alternating bevels. The staggered teeth on these blades are beneficial because they score the fibers before hogging out the stock.

Avoid Trim Cuts Sometimes tearout occurs by taking too light of a trim cut. It often is better to have material on both sides of the blade; that way, the wood fibers are supported across the full width of the kerf and onto the offcut. This tension keeps the fibers from ripping away. On trim cuts, the fibers are more inclined to break away, which can be a real problem when working with man-made panel products, such as plywood, and with porous woods, such as oak.

Raise the Blade to Reduce Tearout

The height of the tablesaw blade also is an issue, although a controversial one. The rules of safety declare that the blade should project above the surface about the height of a tooth. Regretfully, a low blade height can lift fibers away from the surface, especially toward the end of the cut.

Raising the blade higher than normally recommended transfers the forces of blade rotation in such a manner that the fibers are pressed into the surface, resulting in a cleaner cut. In many applications, I raise the blade at least an inch above the workpiece and take extra precautions to ensure safety, such as clamping the workpiece to a

Shop Aids to Prevent Tearout

Tearout mostly occurs on a crosscut when the sawblade breaks the wood fibers rather than "splitting" them. Once you understand the common causes of tearout, you can follow a few simple guidelines to prevent it.

IDENTIFY TROUBLE SPOTS

Tearout is most likely to occur on the underside of the workpiece as well as on the back edge and back corners. A wide kerf in the tablesaw insert or crosscut sled also can allow tearout.

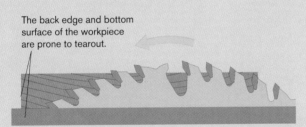

The back edge and bottom surface of the workpiece are prone to tearout.

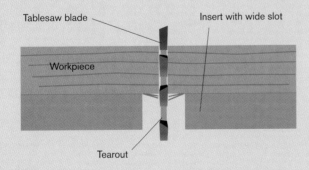

Tablesaw blade

Insert with wide slot

Workpiece

Tearout

INSTALL A ZERO-CLEARANCE INSERT

A zero-clearance insert increases the support area under the workpiece and reduces the chance of tearout.

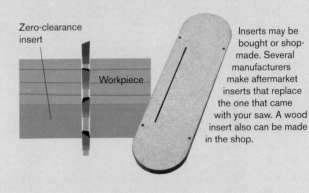

Zero-clearance insert

Workpiece

Inserts may be bought or shop-made. Several manufacturers make aftermarket inserts that replace the one that came with your saw. A wood insert also can be made in the shop.

USE A CROSSCUT SLED

Another solution is to use a crosscut sled. If the original kerf has become too wide, add a fresh auxiliary deck and fence and make zero-clearance kerfs in them.

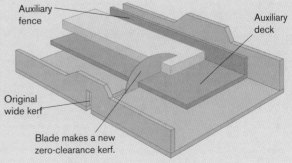

Auxiliary fence

Auxiliary deck

Original wide kerf

Blade makes a new zero-clearance kerf.

Orient the Workpiece to Hide the Tearout

IDENTIFY THE INSIDE EDGES OF TABLE LEGS. With the legs oriented with the exposed faces outward, mark the unexposed sides of the legs with a crayon.

1. TABLE LEGS

PLACE THE HIDDEN SIDES OF THE LEG AGAINST THE FENCE AND DECK. Orient the leg on the tablesaw so that the blade exits the workpiece on a surface that won't be visible on the finished furniture piece.

2. DRAWER FRONTS

ORIENT DRAWER FRONTS SO THAT TEAROUT IS RESTRICTED TO THE INSIDE FACE. Crosscut drawer fronts with the exposed face up.

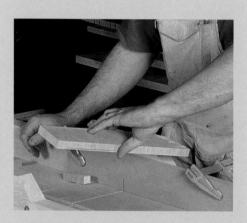

ROTATE, DON'T FLIP THE DRAWER FACE. When crosscutting the other end of a drawer front, make sure the exposed face is still on top.

crosscut sled to keep my hands clear of the heightened blade.

Use a Zero-Clearance Insert or Crosscut Sled

Another common cause of tearout when crosscutting is a tablesaw insert in which the blade slot is too wide—typical on most stock inserts. This slot is a hot zone for tearout because it creates an unsupported surface for the material being cut. The hard edge where the workpiece finally becomes supported serves as a chipbreaker and allows the fibers to tear as far as the hard edge.

A zero-clearance insert ensures that the workpiece is fully supported as it passes across the blade, thus reducing tearout (see p. 139). I've applied this same zero-clearance concept to my crosscutting sled, which has developed a wide kerf from the various thicknesses of blades I've used. Each time I use a sled for a new operation, I affix an auxiliary deck and fence on which a workpiece will rest as it is run through the saw. Once I've applied the fresh deck and fence, I run it through the saw and produce a new kerf that is the exact width of the blade. As an added benefit, the new kerf also serves as a reference point for lining up successive cuts.

Isolate Tearout to Hidden Surfaces

In my woodworking courses, nothing knocks down a student's grade faster than visible tearout on a finished piece. I've often seen this occur on the top of a table leg as a result of the student improperly cutting it to length. You should have a good idea how the legs will be positioned on a table before you make any cuts. As noted earlier, the bottom face, back corner, and back edge of a workpiece are most susceptible to tearout. Therefore, table legs should be oriented on the saw so that the outside faces of the leg make first contact with the blade. This way, any tearout that does occur won't be visible once the table has been assembled. I always mark the inside faces and end grain of a table leg before cutting it to length to remind me of the proper orientation. This same concept can be applied to a cut on the miter saw, which will produce tearout in a similar fashion.

Another example of properly orienting a workpiece to limit tearout is when trimming a drawer front to length. The drawer front should be positioned with its inside face against the tabletop so that tearout is isolated to the unseen face. After making the first cut, rotate the stock and cut the other end rather than flipping it. Rotating the stock places all of the tearout on the back face, while flipping it will result in tearout on the inside and outside faces.

Order Your Cuts to Eliminate Tearout

WHICH COMES FIRST, THE DADO OR THE RABBET?
The dado comes first, if you follow the general rule that end-grain cuts should be made before long-grain cuts.

A RABBET WILL SCOOP AWAY TEAROUT CAUSED BY THE DADO CUT. Cut the rabbet deeper than the dado to ensure a clean edge.

Cut End Grain before Cutting Long Grain

The proper sequencing of cuts also plays a vital role in how clean a project will turn out. In general, when a workpiece needs to be cut across the grain and along the grain, it's best to cut the end grain first. This old standby holds true for most machining processes, from raising panels to rabbeting drawer bottoms. If tearout does occur from the blade (or cutter) exiting the end grain, the long-grain pass will scoop away any blowout that might have occurred.

There are a number of operations where this rule holds true. One good ex-ample is a bookcase that uses dadoes to fix shelves and a rabbet to hold the back boards. Which comes first—the dado or the rabbet? If we follow the rule of end grain first, the dado would need to come first. Rabbeting the back afterward removes any tearout produced along the back end of the dado.

Scoring and Taping Can Help Reduce Tearout

Due diligence also will prevent tearout. For example, when working on large cabinet projects, I always make frame-and-panel doors slightly oversize, then cut them to fit once I can determine the exact dimensions of the opening that the door will fill. However, when cutting a door to height, you encroach on a major problem area: the back edge on the door stile where the sawblade is cutting end grain.

Using a marking knife or an X-Acto® knife, I score a line on the bottom side and back edge of the stile where it will be cut on the tablesaw. This scored line will allow the fibers to break cleanly before they have a chance to tear out.

Applying clear tape to an edge that is to be cut also works well to prevent tearout, but special care has to be taken when pulling off the tape. Peeling it off in the direction of the fibers will lay them down. If you peel it off in the other direction, the tape will lift the fibers. Sometimes a very light film of white glue rubbed over a troublesome area will provide enough support to keep fibers from tearing. Just make sure that all of the glue is removed before it comes time to apply a finish.

STEVE LATTA is an instructor at Thaddeus Stevens College of Technology in Lancaster, Pennsylvania, and a frequent contributor to *Fine Woodworking*.

Score or Tape the Workpiece before Cutting

SCORE THE CUTLINE. When crosscutting a cabinet door to length, score a line around the underside and back edge of the cross-grain stile to reduce the chances of tearout on those trouble spots.

TAPE TROUBLESOME AREAS. The unsupported corners on this workpiece will tear when crosscut on the tablesaw if preventive measures aren't taken.

One-Stop Cutting Station

BY KEN PICOU

T
ablesaws are excellent for ripping stock, but the standard miter gauge that comes with most tablesaws makes them mediocre at best for crosscutting material or cutting joinery. But by making a simple sliding-crosscut box and a few accessory jigs, you can greatly increase the accuracy and flexibility of your saw and turn it into a one-stop cutting station, capable of crosscutting, tenoning and slotting.

The system I've developed consists of a basic sliding-crosscut box with a 90° back rail, a removable pivoting fence, a tenon-

ing attachment and a corner slotting jig, for cutting the slots for keyed miter joints (see the photo above). This system is inherently safer and more accurate than even the most expensive miter gauge for several reasons. First, it uses both miter slots, so there is less side play than with a miter gauge. Second, the work slides on a moving base, so there's no chance of the work slipping or catching from friction with the saw table. Third, the long back fence provides better support than a miter gauge, which is usually only 4 in. or 5 in. across. Fourth, the sliding-

MAKING A CROSSCUT BOX MORE VERSATILE. An accurate sliding-crosscut box makes a good base for cutting accessories, including this corner-slotting jig. This jig mounts or dismounts in seconds and makes for strong miter joints in picture or mirror frames and in small boxes or drawers.

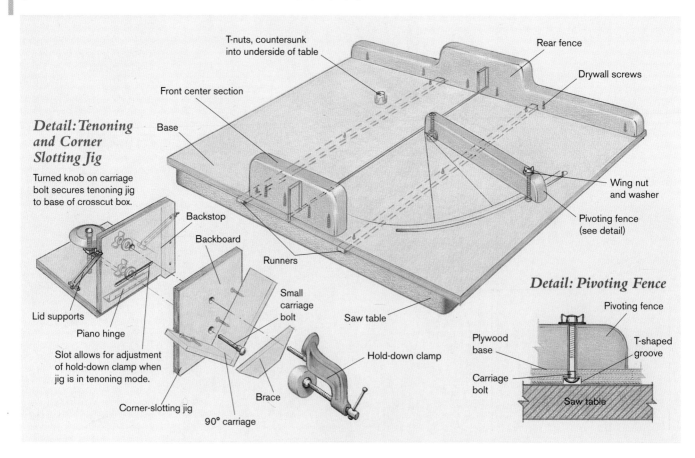

Detail: Tenoning and Corner Slotting Jig

Turned knob on carriage bolt secures tenoning jig to base of crosscut box.

T-nuts, countersunk into underside of table

Front center section

Base

Rear fence

Drywall screws

Backstop

Backboard

Runners

Small carriage bolt

Saw table

Wing nut and washer

Pivoting fence (see detail)

Lid supports

Piano hinge

Slot allows for adjustment of hold-down clamp when jig is in tenoning mode.

Corner-slotting jig

90° carriage

Brace

Hold-down clamp

Detail: Pivoting Fence

Pivoting fence

Plywood base

Carriage bolt

T-shaped groove

Saw table

crosscut box is big, so angles can be measured and divided much more accurately than with a miter gauge (the farther from its point of origin an angle is measured, the greater the precision). Finally, the sliding crosscut box is a stable base on which to mount various attachments, such as a tenoning jig or a corner slotting jig, which can greatly expand the versatility of the tablesaw.

Building the Basic Crosscut Box

I cut the base of my sliding-crosscut box from a nice, flat sheet of ½-in.-thick Baltic birch plywood, and then I make it a little bit wider and deeper than my saw's tabletop. A cheaper grade of plywood also would be fine for this jig, but I decided to use a premium material because I wanted the jig to be a permanent addition to my shop.

The runners that slide in the tablesaw's miter-gauge slots can be made from any

stable material that wears well. I prefer wood to metal because wood works easily, and I can screw right into it. I usually use hard maple, and I've never had a problem. Using a long-wearing, slippery plastic such as an acetal (Delrin®, for example) or ultra-high molecular-weight (UHMW) plastic is also a possibility.

I start with a maple board of sufficient length that is at least as wide as three or four runners are thick. I plane this board, taking off minute increments with each pass, until it slides easily on edge in one of the slots but isn't sloppy. Once the fit's right, I rip the runners from this board, setting the fence on my tablesaw to just under the depth of the miter-gauge slot. Then I drill and countersink them at the middle and near both ends (I check the dimensions of the Baltic birch base to make sure I drill the screw holes so they'll fall near the edges of the base). I usually drill a couple of holes near each end as insurance in case a screw drifts off when I'm screwing the runners to the base.

Next I crank the sawblade all the way down below the table and lay the runners in the miter-gauge slots. I position the base so that its back edge is parallel to the rear of the saw table and the front edge over-hangs by a couple of inches. I clamp the runners to the base in the front. I drill pilot holes in the plywood from below using a Vix bit (a self-centering drill bit available through most large tool catalogs) placed in one of the countersunk holes in the run-ners. Then I screw up through the runners into the base. When I've done both run-ners at the front of the saw, I slide the base back carefully and repeat at the rear (see the top photo at right). I check for binding or wobble by sliding the base back and forth a few times. If the fit is less than ideal, I still have four more chances (the extra screw holes I drilled at both ends of each runner) to get it right. If the fit is good, I drill pilot holes with the Vix bit and screw the runner to the base in the middle, taking care not to let the runner move side to side. I also trim the runners flush with the front and back of the crosscut box.

If the fit's a bit too snug at first, use will tend to burnish the runners so that they will glide more easily. If, after some use they're still a little snug, you can sand the runners just a bit and give them a coat of paste wax. That will usually get them gliding nicely.

Building Accuracy into the Jig An inac-curate jig is useless, so it's essential that as-sembly of this jig be dead-on. Fortunately, this isn't difficult; it just takes a little time and patience.

I made both the back fence and the front center section from straight-grained red oak, but any straight-grained hardwood will do (see the drawing on the facing page). I make sure the center portions of

both pieces are built up high enough to provide 1½-in. clearance with the blade cranked up all the way.

The front section helps keep the table flat and prevents it from being sawn in half. Because this front section is not a reference surface, its position isn't critical, so I screw it on first.

Then I mount the rear fence about ¼ in. in from and parallel to the back of the Baltic birch base. I clamp the fence to the base and drive one screw through the base, which I've already drilled and countersunk, into the fence a couple of inches to the right of where the blade will run. This pro-

REAR FENCE HELPS ALIGN JIG'S HINGE. Using the rear fence as his reference, the author aligns the tenoning jig's hinge with a square. The Vix bit ensures that the screw holes are centered, so the screws will go in true and the hinge will be straight.

vides a pivot point, making it easier to align the rear fence to the blade.

I remove the clamp, raise the blade up through the base and cut through the front section and the base, staying just shy of the rear fence. So far, there's only one screw holding the rear fence in place. To set the rear fence permanently and accurately at 90° to the blade, I place the long leg of a framing square against the freshly made kerf (saw is off) and the short leg against the fence. With the fence flush against the square, I clamp the fence on an over-hanging edge and do a test-cut on a wide piece of scrap. I check this for square with a combination square and adjust the posi-tion of the fence as necessary. When I've got it right, I put another clamp on the fence near the blade on the side opposite my one screw. Then I drill, countersink and screw through the base into the fence right next to the clamp, and I check the fence's position again to make sure screwing it to the base didn't pull it off the mark (see the bottom photo on p. 145). I also make an-other test-cut, and as long as it's still good, I screw the fence down near the ends and the middles on both sides of the blade (see

the drawing on p. 144). If the second cut is not a perfect 90°, then I'll fiddle with the fence until the cut is perfect before screw-ing it into position permanently. Time spent getting the fence right is time well-spent. If, for aesthetic reasons, you want the rear of the base to be flush with the fence, you can trim the base flush with a bearing-guided, flush-trimming router bit. Either way, the performance of the crosscut box will be unaffected.

Anything from a small wooden hand-screw to a fancy commercially made stop will work as a stop block for this fence. A self-stick ruler can be added to the fence or table.

A Pivoting Fence

I wanted a pivoting fence for making angled cuts, but I also wanted to be able to remove the fence quickly when I need to cut wide boards. I accomplished this first by setting a T-nut for the pivot point into the underside of the jig's base about 6 in. forward of the fixed fence. Then I routed an arc-shaped track for a carriage bolt at the end of the fence (see the drawing on p. 144). The arc runs from 0° to a bit more than 45°, and there's a plunge-routed hole just below the 0° point through which the carriage-bolt assembly can be lifted out to remove the fence. I marked two com-mon angles (22½° and 45°) onto the jig for quick reference using a large pro-tractor and transferring that angle to a bevel square and then to the plywood. These angles can also be checked and fine-tuned by cutting them, setting the result-ing blocks together and checking for 90° with an accurate square.

A slotted screw and washer secure the fence at its pivot point but allow the fence to move, and a wing nut (with washer) fixes the angle of the fence at its outboard end. As with the fixed fence, a stop block may be as simple or sophisticated as you like.

An Adjustable Tenoning Jig

A simple hinged jig that uses the rear fence as a reference surface will allow you to cut both regular and angled tenons, rabbets and angled edges accurately and without too much fuss. I built this jig also from Baltic birch plywood. I crosscut it in the basic jig and routed the slots in it on my router table.

To attach the hinges accurately, I indexed both halves against the fixed rear fence, set a length of piano hinge in place and used a small carpenter's square to align the hinges (see the photo on the facing page). Then I drilled screw holes using the Vix bit and screwed the hinge on.

A small shopmade (turned) knob at the end of a carriage bolt secures the tenoning jig to a T-nut in the underside of the crosscut box's base. The fixed rear fence ensures that the face of the tenoning jig stays parallel to the blade. Two brass lid supports hold a set angle securely (see the right photo above). And a hold-down clamp travels in a slot in the upper portion of the jig, allowing me to hold almost any size workpiece securely (see the left photo above).

Corner-Slotting Jig

Attaching directly to the tenoning jig, the corner-slotting jig is easy to build and simple to use. I screwed two scrap boards to a backboard to form a 90° carriage positioned at 45° to the base of the crosscut box (see the drawing on p. 144). I cut a brace to fit up a few inches from the corner of the 90° carriage and across whatever it is I'm slotting. A hole through the backboard permits a hold-down clamp to bear upon the brace, distributing the pressure of the clamp.

In use, I slide the workpiece into place, then the brace, and then I tighten the clamp. The jig feels solid and works well.

KEN PICOU is a designer and woodworker in Austin, Texas.

Drill Presses and Hollow-Chisel Mortisers

With some projects, drilling holes is crucial for fitting joints, hardware, and making other attachments. As simple an act as drilling is, it demands the same kind of accuracy as does sawing, jointing, planing, and other operations. This makes the humble drill press one of the most important machines in the woodshop. It allows you to repeatedly drill holes easily and precisely to the desired depth and angle—a difficult feat to perform freehand.

A hollow-chisel mortiser bores "square holes" to create mortises for mortise-and-tenon joinery. The cutter is a drill bit that spins inside—you guessed it—a hollow chisel. The bit drills away most of the waste while the chisel cuts the walls square. Formerly restricted primarily to professional shops, hollow-chisel mortisers are now available in benchtop models that are affordable to many amateur woodworkers.

In this section, you'll learn how to make the most of your drill press and hollow-chisel mortiser. In the process, you'll get a great education on what bits work best for particular operations and how to make jigs to expand your tools' repertoire.

Jigs for the Drill Press

BY GARY ROGOWSKI

Like most power tools, the drill press won't tackle too many wood-working jobs without jigs to hold work safely and securely. I make all of my jigs out of wood and wood products such as plywood and medium-density fiberboard (MDF). I make the jigs as simple as can be and use them to handle stock of odd shapes and sizes and to bore at any angle.

The drill press is primarily designed for metalworking. Its metal stock table is too small for clamping large boards. So the first order of business is to add a larger auxiliary table made of MDF or plywood. A simple solution is to screw the auxiliary table to the stock one. Or if you prefer a table that's fast to remove, make one that can be clamped to the metal table (see the photos on p. 150).

Vertical Boring Jig

For boring into end grain, an adjustable table and fence provide a solid clamping surface. Wedges may be placed between the stock and base of the drill press for additional stability.

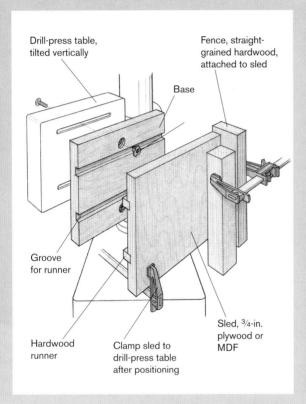

Drill-press table, tilted vertically

Fence, straight-grained hardwood, attached to sled

Base

Groove for runner

Hardwood runner

Clamp sled to drill-press table after positioning

Sled, ¾-in. plywood or MDF

Use a Two-Part Jig to Drill into End Grain

Drilling into long boards requires one of two things: great patience or another indispensable jig. You can simply tilt your drill-press table to 90° and maneuver the stock into position and clamp it. That usually entails a lot of fiddling.

Here's a better way. Make up a vertical two-part drilling jig (see the sidebar above). The jig is similar to the mortising jig in that it consists of a base and a movable sled with a fence. Stock clamped to the fence and the workpiece can be moved fore or aft and remain plumb (or at whatever angle the jig was set to).

Just like a tablesaw, the drill press can handle a lot of jobs in the workshop, but the machine demands a host of jigs before it truly performs to capacity.

GARY ROGOWSKI is a contributing editor to *Fine Woodworking* and an author and teacher in Portland, Oregon.

Best Practices for Drilling

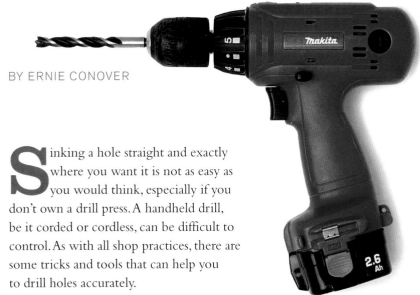

BEFORE DRILLING, MARK AND CENTER-PUNCH.
The dimple punched into the workpiece will guide the bit.

BY ERNIE CONOVER

S inking a hole straight and exactly where you want it is not as easy as you would think, especially if you don't own a drill press. A handheld drill, be it corded or cordless, can be difficult to control. As with all shop practices, there are some tricks and tools that can help you to drill holes accurately.

Find the Center to Drill on Target

Layout is the first step in drilling a hole. To determine the precise location of a hole, draw or scribe cross lines. Then use a center punch to make a 90° dimple in the wood at the intersection of the lines. The dimple will prevent the bit from wandering when you start drilling.

Another way to drill in an exact location is to use a self-centering bit. These bits most commonly are used to drill holes when installing hardware that needs flat-head screws, such as hinges. The bit is housed inside a metal casing, which has a tapered end. To use it, fit the tapered end of the housing into the hole on a piece of

SELF-CENTERING BITS HELP WHEN INSTALLING HARDWARE. Drilling for hinge screws requires precision. Self-centering bits have a tapered end on the metal housing, which centers the bit in the hinge's machined hole.

If the flutes of a bit get clogged with wood chips, they can cause the bit to burn or wander, to create oversize holes, or even to get jammed completely in the workpiece. It is important to withdraw the bit from the work periodically to clear the chips. This also is a matter of safety, as impacted bits are more prone to spin the work or the drill motor in the hands of the operator.

POSITION A SACRIFICIAL BOARD UNDERNEATH THE WORKPIECE. When wood fibers are supported, they don't tear as the bit exits the workpiece.

hardware. The tapered end automatically centers itself in the hole. As you apply pressure to the bit and begin drilling, the housing retracts and exposes the bit, allowing it to drill centered into the workpiece.

Back up the Workpiece to Prevent Tearout

The best way to prevent tearout when drilling through-holes is to place a sacrificial backer board underneath the workpiece to support the wood fibers where the bit exits (see the photo at left).

When using a bit with a brad-point tip, you can prevent tearout by drilling until the point just peeks through the back side of the workpiece. Then turn over the work and use the resulting pinhole as the center point to finish drilling.

A power drill with a variable-speed motor can be especially useful when it comes to drilling without tearout. Drill slowly at first, and increase the speed as the bit finds center and starts to bite in.

Square the Bit for Perpendicular Holes

If your shop lacks a drill press, it can be a challenge to drill a perpendicular hole in a workpiece. Some power drills have embedded bubble levels on them that can be used to help align a bit. If your drill doesn't, one simple trick is to place two squares on the workpiece next to the area where a hole is to be sunk. Use the squares to sight your bit (see the left photo on the facing page). If it is parallel with the squares when looking from all sides, the bit should drill perpendicularly into the workpiece. Continue sighting the bit until the hole is complete.

When you want to be more precise than is possible by sighting a bit, there are several commercial jigs that can be used to keep a bit square to a workpiece. Many of these jigs convert a handheld drill into a miniature drill press (see the right photo on the facing page).

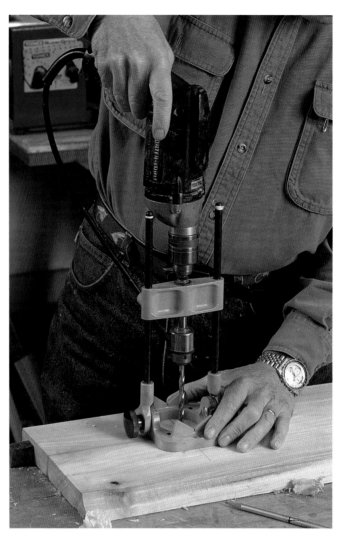

YOU DON'T NEED A DRILL PRESS TO MAKE STRAIGHT HOLES. Sight the bit against two squares to ensure that the hole is drilled perpendicular to the workpiece (left). Or you can use an accessory, like this drill guide from General (right), which turns the handheld drill into a mini drill press.

Use a Shopmade Jig for Angled Holes

For drilling angled holes, I like to use a shopmade jig that consists of a block of wood with a hole drilled through its center. The end of the wood block that makes contact with the workpiece is crosscut at an angle so that it can rest on the workpiece in the correct position. Glue two support blocks to the sides of the jig to create a larger base. Finally, mark the bottom of the jig with lines that intersect at the center of the hole. Continue the lines around the sides of the jig so that they will be visible when drilling.

To use the jig, line up the cross lines on the jig with the cross lines that mark the location of the hole on the workpiece. If your lines are accurate, the hole in the jig should line up dead center with the desired location of the hole on your workpiece. Hold the jig steady with your hand or with clamps, and drill through the jig and into the workpiece.

Use a Stop to Control Depth

Sometimes it is necessary to control the depth of a drilled hole. A variety of drill stops can help you do this. For example, you can buy a locking collar that fits over the drill bit. Once the bit cuts into the wood to the desired depth, the collar prevents it from going any deeper.

Drill in the Right Order

When countersinking for bolts or screws, you often need to drill stepped holes. In most cases, you must drill the bigger-diameter hole first and then follow that up with the smaller-diameter hole. The smaller bit can be centered in the larger hole using the dimple created by the tip of the larger bit as a center point. Common twist bits are the exception. They can be used in the opposite sequence; large twist bits will self-center in a hole drilled with a smaller bit.

LAG BOLTS REQUIRE STEPPED HOLES. Using brad-point bits, drill the larger hole before the smaller one.

MAKE A JIG FOR DRILLING AT AN ANGLE. A block of wood cut at an angle helps guide the bit into the workpiece at a consistent angle.

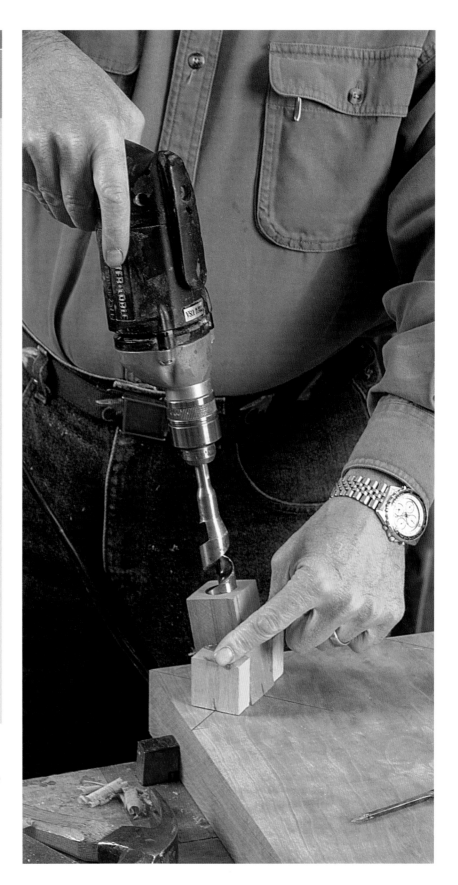

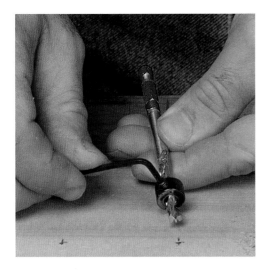

THREE WAYS TO CONTROL HOLE DEPTH.
A commercially available collar (top left) is one type of depth stop. A block of wood cut to a precise length and fitted over a drill bit (right) will prevent overdrilling. A piece of duct tape (bottom left) also can be used; stop drilling when the tape brushes away the chips.

A wood block also can be used as a drill stop. Drill a hole in a small block of wood so that the bit is completely buried in the block. Then cut the scrap to length so that the bit protrudes from the block equal to the desired depth of the hole. When you drill into a workpiece, the block will stop the bit from going in any deeper than you intend.

In many situations I have found that wrapping a piece of masking or duct tape around the bit at the desired depth works fine. However, the tape will become unreliable after drilling five to 10 holes.

ERNIE CONOVER is a turner and teacher in Parkman, Oregon.

Using a Hollow-Chisel Mortiser

BY JOHN WEST

Some time ago, fresh out of school, I practiced architecture for several years. I discovered early on that I had to make too many compromises to practice my trade. Now I own and run a small custom woodworking business, and I'm often awarded jobs that demand we make things in limited production quantities. It's not unusual to get an order for two or three dozen large doors or to do a kitchen requiring 50 to 60 cabinet doors. For these jobs, I'd be lost without my mortiser.

I use a manual, foot-operated hollow-chisel mortise machine. There have been times when I would have appreciated the brute strength and speed of a pneumatic-operated chain or oscillating mortiser. But the one I use will produce a square-bottomed, square-ended mortise. It's easy to set up for angled or canted mortises, and it's the only type that will make a single square hole, like those in window-sash bars and louvered doors.

With a little ingenuity and some jig making, the hollow-chisel mortise machine will handle any angle or curve. I've used mine for cabinet face frames, chairs and benches, curved windows, lock sets, miniature fretwork, and 10-ft.-high by 2½-in.-thick doors. I could cut mortises by hand or use either a drill-press attachment or one of the benchtop mortisers that have come onto the market in the past few years (see the photos on the facing page). Neither of those would do the job as quickly or as accurately, but they are options.

How the Tool Works

The cutting tool consists of a square hollow tube with a relief, or emptying slot, cut out of one face (sometimes two slots on opposing faces). The tool is internally flared and sharpened at one end and turned down at the other end to fit into a collet (see the drawing on p. 162). Within the tube is a double-spur machine bit (with no point) that telescopes through the chisel and fits into a drill chuck. The way it works is simple: As the tool plunges into wood, the bit drills a hole and the chisel cleans out the corners by scraping the side walls, producing a square hole. Multiple plunges in line produce a rectangular mortise slot. Chisel sets come in square sizes from ¼ in. to 1 in. and in various lengths.

Setting Up and Troubleshooting

There are two ways to set up the tool in the machine. Most manufacturers recommend this procedure: Slide the bit into the chisel, install both through the collet and

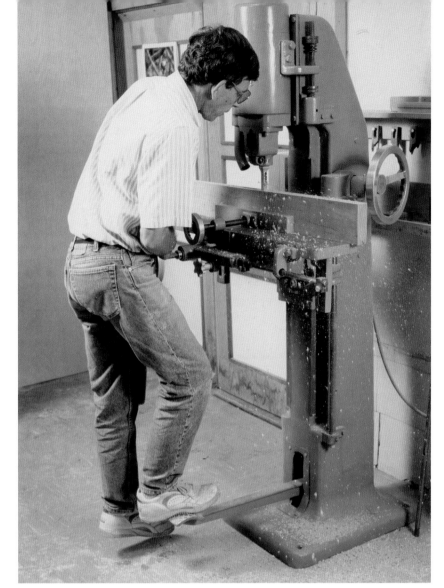

THREE WAYS TO CUT MORTISES.
The author uses a large foot-operated mortiser (left), a capable but expensive tool. Alternatives for smaller shops include dedicated benchtop mortisers like this Multico (top right) and an attachment for a drill press (bottom right).

place a ¹⁄₃₂-in. spacer (¹⁄₁₆ in. for sizes ¾ in. and larger) between the chisel shoulder and the collet. Push the bit tight to the bottom of the chisel tube, and tighten the bit in the drill chuck. Then remove the spacer, push the chisel shoulder tight to the collet and tighten the collet clamp. This method provides the recommended clearance between the bit tip and the chisel tip, which prevents heat buildup from too much friction.

I prefer another method: Install the bit and the chisel assembly through the collet, push the chisel shoulder tight to the collet and tighten the collet clamp. Push the bit into the drill chuck, and sight the bit tip and chisel tip, adjusting the bit up or down until the straight cutting edge—not the spurs—of the bit is in line with the pointed corners of the chisel (see the drawing on p. 162). Tighten the bit in the drill chuck. I like this method because it's easier for me to get the cutting edge in line with the chisel points. And even though I risk more heat buildup, I'm convinced I get less wear on the tool.

When I have to cut mortises ½ in. or larger into hardwoods like ash or white oak, I set up the tool a little differently. I keep the bit's cutting edge as much as ¹⁄₁₆ in. below the corners of the chisel. This produces a little less resistance in the plunge. Under too much stress, tips will snap off. However, I have found that the incidence of tip breakage is the same for either method and is very rare. Allowing the bit to stick out much more than ³⁄₃₂ in. from the chisel tip may cause it to begin oscillating within the

A MORTISE CHISEL AND BIT

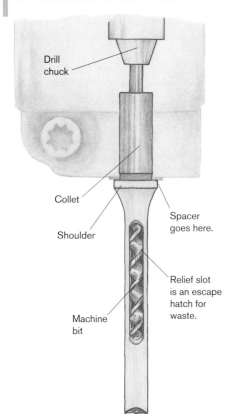

Drill
chuck

Collet

Shoulder

Machine
bit

Spacer
goes here.

Relief slot
is an escape
hatch for
waste.

The Cutting Edges
When setting up his machine,
the author takes pains to align
the cutting edge of the bit with
points of the chisel. Notice that
the spurs of the bit make the
first contact with the wood.

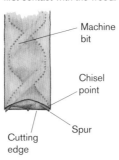

Machine
bit

Chisel
point

Cutting
edge

Spur

A Chisel Gone Bad
The heat and
pressure of clogged
debris may cause the
steel to crack, usually
on the weaker relief
side of the chisel.

hollow shaft, causing scoring and damage to
the interior of the chisel.

Bits do rub against the inner wall of
the chisel during normal operation. Older,
much-used bits occasionally will begin
oscillating, but they will stop when the
plunge is started. This doesn't seem to affect
performance, until the oscillating becomes
so severe the bit tip wanders when the
plunge is started. The only cure for that is
to buy a new chisel.

Another serious problem can occur
when the chisel overheats (see the photo
at left). This happens most frequently with
smaller tools (1/4 in. to 3/8 in.) when mortising deeply into resinous wood like cherry
or sugar pine. Hot debris collects in the
flutes of the machine bit between the chisel
tip and relief slot. If the material is not
forced out the emptying slot with the next
plunge, enough heat and pressure can build
up to split the chisel. This usually happens
on the weaker relief slot face at the thinner
tip area (see the drawing at left). Plunging
quickly helps prevent the problem.

When installing the tool into the machine, place the relief slot (as you face the
machine) 90° to the right. The waste emp-
ties away from the direction of the plunging and away from the operator (hot debris
can hurt). The weakest axis of the chisel
is captured between the side walls of the
mortise, decreasing chisel flex. Plastic drafting triangles work well for squaring up the
chisel to the fence, as shown in the photo
on the facing page, or for setting the chisel
on an angle.

Plan Your Joints First

You must allow for the seasonal movement
of a rail when laying out mortise-and-
tenon joints. A wide rail locked tightly between both ends of a mortise will be forced
to cup when expanding in high humidity.
This may create a bulge or even a split in
the stile around the mortise area. I've seen
stiles split out at the ends because the rails

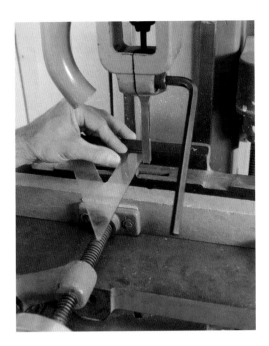

SET THE CHISEL SQUARE TO THE FENCE OR AT WHATEVER ANGLE THE JOB DEMANDS. The author likes small plastic drafting triangles for this task because they're light and true.

were locked in too tightly. It is best to accommodate movement so that as the rails expand, they'll move toward the inner part of the frame, as shown in the drawing on p. 164. This is especially important for inset cabinet doors, so they won't bind.

I've always been dead set against gluing opposing grains. The joints break down after many years of service. I've never glued a mortise-and-tenon joint in a large interior or exterior door because I know it will last a lifetime. But narrow rails, depending on the species, won't move too much, so I glue these joints. (I prefer white glue; it has some elasticity when dry.) I usually pin the joint in some fashion.

Mark the Joints Precisely

After I've processed and sized the materials, I pair up the stiles, mark their faces and mark the faces of the rail stock. Machining of all the parts should be done with the faces against a fence, table, or other fixed

platform so that all parts are indexed from the face surface. This ensures that the relationship between the mortise and tenon will be the same on all pieces.

Establish and mark where mortise slots and haunch cuts begin and end. Using a sample piece, make a mortise to the desired depth (about 1/8 in. deeper than the tenon length) in its approximate location front to back. Use scrap from the materials being used.

Next make a tenon (with or without a cope) to the desired length, position it front to back on the rail (tenons are rarely centered on the stock) and thickness to fit the mortise. Then fine-tune the front-to-back position on the mortise machine so that the fit is flush on the face, or whatever position is desired. Remember that when you assemble frames with a coped and molded stile and rail, most copes will have a tendency to pull the tenon toward the face as the frame is clamped up, as shown in the drawing on p. 164.

Making the Plunge

Plunging methods vary depending on the size and type of mortise and the material used. Facing the machine, I make the first plunge at the left end of the mortise. If I need to make a really deep mortise—too much work for the first plunge—I'll go as deep as possible, move to the right one-half the chisel width and plunge just short of the first hole's depth.

I return to the first hole and plunge deeper, repeating this process until the first hole is to the desired depth. I move to the right end of the mortise and make a full-depth plunge (or repeat the above process in reverse). Then, starting from the right and working to the left, I plunge one-half to three-quarters the width of the chisel with each overlapping plunge, until I reach the first hole on the left. I replunge in line from left to right. This cleans off the side walls and the bottom of the mortise. It's

Plunging methods vary depending on the size and type of mortise and the material used.

LOCATING MORTISES

Plan the Joint for Movement

Seasonal expansion of rail will cause this door to bind.

Seasonal movement won't affect fit of this door.

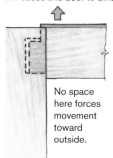

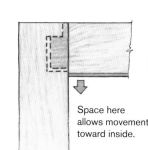

No space here forces movement toward outside.

Space here allows movement toward inside.

Shape Affects the Fit

Coped rails tend to move toward the front face under clamp pressure. To avoid this problem, snugly fit the tenon to the mortise.

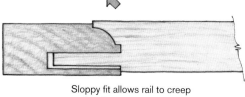

Sloppy fit allows rail to creep under clamp pressure.

Sources

Garrett Wade Co.
161 Avenue of the Americas
New York, NY, 10013
800-221-2942
www.garrettwade.com

a little dangerous to drag the chisel across the bottom of the mortise to clean it; snagging may snap the bit tip, bend the chisel or both. But I do use this process for cleaning a tenon haunch, which isn't as deep.

When the mortise slot is six or more times (my own rule of thumb) longer than the chisel size, I will make one or more midway holes between the left and right ends. This keeps the tool cutting straight on long mortises, especially when the edge of the mortise is close to the face of the stock. On very long mortises (for large door bottom rails, for example), I will split the tenon and make two mortise slots.

Cut Haunches Cleaner On most frame-and-panel doors, a groove is cut in the rails and stiles to hold the panel. If this groove is the same width as the tenon, it can serve as the cut for the haunch. If not, a haunch cut must be made with the mortise machine. When the machine is set up for the regular mortise, a stop controls the depth of the mortise. A second stop will serve to cut the desired haunch depth. Rather than reset the machine stop, I use a block of wood (see the photo on p. 166) as a spacer to save time and trouble.

After the mortise is made, I plunge the haunch, working toward the end of the stile. Then replunge the haunch from the outside back toward the mortise. And, with the chisel pressed to the bottom of the slot, I slowly scrape the bottom of the slot clean with a side-to-side motion of the chisel. This produces a clean haunch cut, which may be visible at the end of a frame or top of a cabinet door.

Frames with No Panels Have Joints That Show When making frames that have no panels, such as a cabinet face frame, a tight joint is required at the intersection of the mortise and tenon because the joint is not hidden inside a panel groove. Before cutting the mortise, I score the ends of the slot with a hand chisel the same width as the mortise. That helps prevent chipping.

I've noticed that the bit has a tendency to leave a slightly ragged edge as it plunges. I also use the chisel to shave back the tenon slightly, so it will go into the mortise easily but draw up tightly at assembly. Also, when the bit is exiting from the end plunge, it will sometimes snag on the edge and lift up some material with it. To keep that from happening, I exert slight pressure on the stock, with the wheel that controls the left-to-right movement of the table, keeping the chisel away from the edge of the mortise.

Large Mortises Need More Passes If you have to make a wide mortise and don't have a big enough chisel, make two separate mortise slots, leaving ⅛ in. or so of mate-

Sharpening Hollow Chisels

BY JOHN LIVELY

You probably can get by with a slightly dull blade on your tablesaw or a less-than-exquisitely sharp slotting bit in your router. But if you're punching out mortises in oak or cherry with a hollow chisel, very sharp is a required condition. A dull hollow chisel just won't work. It takes lots of muscle to force a dull bit into the cut, and once buried in the stock, the bit sticks there. This is why you'll find more hollow-chisel mortising rigs in storage than in actual use.

But if you keep your hollow chisels really sharp all the time, they'll cut crisply with minimal effort and back out of the hole with ease. With the right tools, sharpening hollow chisels can be an uncomplicated, uncluttered, quick affair.

HONE THE OUTSIDES FIRST

All four outside faces of the hollow chisel should be honed before you tackle the cutting edges of the tool. There are two reasons: First, you get sharper cutting edges, and second, you reduce binding in the cut. Honing polishes all those grinding scars, which act like treads on a tire, and reduces friction during cutting and withdrawal.

For honing the sides, I clamp the hollow chisel in my vise and use a medium-india slip stone (see the top photo at right). You could hone them on a benchstone just as you would the back of an ordinary chisel. Make sure you get a nicely polished surface on all four faces of the chisel—smooth and slick.

THEN GO AFTER THE BEVEL

Now that you've honed the four faces of the chisel, how do you get into the hollow of the tool to sharpen those bevels? Without the correct tool, that can be a big problem. A look through the stack of woodworking catalogs teetering on the back of your commode will reveal that almost every mail-order supplier offers hollow chisels. But few offer the simple little device you need to sharpen them.

This thing is a reamer, basically. Its body is a fluted conical cutter (sort of like a countersink). The reamer has a tapered square shaft on one end for chucking into a bit brace and a hole in the pointy end for accepting interchangeable pilots (see the middle photo at right). You insert the correct pilot into the reamer, insert the pilot into the hollow chisel and crank away gingerly (see the bottom photo at right) to remove enough tool steel to establish clean, sharp interior bevels. Return briefly to your stone to hone off any burrs, and you're finished.

I use a Clico reamer, which is available through Garrett Wade Co. Wherever you buy one, make sure you ask whether the pilots fit into the bits you own. The Clico reamer that Garrett Wade sells, for instance, fits Clico's English chisels but may need a masking tape bushing to fit Taiwanese chisels.

JOHN LIVELY is the former CEO of the Taunton Press, Inc.

FIRST, HONE THE CHISEL. Use a small slip stone to hone all four outside faces of the hollow chisel until smooth and polished.

THEN REAM THE INSIDE BEVEL. Interchangeable pilots fit different chisels. After selecting the correct pilot and mounting the reamer in a brace, gently grind the inside bevel. Any burrs may be removed with a slip stone.

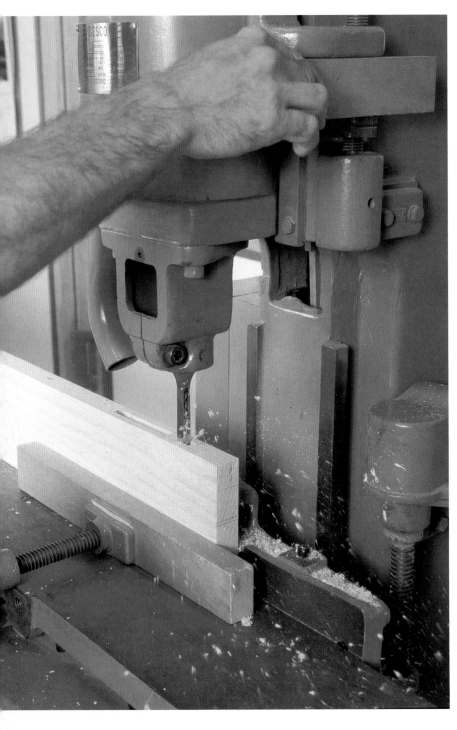

TO LIMIT DEPTH, USE A BLOCK. Instead of resetting the machine for
the shallow haunch, the author inserts a block of wood as a spacer.

rial in between. Go back and plunge out the middle. This is time-consuming. But if you overlap the first slot, the chisel will flex into it and produce a tapered mortise, and you'll have to taper all your tenons. In some cases, this routine may be your only choice because you'd have to be Godzilla to push a 1-in. chisel into a piece of hard maple.

Cut Sash Bars on Both Sides If I have to make a through mortise for sash bars, I'll plunge from both sides to keep the mortise tracking straighter vertically and to eliminate tearout, which seems to occur even when I use a back-up piece.

Cut for Lock Sets before Assembly If I'm making a batch of passage doors or a lot of cabinet doors that require full-mortise locks, I'll mortise all the stiles for the hardware before the doors go together. It's easier and more accurate than using a hand drill and chisels later on.

The Benchtop Versions

I don't use a drill-press mortiser, but I did try a few of the benchtop mortisers to see how the smaller machines compared to industrial-grade mortisers. Without going into a full-fledged tool review, I should say that I was skeptical of these machines before I got my hands on them. But I was surprised to learn how well a little ½-hp motor with a hand-lever driven, pinion-geared plunger could cut a fine mortise. The design is similar to the industrial-grade versions, but the devil is in the details. Driving the plunge by hand is more cumbersome and tiring, and the benchtop versions don't offer the same conveniences of table movement. The hold-down mechanisms are not nearly as strong and somewhat difficult and time-consuming to adjust.

If you're not in the market for a large mortise machine, I think you may be better off using a router. Unless, of course, you just want a new toy to play with.

JOHN WEST owns Cope and Mould Millwork Co. in Danbury, Connecticut.

Choose the Right Drill Bit for the Job

BY BRIAN BOGGS

Drilling is serious business. When I drill a hole for a rung in one of my chair legs, the leg I'm drilling is already sanded and oiled. The rung is turned to fit. Any mistake now would be very expensive, so I'm betting a lot on the performance of my drill. But why not? Drilling clean, accurate holes should be a simple task. A drill bit spinning in a chuck can be jigged to cut a hole in just about any material woodworkers use at just about any angle. But with all of the drill bits to choose from in all of the catalogs overloading our bookshelves, selecting the right bit for the task at hand can be pretty complicated.

While there is a huge variety of bits available, there are three things that all bits need to do: (1) Stay centered, (2) cut the wood loose to form a round hole, (3) eject the chips. Bits vary in how they accomplish each of these tasks. Improving performance in one area invariably diminishes it in others. No single bit covers all of the bases, but it's not likely you'll need every type available. To know which bit to use when, I think it's important to understand the anatomy of each bit—just how it is designed and how that design affects its performance. I hope this article will steer you toward the bits that best cover the range of your drilling needs.

Twist-Drill Bits

The most common bit, the twist drill, is also one of the simplest. It covers the widest range of cutting possibilities in wood, sheet goods, metals, and plastics and is also available in the widest variety of sizes. A twist-drill bit performs adequately or well in practically all general drilling situations for woodworkers. A couple of exceptions: drilling at angles over 45° and drilling perfectly flat-bottomed holes. A twist drill is excellent for cutting holes into end grain, where the cutting action of the bit yields the cleanest, fastest, and most accurate holes of any of the bits. I keep an index of inexpensive twist drills handy for general shop use, such as making plywood jigs and forms. And a few finely tuned twist drills live on a rack by my drill press, ready for more precise work.

A twist drill's lips work both to center the bit and to cut the wood. With most other precision bits, the cutting action is divided in two: They'll have cutters that score the perimeter of the hole and lips that lift the chips within the perimeter. The sharpness of the lips is more critical with twist drills than with most bits, especially at the outer corners, where any tearout will show in the finished hole. Some tearout is inevitable with a twist drill in all but end-grain drilling; the

Twist-Drill Bits

ADVANTAGES

- Exceptional for drilling into end grain

- Good general-purpose bit for solid wood and sheet goods

- Easy to sharpen

LIMITATIONS

- Poor for severe angles

- Leaves some tearout at perimeter of hole

- Tendency to walk at start of cut

Flute   Land   V-angle

Shank

Margin   Lip

Lip clearance is the surface behind the lip that is ground away to permit the lip to cut the wood at its edge—like the end of a chisel—rather than the whole tip contacting the wood at the same time.

Lip clearance   Web

Lip

118°

118° Twist drill

90°

90° Twist drill

BEST BIT FOR END GRAIN. A twist drill, which cuts like a ripsaw, bores into end grain beautifully. Brad-point and Forstner bits, which score the hole at the perimeter, act more like crosscut saws and perform better than twist drills in cross-grain but not as well in end grain.

only way to reduce or prevent it is to use a relatively slow feed rate and a very sharp lip.

The V-angle at the tip of the bit can vary from 60° to 118° for drilling wood. Most bits in the catalogs are ground to 118°, which is standard for drilling metals. Twist drills with 90° V-angles are available (I buy them from Morris Wood Tool; see Sources), but for anything more acute, I grind them myself. When working in wood, the sharper the V-angle, the better the bit centers and the cleaner entry and exit it makes. The longer point that results when the V-angle is sharper reduces the usable depth of a hole, however.

At the very tip of the twist-drill bit, the two lips meet and form a chisellike web rather than a true center point. The web is more durable than a center point, but it can cause the bit to wander just as the bit starts to cut. The web doesn't actually cut any wood; it sort of mangles the fibers as

it spins, making it possible to force the bit into the wood. On larger bits a pilot hole is sometimes recommended to accommodate the large web. The smaller the web, the less force is required, the better the bit centers, and the less it walks at the entry. Manufacturers sometimes minimize, or thin, the web for this reason. I like to grind the tips to eliminate the web on my bits, sacrificing durability for performance.

A bit's clearance angle also affects its performance. The clearance angle is the amount of relief behind the cutting edge of the lip. Just as you can't do much chiseling if you hold the chisel flat on the workpiece, you would struggle to drill a hole if the whole tip of the bit—the cutting edge of the lip and the area behind it—contacts the wood at the same time. If there's not enough clearance, too much pressure is required to enter the wood and the bit gets hot from the friction. Too much clearance,

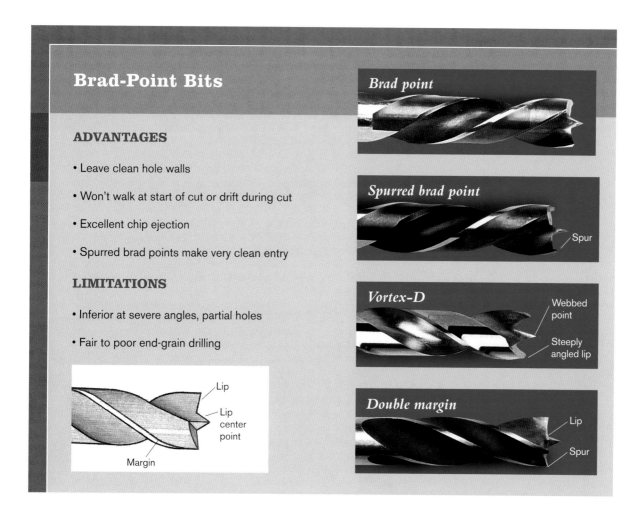

Brad-Point Bits

ADVANTAGES

- Leave clean hole walls
- Won't walk at start of cut or drift during cut
- Excellent chip ejection
- Spurred brad points make very clean entry

LIMITATIONS

- Inferior at severe angles, partial holes
- Fair to poor end-grain drilling

Brad point

Spurred brad point

Spur

Vortex-D

Webbed point

Steeply angled lip

Double margin

Lip

Spur

Lip

Lip center point

Margin

and the bit vibrates in the cut for lack of support. When you sharpen your own bits, these angles should be maintained carefully.

Although it's true that all of the cutting takes place at the tip of the bit—those sharp-edged spiral flutes are merely passive conductors of chips—the flutes of a twist drill are still as important as any other aspect of the bit. In machinist's catalogs there are bits with a variety of flute (helix) angles to more effectively eject shavings of difficult materials. The bits I've seen in woodworking catalogs have moderate spiral flutes, and they work just fine in wood as long as they are kept clean and rust free.

Brad-Point Bits

A brad-point bit is basically a twist drill with a modified end. The brad-point design addresses two shortcomings of the twist-drill bit when used in wood: The bit overcomes the tendency to walk at the start of a hole,

and it reduces tearout at the perimeter of the hole. These modifications make brad-point bits better than twist drills for precision cutting in virtually all cases, with the prominent exception of drilling into end grain.

There are two basic types of brad-point bits—those with scoring spurs and those without. Brad points without spurs—plain brad points—have lips that angle down and outward from the center, so they first contact the wood at the perimeter of the hole. A long point in the center engages the wood before the lips begin to cut. This style still has some tendency to tear the wood at the perimeter of the hole, but tearout can be prevented with a sharp bit and a light cut.

A fairly new variation on this plain brad point is the Vortex-D® bit. It has lips that are ground at a severe downward angle and a center point that is ground on only two sides, leaving a flat, chisellike web across the center rather than the standard four-sided

| 118°
Twist drill | 90°
Twist drill | Brad
point | Spurred
brad point | Forstner | Power
bore | Auger | Spoon |

MODERATE ANGLES ARE NO PROBLEM FOR A BRAD-POINT BIT. Angles like this can be handled by a brad point because the spurs and center point are engaged before the lips begin cutting. The Austrian double-margin brad point (shown here) has separate margins for its spurs and its lips.

point of the other brad points. The bit's steeply angled lips perform like spurs to cut a clean entry, but the web at the end of the point can cause the bit to walk across the surface of the workpiece when drilling freehand. In my testing I could not find any situation where this type of bit outperformed the other brad points.

A spurred, or lipped, brad point is far superior to its spurless cousin. The spurs are extensions of the margins that score the perimeter of the hole, preventing any tearout as the chips are lifted by the cutting lips. A spurred brad point is excellent for its clean entry and clean walls and for drilling at angles. A spurred brad point will even cut a reasonably clean hole after it has dulled slightly, an important feature, especially in production situations.

An interesting variation on the spurred brad point is a double-margin bit made in Austria (available from Woodcraft[SM]; see Sources). Instead of the spurs being at the ends of the lips, they are located on their own margins. This allows the lips and the spurs to be ground separately, which makes sharpening easier. Performance is virtually identical to a regular spurred brad point.

I use plain brad points for all of my pinning, because they are easier to sharpen than spurred brad points, especially in the smaller sizes. Were I to work with medium-density fiberboard (MDF) and melamine, I would choose these simpler bits over the spurred

bits because they cut just as well in this application, and I don't have to risk dulling and burning the spurs on my good bits. I also prefer plain brad points over spurred brad points when drilling end grain. Without the spurs, a brad point cuts more like a ripsaw, leaving very clean walls, even with an aggressive feed. In general, you can think of any bit with a spur or cutting rim to be a crosscutting bit (like a crosscut saw). Choose spurless bits for end grain.

A spurred brad point is the bit of choice for the bulk of the joinery in my chairs because the bit cuts a beautiful hole, even at an angle, and I can feed a little faster than with a twist drill or a plain brad point. Also, the flutes clear the chips well enough that I can plunge to the bottom of a 1½-in.-deep hole in one pass without worrying about clogging.

Forstner and Multispur Bits

Most bits we use are centered as they cut by contacting the workpiece with the center of the bit. A Forstner bit is unique in that it uses a peripheral rim to keep the cut running true. The rim is so effective in guiding the bit that the center point is optional. For cutting through very thin stock or anywhere a perfectly flat-bottomed hole is critical, a Forstner is the bit of choice. The bit also has the ability to cut overlapping holes, which is handy in mortising and other situations where stock removal is most easily done on the drill press. (Center-guided bits, such as twist drills and brad points, because they need to engage wood at the center of the cut to run true, have trouble with overlapping holes.) A Forstner bit is also very good for drilling at severe angles and for angled partial holes, two more operations that are very difficult for a center-guided bit. All off-angle and overlapping holes cut with a Forstner bit should be drilled on the drill press.

Most of what a Forstner bit is good at requires that the rim be extremely sharp, especially at the leading edge. The rim serves the same function as the spurs on a brad point—it scores the fibers ahead of the cut. Because the rim is continuous and stays engaged in the cut, the bit won't drift laterally. The rim also keeps the bit from taking a heavy cut. This helps prevent tearout at the beginning of a cut, even when drilling into round stock or drilling angled holes, situations where the rim can't cut the entire periphery before the lips start lifting out chips.

The multispur, or sawtooth, bit is a variation on the Forstner. The multispur bit lacks the finesse and slick cut of a regular Forstner in some situations, like overlapping holes, but it cuts more aggressively. This is particularly helpful in larger holes. With larger-diameter Forstners, the rim is quite long and heat build-up gets to be a problem. The multispur design reduces friction and provides much faster entry into the wood. Most sets of Forstners come with solid rim bits up to 1 in. diameter and switch to the multispur design for the larger sizes.

For all of its advantages, the Forstner has some serious drawbacks. First, because of the design of the rim, the chip chute narrows at the opening, which makes chip ejection almost impossible in holes deeper than the height of the chute. For deeper holes the bit must be lifted nearly out of the hole every ⅛ in. or so to clear chips.

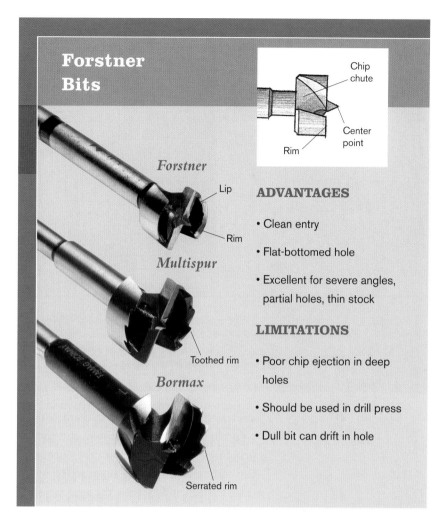

Forstner Bits

Forstner

Lip

Rim

Multispur

Toothed rim

Bormax

Serrated rim

Chip chute

Center point

Rim

ADVANTAGES

- Clean entry
- Flat-bottomed hole
- Excellent for severe angles, partial holes, thin stock

LIMITATIONS

- Poor chip ejection in deep holes
- Should be used in drill press
- Dull bit can drift in hole

Having a clogged bit going up and down is risky and affects the quality of the hole. Also, while a new Forstner tracks well, with any amount of wear the bit starts to drift slightly through the cut, especially on end grain. This is probably the worst problem with Forstners, and it is compounded by the fact that the bits are a bear to sharpen.

Because of the way the rim works on both Forstners and multispurs, they are well-suited for cross-grain cutting and perform pretty poorly on end grain. A Forstner cuts well in plywood, but a multispur is a better choice for manufactured sheet goods like MDF and oriented-strand board (OSB). Both bits make an ugly exit if unsupported, so use a backer board.

There is a type of multispur on the market, a German-made bit called Bormax®. Its teeth are formed by grinding the outside of the rim in a pattern that looks like

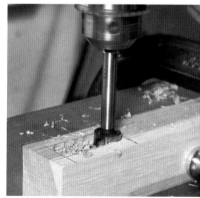

ALL-TERRAIN BIT. Steep angles, overlapping holes, very thin stock—none of these situations poses a problem for the Forstner bit, with its continuous rim guiding the bit. Unless the bit is backed out of deep holes every ⅛ in. or so, chips become impacted above it and can cause burning.

Spoon Bits

ADVANTAGES

- The link to yesteryear

- Fairly clean holes with an unusual bit

LIMITATIONS

- Centering the bit is an acquired skill

- Hole is somewhat oval

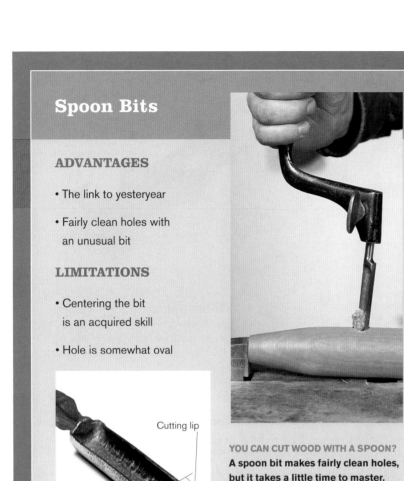

YOU CAN CUT WOOD WITH A SPOON?
A spoon bit makes fairly clean holes, but it takes a little time to master. The bit won't drill exactly where you start it, but you can learn the bit's eccentricities and even come to enjoy them.

Cutting lip

Hollow serves as chip chute.

Sources

Morris Wood Tool
423-586-0110

Woodcraft
800-225-1153
www.woodcraft.com

Wharton Valley Chair Works
607-965-842

tear at the opening. Starting the hole perpendicular to the work to score the hole first and then restarting at the desired angle can prevent this, but this operation is less than ideal.

Another downside of this bit is that on the larger sizes (5/8 in. and up) the lead screw is big enough to start a split in the wood. I've had such splits go unnoticed until a chair rung is driven into its hole. A most disappointing sight in an otherwise fine chair.

Spoon Bits

A spoon bit is unlike any other in several ways. Probably the most important is that it requires far more skill to use. Not only does the bit need to be powered with a bit brace, but it also requires quite a lot of practice to get it to drill a hole exactly where you want. (Wharton Valley Chair Works makes excellent spoon bits, see Sources.)

The spoon bit's cutting action is similar to that of a twist drill. But it lacks the symmetrical balance that helps hold a twist drill centered, so a spoon bit pulls itself off center at the beginning of the cut. This sounds awful, but it is quite predictable, and with practice you learn where and how to begin your cut so that the hole ends where you want it to. And because the feed rate is determined by pressure, you can take a light cut for a clean entry. Once the bit is in the hole, it follows itself. But more than with any other bit, the quality of the result depends on the skill of the user.

Because of the initial skill development required to use this bit well, and the fact that it has no advantages over the twist drill, I can't recommend it as a practical requirement in your drilling arsenal. But for those of us who enjoy the challenges of mastering traditional woodworking techniques for benefits we can't take to the bank, the spoon bit is definitely a kick.

BRIAN BOGGS builds chairs in Berea, Kentucky.

an efficient bit to get to know. And for folks in the timber-framing trade, the long, fluted sections of the bit are essential for the deep holes needed for trunnels. But the list of problems with the auger is long. None of the new bit-brace augers I have encountered was machined accurately, and most cut an oversize hole. They all require tuning up before they cut very well, and the quality of cut of even a well-tuned bit pales in comparison with all of the previously mentioned bits.

Drilling angled holes with this bit is something of a trick, too. Because the lead screw regulates feed rate, you can't take a light cut at the entry to the hole. Because the spur can't score the entire hole before the lips engage, you can get a pretty nasty

Bandsaws

The bandsaw is a remarkably versatile tool. In fact, some woodworkers would choose it over the tablesaw if forced to decide between the two. A bandsaw can make straight and curved cuts as well as circles. It can rough out bowl blanks, slab small logs, and slice thin veneers, among other operations. But for a bandsaw to perform well, it must be tuned properly and fitted with the right blade for the job.

One operation the bandsaw performs better than any other tool is resawing, which allows you to cut book-matched panels or thin slices of veneer. For successful resawing, though, the saw must be adjusted perfectly, and your feed technique and fence have to account for blade drift. Otherwise, you're looking at a setup for frustration. But not to worry. In this section, you'll find out exactly what you need to do to make the operation go smoothly. You'll also see how to soup up your bandsaw to go above and beyond its usual abilities.

Bandsaw Tune-Up

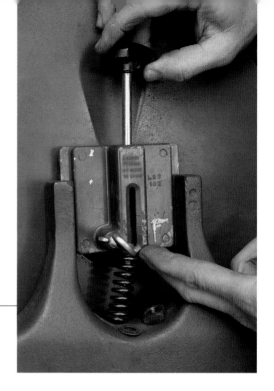

BY JOHN WHITE

A poorly tuned bandsaw will cause nothing but frustration. But the tune-up process is straight-forward, takes only a few hours, and is certainly worth the trouble. The procedure of making a bandsaw behave consists of two basic steps: tuning up the machine and then adjusting it for the blade being used and the work being done.

In this chapter, I've broken down the tune-up process into its main components, allowing you to go through the whole machine step by step. During tune-up, the machine's wheels, drive pulleys, and table are brought into alignment and the guide assemblies are cleaned and lubricated. Also, the machine's tires, drive belts, guide components, and bearings are checked and, if

TROUBLESHOOTING GUIDE

Symptom	Possible Cause	See
Vibration at high speed	• Pulleys on motor are worn or bent • Drive belt is stiff or worn • Wheel-bearing failure • Thrust-bearing failure	Wheels, Blade Guides
Vibration at low speed	• Wheels are bent or misaligned • Dust buildup on tires • Tires are cracked or worn • Tire is lifting off wheel • Blade is cracked or kinked or has a bad weld	Wheels, Tires
Blade doesn't stay centered on wheels	• Tires are grooved, hardened, or worn • Wheel-bearing failure • Wheels are misaligned • Tracking mechanism is slipping or bent	Tension, Wheels, Tires
Blade doesn't cut straight	• Blade is dull • Fence is not aligned for drift • Worn guide blocks • Low blade tension • Poorly adjusted guides	Tension, Blade Guides
Cut is barrel shaped	• Blade is dull or too narrow • Feed rate is too fast • Low blade tension • Poorly adjusted guides	Tension, Blade Guides

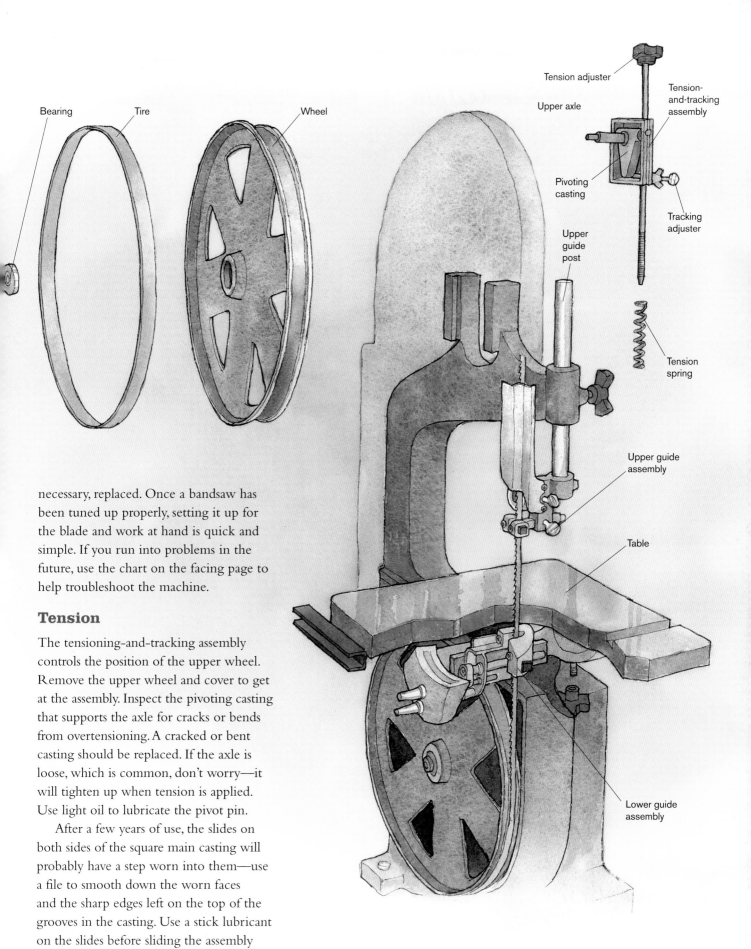

Bearing

Tire

Wheel

Tension adjuster

Upper axle

Tension-and-tracking assembly

Pivoting casting

Tracking adjuster

Upper guide post

Tension spring

Upper guide assembly

Table

Lower guide assembly

necessary, replaced. Once a bandsaw has been tuned up properly, setting it up for the blade and work at hand is quick and simple. If you run into problems in the future, use the chart on the facing page to help troubleshoot the machine.

Tension

The tensioning-and-tracking assembly controls the position of the upper wheel. Remove the upper wheel and cover to get at the assembly. Inspect the pivoting casting that supports the axle for cracks or bends from overtensioning. A cracked or bent casting should be replaced. If the axle is loose, which is common, don't worry—it will tighten up when tension is applied. Use light oil to lubricate the pivot pin.

After a few years of use, the slides on both sides of the square main casting will probably have a step worn into them—use a file to smooth down the worn faces and the sharp edges left on the top of the grooves in the casting. Use a stick lubricant on the slides before sliding the assembly back into the frame.

REMOVE COVER AND CLEAN UP TENSIONER. With the cover removed, it is easy to access the tensioner. Once the tensioner is removed, check to be sure the axle isn't bent, and then file the slides on both sides smooth.

The original tensioning spring on a 14-in. bandsaw is almost always crushed, making it impossible to tension the blade properly. The spring can be replaced with a heavy-duty version from Iturra Designs (888-722-7078) without having to remove the upper wheel and blade cover.

The last step in servicing the top end of the saw is to remove the tension and tracking bolts—clean the threads with a wire brush, and round off the ends with a file. Use a stick lubricant on the bolts before you reinstall them.

Wheels

Having the upper wheel aligned directly above the lower wheel allows the bandsaw blade to track better and puts less stress on the saw and the blade. On a 14-in. bandsaw, checking the alignment is easy. Remove the table and lay a long straightedge across the faces of both wheels. If the wheels are out of alignment, you'll see a gap between the straightedge and one wheel. On a Delta saw, the wheel alignment is adjusted by adding or removing shims on the upper axle. On Jet and most other Taiwanese-made saws, the upper wheel

CHECK THE ALIGNMENT. Begin by placing a long straightedge (White uses a 4-ft. level) across both wheels. Then adjust the tracking mechanism to bring the upper wheel parallel to the straightedge.

SHIM OUT THE UPPER WHEEL. **If the rims of both wheels aren't touching the straightedge, use shims to bring them into alignment. On Delta saws you can shim the upper wheel; for Taiwanese-made saws, shim the lower wheel.**

can't be shimmed without placing excess pressure on the wheel bearings. These saws are aligned by shimming behind the lower wheel. Iturra Designs sells inexpensive sets of graduated shims for both Delta and imported bandsaws.

Tires

Tires are simply oversize rubber bands. But they should be checked regularly, because the rubber becomes worn, cracked, or hardened and can cause tracking problems and vibration. A tire should have an obvious crown and be smooth and free of grooves. Press your thumbnail into the tire; it should press in easily, and the surface should spring back. A lack of springback is a sign that the tire has hardened and needs to be replaced. To remove a tire, use a screwdriver to lift it over the rim. If the old tire was glued on, clean off the adhesive using acetone. The new tire should snap into a groove in the rim of the wheel (see the photos on p. 180).

Table

To get square cuts on a bandsaw, the table must be aligned square to both the sides and back of the blade. To align the table,

Checking and Replacing Wheel Bearings

To test the wheel bearings, remove the saw's blade and rotate the wheel through several revolutions with the tip of a finger against one of the spokes. You may feel a slight drag, but the motion should be smooth and silent. Even small amounts of roughness or a grinding sound indicate a contaminated bearing. If there is only a small amount of catching, the saw is still usable, but new bearings should be installed soon. If there is continuous roughness or grinding noises, the saw shouldn't be used until new bearings have been installed.

OUT WITH THE OLD, IN WITH THE NEW. **A bandsaw wheel has two bearings: Even if only one is failing, they should both be replaced. The wheel bearings must be tapped out with a hammer and punch (top). When installing a new bearing, gently tap it into place using a soft hammer against the outer race (bottom).**

Installing a Bandsaw Blade

A bandsaw is not properly tuned until you have installed the blade and made sure it is tensioned and tracking properly and that the guides are set correctly. Following the steps here makes this a quick and straightforward process.

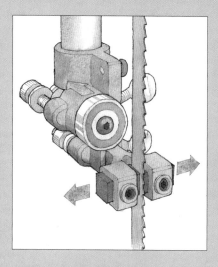

Step 1: Position the Blade

With the saw unplugged, pull back the guides and the thrust bearings and place the new blade on the wheels. Raise the upper guide assembly to clear the stock you'll be cutting by ¼ in. to ½ in.

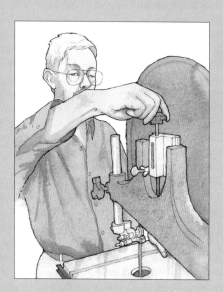

Step 2: Tension and Track

Rotate the upper wheel by hand while alternately increasing the tension and adjusting the tracking to keep the blade centered on the upper wheel.

Turning the tracking adjustment in adjusts the blade toward the back of the wheel.

Step 3: Adjust the Guide Assemblies

Move the upper and lower guide assemblies forward or backward to align the leading edge of the guide blocks or bearing with or just behind the back of the sawblade's gullets.

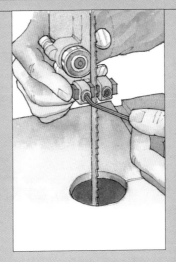

Step 4: Adjust the Guide Blocks

Move one of the guide blocks or bearings in each assembly so that it just touches the side of the blade. Lock it in place. Double-check that the block or bearing doesn't reach beyond the back of the blade's gullets. Bring the second block of each assembly against the blade. A soft block can be locked in place touching the blade. Hard blocks or ball-bearing guides should be spaced away from the blade with a single piece of paper. Rotate the blade by hand to check that a bad weld or kink in the blade won't cause problems.

Step 5: Position the Thrust Bearing

Bring the upper and lower thrust bearings forward to just barely touch the back of the blade. Rotate the blade by hand to make sure everything turns smoothly.

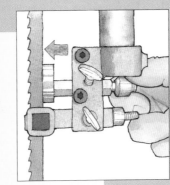

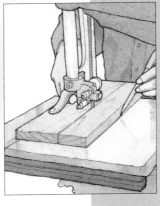

Step 6: Align the Fence for Drift

Begin by drawing a straight line parallel to the edge of a test board. Rip the board freehand, adjusting your feed angle until the blade naturally follows the line. Once the blade is following the line, hold the stock in place and turn off the saw. Use a marker to draw a line on the tabletop along the edge of the stock. Reinstall the fence and adjust its angel parallel with the mark on the table.

ALIGN THE UPPER THRUST BEARING. The blade should ride along only the outer edge of the bearing. If one face is scarred from use, flip over the bearing and use the back face.

Blade Guides

The guide assemblies on a 14-in. saw are mechanically simple but have a number of parts that can wear out or jam up. Start by replacing any thrust bearing that is noisy or won't rotate freely. Then remove the bearing support and guide-block holders, file off any paint and burrs and inspect all parts for cracks or worn threads. Remove all of the setscrews and round off their ends with a file—the smoothed ends will hold better. Remove the knob that locks the guide post and shape the tip of its threaded end to match the groove in the guide post. Clean

and lubricate the threads and the other parts of the guides as you reassemble them.

The guide blocks should be smooth, flat, and square. Clamp the blocks in the holder with their faces touching; there should be no gaps between the blocks.

The lower guide assembly on the Delta 14-in. bandsaw is more complex than the upper guide assembly, but the same logic applies to tune-up. The lower guide assembly on a Taiwanese-made saw is tuned up the same way as the upper guide assembly.

JOHN WHITE is the shop manager for *Fine Woodworking.*

ADJUSTING THE BLADE GUIDES

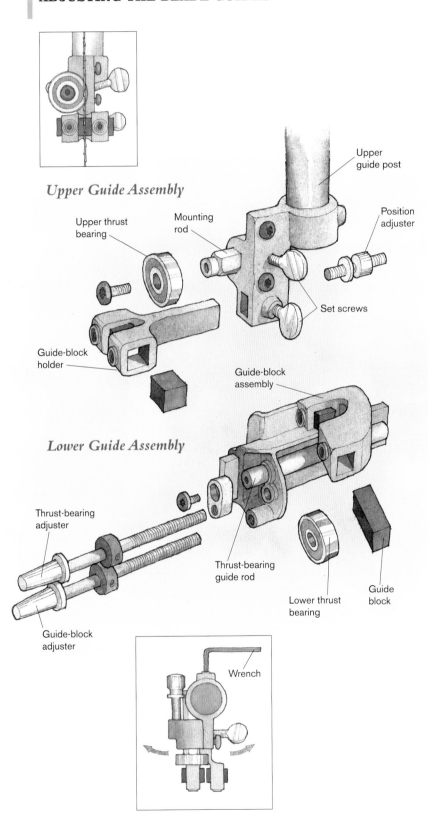

Upper Guide Assembly

Upper guide post

Upper thrust bearing

Mounting rod

Position adjuster

Set screws

Guide-block holder

Guide-block assembly

Lower Guide Assembly

Thrust-bearing adjuster

Thrust-bearing guide rod

Guide-block adjuster

Lower thrust bearing

Guide block

Wrench

ALIGN THE GUIDE ASSEMBLY WITH THE BLADE.
Loosen the Allen screw on the upper guide assembly and adjust the assembly until the faces of the guide blocks are parallel to the blade.

REPLACE THE LOWER THRUST BEARING. Remove the nut on the end of the guide rod and slide off the tube to free up the bearing. Clean up everything and, if necessary, slide a new bearing into place.

Resawing on the Bandsaw

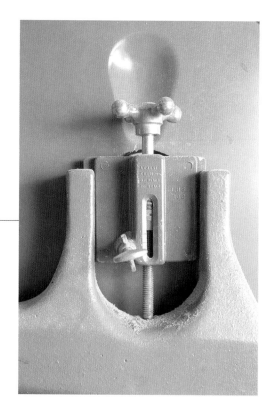

BLADE-TENSION SCALES AREN'T EXACT. **The author tensions the blade by ear, not by the calibrations on the saw.**

BY RONALD VOLBRECHT

I buy quilted maple for the backs and the sides of the guitars I make from a friend who is a lumber grader. Each year he inspects more than a million board feet of lumber, and if I'm lucky, he will find three good 2½-in.-thick planks. Some of the hardwoods and old-growth spruce I use are no less rare.

When it comes time to resaw these irreplaceable planks, I don't want anything to go wrong. Over the years, I've learned to adjust my bandsaw for consistent re-sawing with very little waste. I can get finished, ³⁄₃₂-in.-thick guitar backs from resawn boards that are only ⅛ in. thick.

I do all my resawing on a 21-year-old Delta 14-in. bandsaw. It has a 6-in. column extension, which allows me to resaw planks that are up to 12¼ in. wide. The boards I resaw are usually 8 in. to 10 in. wide. I use a ½-in. blade with 3 teeth per inch (tpi).

Other than replacing the motor, I have not made any modifications to the saw, and I have no magic tricks. But there is more to getting good results than just running a board through the saw. I tune my blade, set the guides close to the blade, and then make sure that the blade is good and tight (for more on this, see the story on p. 193). I use wrenches to lock down all the adjust-ment points on the saw so that they can't vibrate loose. Then I feed the plank slowly against a high fence (see the photo on the facing page), judging the feed rate by the sound of the blade.

A heavy-duty Motor and New Pulleys

When I bought the saw, it had a ½-hp, 1,750-rpm motor, but I soon replaced it with a ¾-hp, 3,450-rpm motor. Because the bigger motor turned faster, I had to change the pulleys to keep the blade run-ning near the factory speed of 3,000 feet per minute (fpm).

I used the formula given in the box on p. 188 to determine the right combination of pulleys. I kept the 2-in. pulley that came with the motor. That pulley and an 8½ -in. pulley on the saw would have given me the right blade speed, but the big pulley wasn't in stock locally. I tried a 12-in. pulley, but

PRESS THE PLANK AGAINST THE FENCE WHILE PUSHING IT THROUGH THE BLADE. The right hand pushes the board while the left hand is positioned down low to press the workpiece against the fence. Use a push stick at the end of the cut.

the blade ran too slowly (about 2,100 fpm). I ended up with an 11-in. pulley, which turns the blade at about 2,300 fpm. That's just about right for the work I do.

Choose a Good Blade, and Keep It Tight

I use the same type of blade for every cut I make on the bandsaw. It's a ½-in. skip-tooth blade with 3 tpi and a thickness of .025 in. I don't think the brand of the blade matters, but the quality of the welds does. I look for blades with good alignment at the weld and no blobs of metal. I check the back of the blade at the weld to make sure there is no offset. Problem welds cause the bandsaw to vibrate, and that makes the results inconsistent. I can tolerate a little offset or lumpiness because I carefully grind these defects smooth with a Dremel Moto-Tool and then dress the blade with a diamond stone.

I determine the correct tension by removing the blade guard on the left-hand column and plucking the blade as if it were a giant guitar string (see the left photo on

the facing page). The sound will go from a sloppy vibration to a smooth, low tone. At that point, you've reached the proper tension. For guitar players, the tone roughly corresponds to an E note on a bass guitar. When the blade sounds right, I replace the guard.

I've never bothered to release the blade tension when the saw's not running. In theory, constant tension will shorten the life of the saw's bearings, but I'm still using the originals. I'd rather keep my saw ready to roll than fiddle with blade tension every time I want to use it.

After the blade is tight, I turn the upper wheel by hand to check the blade tracking. I spin the wheel and adjust the thumbscrew near the blade tensioner until the blade runs in the middle of the tires. When the blade tracks true, I tighten the thumbscrew and its locknut with Vise-Grips®.

Next I set the table perpendicular to the blade. I raise the guides full height and use a long combination square. I put a light behind the square so I can detect and correct even small discrepancies (see the photo on p. 190). I tighten the knobs that lock the table in place with a wrench, so they don't loosen while I'm resawing. Before the next step, I check the squareness again.

Use a Wrench to Tighten the Adjusting Screws

Before I set the blade-guide adjustments, I raise the guide bar so the upper guides are about 9½ in. off the table—high enough to clear my resaw fence. I tighten the thumbscrews that hold the guide bar in place as tightly as I can. For leverage, I use a pair of Vise-Grips. With this kind of pressure, the end of the thumbscrew becomes slightly mushroom-shaped over time. This can cause the guide bar to rotate slightly each time the thumbscrew is tightened, and the motion can twist the blade. To prevent this, I

PLUCK THE BLADE TO CHECK THE TENSION. **Listen for a clear note, roughly an E on a bass guitar. The author replaces the blade guard after tensioning the blade.**

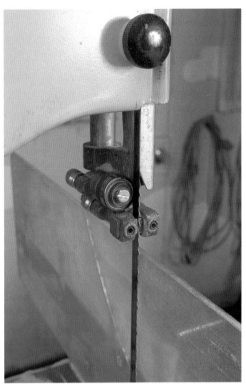

RAISE THE GUIDE BAR, AND ADJUST THE BLOCKS AND THRUST BEARING. **Set the gap between guide blocks and blade to .002 in., and bring the thrust bearing in light contact with the back of the blade.**

periodically remove the thumbscrews and file the ends square. With the guide bar set, I turn my attention to the guide blocks and thrust bearings. I usually adjust the lower guides first and then the uppers.

Some woodworkers prefer aftermarket guide blocks made of phenolic resin, but I've kept the original steel guide blocks that came with the saw. I prefer that the blade bear against a hard, flat surface, so I grind the guide blocks square and set them close to the blade to minimize its side-to-side motion. Because I clean up the welds on the blades, I can position the guide blocks only .002 in. from the blade. I use a feeler gauge to set the gap, and I tighten the setscrews carefully against the guide blocks so they don't shift. After they're locked in place, I double-check the gap. I locate the blocks just behind the blade gullet (see the right photo above).

Before moving the bearing, I spin it to make sure it turns freely. If necessary, I give it a little oil. If one side of the bear-

ing shows wear on the outer rim, I turn the bearing around. Then I move the bearing up to the back of the blade. It should just touch the blade but not spin until the saw is cutting wood.

When I first started resawing, I ruined a few boards because my carefully set adjustments vibrated loose. I tightened the adjustments as much as I could by hand, but that wasn't enough. I finally added locknuts to the lower guide adjusting screws. The nuts won't vibrate loose even after hours of resawing. I make them wrench-tight, which would be 20 ft. lb. to 25 ft. lb. on a torque wrench. On the upper guide adjustments, I use Vise-Grips locked onto the thumbscrews to torque them tightly enough to be vibration-proof. These adjustments make my cuts very precise, but the tolerances are so close they have to be reset each time the guide-bar height is altered.

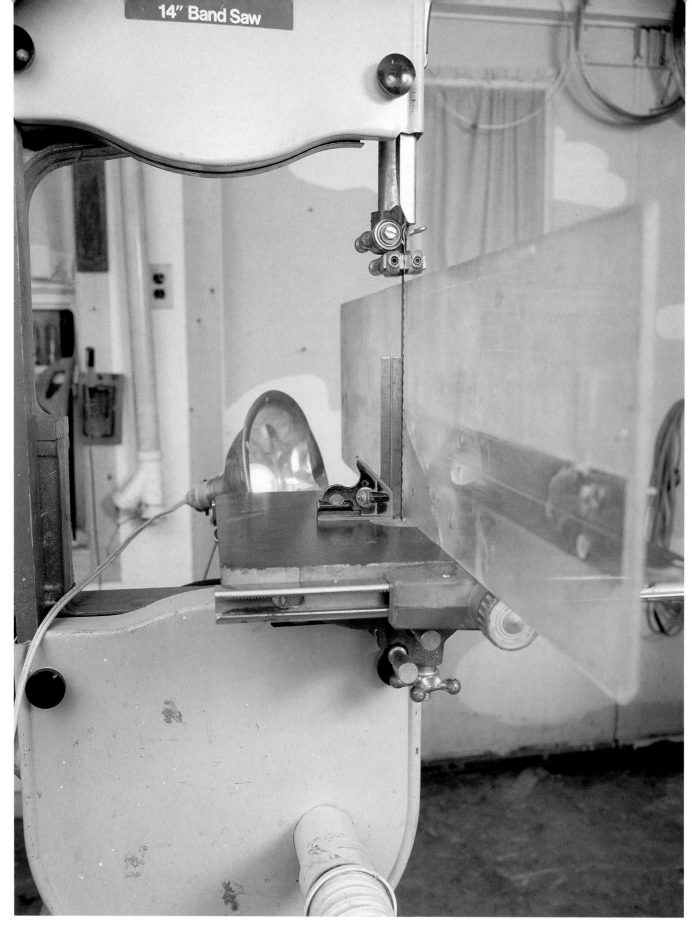

MAKE THE TABLE PERPENDICULAR TO THE BLADE. **The author uses a light behind the square to highlight small misalignments. An out-of-square adjustment can ruin stock.**

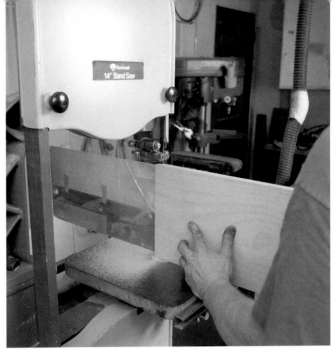

A WIDE BOARD NEEDS A HIGH FENCE. A length of angle iron bolted to the top of the bandsaw's original fence supports a facing of ¼-in. Plexiglas. Wedges help square the Plexiglas to the table.

SLOW, STEADY PRESSURE. The author maintains a steady feed rate as he moves the workpiece through the saw. Stopping even briefly will produce a thin spot in the board.

A High Fence Supports the Plank

The resaw fence needs to be almost as high as the piece being sawn. If the fence is too low, when feeding a plank through the saw, the bottom of the board will tend to move away from the fence. The face of the fence must be 90° to the table. Even if the fence is out of square by only ½°, finished boards resawn from wide planks will have a pronounced wedge shape.

I built my resaw fence by adding a 9-in.-high piece of ¼-in. Plexiglas® to the face of the rip fence that came with the saw. I used Plexiglas simply because it was handy. Plywood, Lexan® (similar to Plexiglas but stronger) or aluminum might be better. Even a crack in the resaw fence hasn't affected its performance. To better support the Plexiglas, I bolted a length of 3-in. by 3-in. angle iron to the top of the fence (see the left photo above).

When I first set up my resaw fence, the original rip fence wasn't square to the table. As a result, the top edge of the resaw fence was out of square. I fixed it by inserting wooden wedges between the Plexiglas and the angle iron (see the left photo above).

The wedges are about 1½ in. long and taper from ³⁄₁₆ in. to ¹⁄₁₆ in. along their length. Each time I set up the fence, I make sure the Plexiglas is square to the table and adjust the wedges as necessary.

You may have to adjust your bandsaw fence for lead or drift. That's when the blade won't make a cut parallel to the edge of the table. To adjust the fence to account for it, I draw a line parallel to the edge of a jointed board and make a freehand cut along the line for about half the length of the board. Then I stop sawing, clamp the board to the table and set up the fence along the jointed edge of the board. Now the fence is parallel to the cut, and the blade will have no drift. I periodically check for drift, but I've never found any on my saw. I hear the same from other woodworkers who use the same saw.

When I'm ready to resaw, I install the fence ⅛ in. to the right of the blade and lock it to the table at both ends with the clamps on the original fence. Then I prepare the plank by jointing both edges and one face. I run the jointed face against the

THE PROOF IS IN THE PUDDING. By adjusting his bandsaw carefully and feeding the workpiece through the cut steadily, the author gets consistent results like this.

fence. When using rare woods, it's important to waste very little. So I run the plank through a thicknessing sander to resurface it after each cut. The sander takes off less wood than a planer and without tearout.

Feed Slowly, and Support the Piece

When resawing, I keep both hands on the piece, as shown in the right photo on p. 187. My right hand is on the end grain, pushing the board through the saw (use a push stick for the last few inches of the cut). I keep my left hand low, and I spread out my fingers to press the planks against the fence across a wide area. Slow, constant feed pressure is the key to success. If you stop sawing for a moment, the blade will bite a little deeper.

I start out sawing slowly, listening to the sound of the blade. It should make a smooth, steady rasp with a light blip as the weld goes through the guides. I gradually increase the rate of feed, still listening. I feed steadily and strive to keep the sound of the blade steady as well. If I feed too fast, the sound switches to an uneven scraping as the saw vibrates more rapidly. If I push faster still, the vibration will smooth out, but the blade will wander, making an uneven kerf. I just keep the feed rate slow. It takes me about 6 minutes to resaw a quilted maple plank 8 in. wide by 3 ft. long.

RONALD VOLBRECHT builds and repairs guitars. He has built instruments for John Mellencamp, Richie Sambora, Hoyt Axton, and other artists. He lives and works in Nashville, Tennessee.

Keep Your Bandsaw Singing, not Whining

BY ANATOLE BURKIN

Like a stringed instrument, a bandsaw likes being under tension to perform well. But too much tension can de-tune your machine. We asked two tool manufacturing representatives to comment on what happens to a bandsaw when too much tension is applied. And we asked how to keep a bandsaw running smoothly.

Louis Brickner, vice president of engineering and product development for Delta International Machinery, says one way to spot overtensioning is to slide the guide bar up and down after tensioning the blade and setting the guide blocks. "If you have to readjust the blocks, it's a clue that you're bending or flexing the machine beyond its design capability," says Brickner.

Most woodworkers adjust blades by using the markers on the machine's tensioning adjustment screw and/or listening for a low tone by plucking the blade as it's tightened. Either method should get the blade in the 7,000 to 15,000 psi tension range (the low figure is bare minimum, and the high number is optimum). These numbers apply to carbon steel blades and bimetal blades, which make up the bulk of what's sold for small- to medium-size bandsaws. If you have an industrial-grade saw, higher tensions may be possible.

The only way to measure the precise tension of your blade is with a tension gauge. You can order one through Starrett®, but it will set you back $294*.

Brickner also advises against keeping a guide bar raised too far above the work. The upper guide

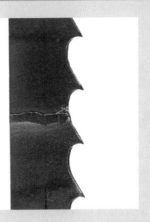

GET RID OF THE BUMPS. Ronald Volbrecht uses a diamond stone to smooth out a rough weld (left) or a Dremel Moto-Tool to feather out a misaligned blade (right).

should just clear the surface of what's being cut. That greatly reduces the risk of injury.

A common problem customers have is tires flying off the bandsaw because the motor they installed runs too fast, says Brickner. To upgrade the motor, pick one that runs at the same speed as the original (1,750 rpm), or change the pulleys after installing a faster motor (see the box on p. 188).

Another problem is using a blade too wide for a 14-in. bandsaw. Machines of this size are not meant for 1-in. or wider blades. Tensioning them can bend or twist the machine. Best results are obtained with blades ½ in. wide or less.

As with all machines, proper maintenance can prevent problems and injuries. Brickner says it's important to inspect for wheel-bearing wear regularly. Unplug the machine, take off the blade and pulley belt, and spin the wheels. A clicking noise in the shaft spells bearing trouble.

Ray McPherson, product safety manager at Powermatic®, says it's important to inspect the spring in the blade-tensioning screw occasionally. A broken spring can make it easier to overtension a blade.

Some woodworkers touch up bandsaw blade welds with a file or grinder. McPherson cautions against taking off too much metal. "A welded joint is stronger than the rest of the blade simply because there's more metal there. Just don't overdo it (grinding). Make sure the weld is complete and there's metal-to-metal contact," says McPherson.

For a comprehensive book on using and tuning bandsaws, a good source is *Band Saw Basics* by Mark Duginske (Sterling Publishing Co., 1989).

*Note price estimates are from 1997.

ANATOLE BURKIN is the publisher of *Fine Woodworking*.

Terms You Need to Know

Bladeback: The body of the blade not including the teeth. The bladeback must be both tough and pliable to withstand the continuous flexing as the blade runs around the wheels of the saw.

Gullet: The curved area at the base of the tooth that carries away the sawdust. The size and efficiency of the gullets decrease as the pitch is increased.

Pitch: The number of teeth per inch (tpi) as measured from the tips of the teeth. The pitch determines the feed rate at which the blade can cut and the smoothness of the sawn surface. Pitch can be either constant or variable.

Rake angle: The angle of the face of the tooth measured in respect to a line drawn perpendicular to the cutting direction. Regular- and skip-tooth blades have a 0° rake angle, which gives them a slow, scraping action. A hook-tooth blade has a positive rake angle, which causes it to cut more aggressively.

Set: On blades designed for woodworking, every tooth is set (or bent) left or right, in an alternating sequence, to create a kerf wider than the bladeback. The set of a blade helps prevent binding during cutting. Although carbide teeth are not bent, they are wider than the steel body to which they're brazed. Then they're ground to create a set pattern that helps keep the blade running true.

Thickness: The thickness of the steel band measured at the bladeback. (In general, thick blades are wider and stiffer than thin blades.) Thick blades require larger-diameter bandsaw wheels to prevent stress cracks and premature blade breakage.

Teeth: The cutting portions of the blade. Teeth must be sharp, hard, and resistant to both heat and wear. The tip

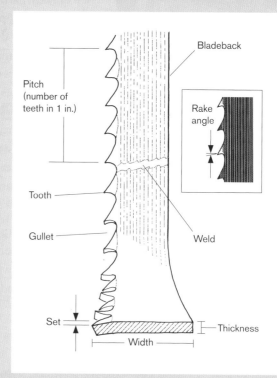

is the sharp part of the tooth that shears away the wood fibers. During sawing, the tooth tip is under tremendous stress and is subject to both heat and wear. The heat produced from friction during sawing can sometimes rise to 400°F on the tip. This occurs because the wood insulates the blade during cutting.

Width: The dimension of a blade from the back of the band to the tip of the tooth. Wider blades are stiffer and resist side-to-side flexing, making them the best choice for resawing. Narrow blades can cut tighter contours.

Spring steel is soft and flexible, which allow it to bend around the small-diameter wheels of benchtop saws. But because spring steel is so soft, it doesn't hold an edge for very long.

Several years ago, however, a unique spring-steel resaw blade—marketed under the trade name Wood Slicer® and sold by Highland Hardware℠ (see Sources)—was introduced. Instead of being stamped, the teeth on this blade are carefully ground, hardened and polished. The teeth have a variable spacing that limits harmonic vibration. These blades make smooth cuts, and best of all, the kerf is a mere ¹⁄₃₂ in. —approximately half the kerf width of a typical carbide or carbon-steel blade. This means you'll get more veneer and less waste out of each plank. Additionally, because the Wood Slicer blade is only .022-in.-thick spring steel, it easily flexes around the medium-size wheels of bench-top bandsaws.

Bimetal Blades Offer the Best of Two Worlds The methods used for making bimetal blades are very different from those used for making most carbon-steel and carbide blades. A bimetal blade is actually two steel ribbons that are welded together. The back of a bimetal blade is composed of soft, flexible spring steel; the blade front, where the teeth are milled, is made of much harder high-speed steel. This strip of cobalt steel is welded onto the spring-steel blank before the teeth are cut. When the teeth are cut, all that remains of the cobalt steel is the tooth tip.

This combination produces a relatively inexpensive blade with longer wear than an ordinary carbon-steel blade. Unlike a carbon-steel blade that loses its sharpness and set at 400°F, the cobalt-steel teeth of a bimetal blade can withstand 1,200°F.

Another advantage of a bimetal blade is the beam strength of its spring-steel back, which can withstand great tension. The beam strength (see the top drawing on p. 198) of a bimetal blade, combined with its resistance to heat, has endeared this type of blade to many woodworkers.

Carbide Blades Are Pricey but Will Last
I'm sure that almost every woodworker is familiar with carbide. Carbide cutting tools have almost made high-speed steel a thing of the past. A significant difference between carbide and steel blades is that each carbide tooth is individually brazed onto a strong, flexible spring-steel bladeback. In fact, the recommended tension for a carbide blade is almost twice that of a carbon-steel blade,

Stock Thickness Dictates Blade Pitch

Pitch, the number of teeth per inch (tpi) on a blade, determines the feed rate and the smoothness of the cut surface. A blade with a continuous pattern of teeth has a constant pitch. A blade with teeth that vary in size has a variable pitch.

A blade with a fine pitch has more teeth per inch than a blade with a coarse pitch. A greater number of teeth means that each tooth is small, taking a small bite that leaves a smooth surface. A greater number of teeth also reduces the size of the gullets. Because small gullets can't haul away dust very quickly, a fine-pitch blade cuts slower and tends to get hotter than a coarse-pitch blade.

On a coarse-pitch blade, both the teeth and the gullets are larger, so each tooth bites off a greater amount of wood, and the large gullets can easily remove the sawdust from the kerf.

The major factor to consider when selecting proper tooth pitch is the thickness of the stock. In general, you want a blade that will have no fewer than six and no more than 12 teeth in the stock at any given time (see the drawings below). For example, if you're cutting 1-in.-thick stock, a 6-pitch blade would be a good choice, but a 14-pitch blade would be too fine. However, if the stock were only ½ in. thick, a 14-pitch blade would be best. Although the range of available pitch is broad, from 2 tpi to 32 tpi, wide blades generally have fewer teeth, and narrow blades have a greater number of teeth.

Choosing the correct pitch will substantially increase blade life. Take, for example, a carbon-steel blade, which is easily damaged by overheating. A fine-pitch carbon-steel blade will overheat when used on thick stock because the gullets become packed with sawdust. This causes the blade to dull quickly and lose its set, rendering the blade useless.

SELECTING THE APPROPRIATE PITCH

You'll get the best cuts when there are between 6 and 12 teeth in the stock. The cut is smooth, and because the sawdust is rapidly carried away, the feed rate can be faster.

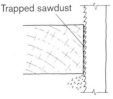

Trapped sawdust

Fewer than 6 teeth in the stock can cause vibration and a rough cut.

Correct pitch for board thickness results in a fast, smooth cut.

With more than 12 teeth in the stock, the small gullets fill with sawdust, and the blade overheats.

Wider Blades Need More Tension

BEAM STRENGTH

A bandsaw blade bows when the beam strength isn't great enough to resist the feed pressure.

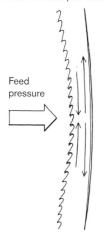

Feed pressure

The front of the blade is in compression, while the back is in tension.

As blades get wider, the steel used for the blades gets thicker. The width of a blade relates to its beam strength—the wider the blade, the stiffer it will be (see the drawing at left).

A wider blade has more beam strength, but the blade must be properly tensioned. Overtensioning can stress and distort the bandsaw frame, possibly beyond repair. Excessive tension also places potentially damaging forces on the saw's wheels, shafts, and bearings. When resawing, use the widest blade that your bandsaw can properly tension. Keep in mind that the widest blade a saw can tension may not be the widest blade it can accept. For smaller saws, you'll most likely get better results from the next-size narrower blade.

The most accurate way to determine the proper tension of a blade is to use a tension meter. But a meter has a price tag of around $300*, so many choose a simpler route. If you set the upper guides about 6 in. off the table, the blade should deflect under the pressure of a fingertip, but no more than ¼ in. For resawing, the tension should be even a little tighter. Bear in mind that the 14-in. saws common in many small woodworking shops work best with blades no wider than ½ in. Each blade width has a minimum radius that it can cut. Squeezing a blade through a turn that is too tight can break the blade, twist the teeth into the guides (which causes them to lose sharpness and set) or pull the blade off of the saw's wheels, which could damage the teeth or bend the blade.

The blade-radius chart below provides the minimum radius that each width of blade can turn. I keep a similar chart posted on my bandsaw.

You may be wondering why you can't mount a narrow blade (such as ¼ in.) and use it for cutting all curves. This does work, but only to a degree. Narrow blades have a tendency to wander. If you try to cut a large radius, such as a 36-in.-diameter tabletop, for example, you'll have a hard time keeping the blade on the line. You'll cut more precisely with a 1-in.-wide blade. However, with practice you'll probably cut a majority of curved work with a ¼-in. or ⅜-in. blade.

HOW BLADE WIDTH AFFECTS THE CUTTING RADIUS

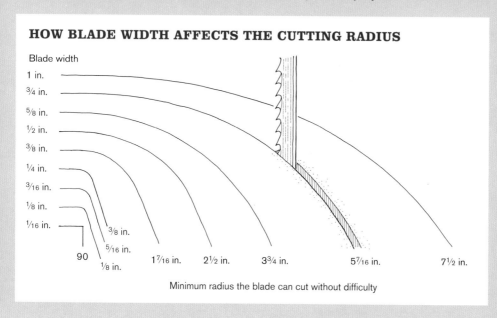

Minimum radius the blade can cut without difficulty

giving a carbide blade much greater beam strength. The carbide teeth are precisely ground on the face, top, and both sides, which results in truer, more precise cuts.

As you would expect, a carbide bandsaw blade is significantly more expensive than an ordinary carbon-steel blade. However, a carbide blade will typically outlast a carbon-steel blade 25:1, and carbide can be resharpened. Although more expensive initially, a carbide blade is much more economical than a carbon-steel blade, especially for resawing.

Stellite Is Softer and Less Brittle Than Carbide Stellite® is the brand name of a unique type of carbide that is reportedly better suited for woodworking applications. Stellite isn't as hard as regular carbide, but it's also less brittle. This gives Stellite greater shock resistance. Like carbide, Stellite promises longer wear and better-quality cuts.

In many other ways, Stellite blades are a lot like carbide blades. The Stellite teeth are brazed onto the band, then precisely ground. And like carbide blades, Stellite blades are expensive.

Different Tooth Forms for Different Jobs

Tooth form refers to the design of the tooth and gullet, specifically the tooth size, shape, and rake, or cutting, angle. The three commonly known tooth forms for cutting wood are regular, skip, and hook. Another form that is gaining in popularity is the variable tooth.

Regular-Tooth Blades The regular-tooth blade, sometimes called the standard form, has evenly spaced teeth for smooth, precise cutting. Teeth and gullets are the same size, and the rake angle is 0°. This combination of features leaves a smooth surface. For cutting curves, a regular-tooth blade is often the best choice because it has the greatest

Blade Types

CARBON STEEL

Pros: Inexpensive; weld or braze your own; readily available

Cons: Dulls quickly; cannot be sharpened

Use: Cutting contours in relatively thin stock

STAMPED SPRING STEEL

Pros: Inexpensive; very flexible for use on bandsaws with small-diameter wheels

Con: Stamped teeth dull very quickly

Use: Light-duty cuts on small bandsaws

BIMETAL

Pros: Cobalt-steel teeth don't readily overheat; high tension means greater beam strength

Con: Don't last as long as carbide

Uses: Demanding applications that generate a lot of heat, such as resawing and cutting thick stock

CARBIDE

Pros: Smooth cut; high recommended tension; outlasts carbon-steel blades 25:1

Con: Initial cost is very expensive

Uses: Resawing and other demanding applications

STELLITE

Pro: More shock resistance than carbide

Cons: Cost; not as hard as carbide

Use: Resawing wide stock

Sources

Highland Hardware
800-241-6748
www.highlandwood-
working.com

number of teeth. This, combined with a 0° rake angle, gives you a smooth finished surface that requires little cleanup.

The disadvantage of a regular-tooth blade is that the gullets are too small to cut thick stock effectively. Remember that the purpose of the gullets is to haul away the sawdust from the kerf. If you attempt to cut thick stock with a regular-tooth blade, the gullets become full before the teeth exit the stock, which slows cutting and overheats the teeth. Obviously, a regular-tooth blade is not designed for fast cutting. In fact, if you push the stock too hard in an effort to increase the cutting rate, the cut actually slows down as the gullets become packed with sawdust.

Skip-Tooth Blades As you might assess from the name, the skip form "skips" every other tooth. A skip-tooth blade has fewer teeth and larger gullets than a regular-tooth blade. The large gullets can efficiently carry the sawdust away from the kerf, making a skip-tooth blade fast cutting. Like a regular-tooth blade, a skip-tooth blade also has a 0° rake angle that scrapes the wood away cleanly. But because it has fewer teeth, a skip-tooth blade doesn't cut as smoothly as a regular-tooth blade.

A skip-tooth blade is best suited for resawing and ripping thick stock. It also works well for cutting softwoods. But because the hook-tooth blade is more efficient, the skip-tooth blade is outmoded. Why do manufacturers still produce skip-tooth blades? One sawblade manufacturer said his company still makes skip-tooth blades mainly because—short of sending people a free hook-tooth blade—it's difficult to convince people to change.

Hook-Tooth Blades The hook tooth is really a further development of the skip tooth. A hook-tooth blade has large gullets and teeth like that of a skip-tooth blade, but the teeth have a positive rake angle that

makes them cut more aggressively. Because of this aggressive nature, a hook-tooth blade has less feed resistance than a skip-tooth blade. It is a great choice for resawing and ripping thick stock. A hook-tooth blade is my choice for general resawing, such as sawing thick planks into thin drawer parts. The coarser pitch and positive rake angle of a hook-tooth blade make quick work of any hardwood.

Variable-Tooth Blades The variable-tooth blade is a hybrid among bandsaw blades. A variable-tooth blade can have regular teeth with a 0° rake angle or a more aggressive, positive rake angle. But the unique feature of this type of blade is that the tooth size and spacing vary on the same blade. This means that both the teeth and gullets vary in size but not in shape. The unique design dramatically reduces vibration; the result is a quieter blade and a very smooth cut.

To understand how this works, it's helpful to think of a bandsaw blade as a string on a musical instrument. A bandsaw blade is under tension, just like the strings on a violin but for different reasons. You want a string on an instrument to vibrate so that it produces a sound. This is called harmonic vibration. But you want to limit vibration on a bandsaw blade because vibrations create a rough surface on the stock. By varying the tooth and gullet size, you effectively limit the vibrations and create a smoother surface.

When sawing veneer from a plank of valuable hardwood, a hook-tooth blade will do a great job, but a variable-tooth blade will leave a much smoother finish. Tooth form affects the performance of the blade more than any other factor. A regular-tooth blade gives the smoothest cut; a hook-tooth blade cuts aggressively; and a variable-tooth blade cuts both smoothly and aggressively.

Which Blade Should You Use?

RESAWING 6-IN.-WIDE POPLAR FOR DRAWER PARTS

Option 1: carbide, 3 pitch, hook tooth
Option 2: bimetal, 2 pitch, hook tooth

Comments: Poplar is soft and cuts easily. The bimetal blade would be less expensive, but the carbide blade would last much longer. For greatest beam strength, use the widest blade that your bandsaw can tension.

SLICING 1/16-IN.-THICK VENEER FROM A 9-IN.-WIDE CROTCH WALNUT PLANK

Option 1: carbide, 2/3 variable pitch, hook tooth
Option 2: spring steel, 3/4 variable pitch, hook tooth
Option 3: carbide, 3 pitch, hook tooth
Option 4: bimetal, 3 pitch, hook tooth

Comments: Walnut crotch has dramatic figure and is expensive. I try to get as much veneer as I possibly can from a valuable plank like this. A carbon blade would be my last choice because it dulls quickly. The variable-pitch carbide blade is very expensive, but the cut is incredibly smooth. Both of the carbide blades are stiff and require a strong frame to tension properly. The spring-steel variable-pitch blade is an excellent choice, particularly for saws with wheel diameters under 18 in. It tensions easily because it's only .022 in. thick. This blade cuts incredibly smoothly, and it's relatively inexpensive compared to carbide blades—although you can't expect it to last as long. Best of all, the kerf from this blade is a slim 1/32 in., half that of the other blades in this category. You'll definitely get more veneer from this blade.

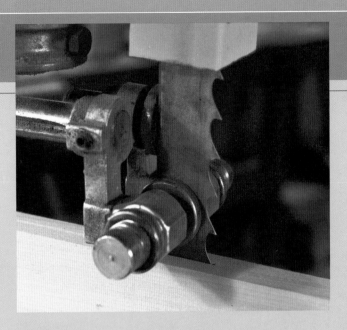

RESAWING POPLAR IS EASY. This 2-pitch bimetal blade makes quick work of softwoods. A carbide blade would also work well but would be more expensive.

SMOOTH OPERATOR. A variable-pitch, hook-tooth carbide blade cleanly slices 1/16-in.-thick veneer from this crotch walnut plank.

The Right Blade Choice

Rather than thumbing through the pages of an industrial bandsaw blade catalog, it's much easier to narrow the blade choices based upon the types of cuts you'll be making. For every job, it's important to consider the blade width, pitch and tooth form.

I always begin by selecting the blade width. Width is determined by the type of cut you're making—whether you're sawing a straight line or a curve. Tooth pitch is dictated by the thickness of the stock you'll be cutting, and tooth form influences how aggressively or smoothly the blade will cut.

RIPPING 2-IN.-THICK HARDWOODS

Option 1: carbide, 4 pitch, hook tooth, ½ in. wide

Option 2: carbon steel, 4 pitch, hook tooth,
½ in. or ¾ in. wide

Comments: If you have a 14-in. bandsaw, you'll probably get truer cuts with a ½-in.-wide, .025-in.-thick blade than with a ¾-in.-wide, .032-in.-thick blade. Your saw stands a better chance of tensioning the thinner and narrower blade.

CUTTING CONTOURS IN ⅞-IN.-THICK MAPLE (MINIMUM RADIUS ⁹⁄₁₆ IN.)

Option 1: carbon steel, 10 pitch, regular tooth,
¼ in. wide

Option 2: carbon steel, 6 pitch, regular tooth,
¼ in. wide

Comments: The 10-pitch blade would create a smoother surface, thus requiring less cleanup of sawmarks.

CUTTING SCROLLS IN ¼-IN.-THICK HARDWOOD (MINIMUM RADIUS ¹⁄₁₆ IN.)

Option: bimetal, 24 pitch, regular tooth, ¹⁄₁₆ in. wide

Comments: This tiny ¹⁄₁₆-in.-wide blade is your only choice for cutting tight contours. You'll need to replace the steel guide blocks with hardwood blocks or Cool Blocks®. This blade can't be used on bandsaws equipped with bearing guides.

THE RIGHT BLADE FOR HARDWOODS. Ripping hardwoods on the bandsaw is easy with a ½-in.-wide, 4-pitch blade.

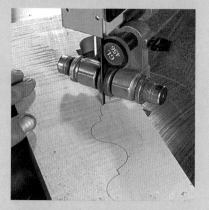

GOOD FOR MOST CURVES. A ¼-in., 6-pitch blade can cut most contours, but a 10-pitch blade leaves a smoother surface.

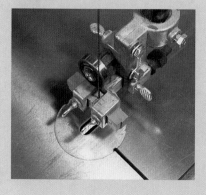

TIGHT CURVES, CLEAN CUTS. A ¹⁄₁₆-in., 24-pitch blade cuts intricate scrolls with little or no cleanup required.

To get the most out of your bandsaw, you'll have to change blades often from wide to narrow or from few teeth to many. Each type of blade is best for a certain kind of cutting. You must decide which is more important to you—speed or smoothness. You can't get the best of both in the same blade. However, you can select a blade that is a good compromise.

Note price estimates are from 2000.

LONNIE BIRD is a woodworking teacher and author. This chapter was adapted from *The Bandsaw Book* (The Taunton Press, 1999).

Soup Up Your
14-in. Bandsaw

BY JOHN WHITE

The classic 14-in. cast-iron bandsaw, developed by Delta Machinery back in the 1930s, was designed mostly for making curved pattern cuts in relatively thin boards. Delta still makes that saw here in the United States. Over the years, it has changed little. Along the way, it even served as a model for several of the Asian-made clones currently sold in the United States, including a couple now marketed by Delta.

Nowadays, though, it seems more woodworkers are looking to push the limits of 14-in. cast-iron bandsaws by using them to resaw wide boards. And many are finding out that it's not always easy to do. The feed rate is annoyingly slow, the motor often bogs down, the blade can drift off line, and the cuts sometimes end up far from square.

But don't trade in the saw yet. I've found that by making some relatively minor modifications, a typical ¾-hp to 1-hp, 14-in. cast-iron bandsaw can be transformed into an effective resawing machine. Indeed, my upgraded machine resaws 12-in.-wide maple boards with little effort.

The Basic Upgrade

The basic upgrade adds a riser block to increase the resaw capacity, a resaw blade, a heavier tension spring, and a tall fence. This upgrade will enable you to start resawing stock as wide as 12 in.

Riser Block Doubles the Capacity Most manufacturers of 14-in. cast-iron bandsaws offer a riser-block kit as an optional accessory that increases the resaw capacity from roughly 6 in. to about 12 in. The kit also includes a longer guidepost and a pair of longer blade guards. The block is bolted between the upper and the lower frames. All of the kits include extralong bolts to account for the added length.

A Good Resaw Blade Is a Must Perhaps more than anything else, a good-quality resaw blade can go a long way toward improving the resawing capabilities of a bandsaw. Resaw blades have large gullets that carry away the considerable sawdust that's generated when cutting through wide boards. Avoid blades with small gullets and lots of teeth because they aren't designed to cut wide stock.

A Riser Block Increases Cutting Capacity

Most 14-in. cast-iron bandsaws can be outfitted with a riser-block kit that's available as an option. Adding a riser block increases the resaw capacity of the machine from about 6 in. to 12 in. With this increased capacity, though, you'll also need longer blades.

ATTACH THE REPLACEMENT BLADE GUARDS AND THE GUIDEPOST. The riser-block kit includes longer blade guards for both the back and the front of the saw, and a longer guidepost.

THE RISER BLOCK MOUNTS BETWEEN THE UPPER AND LOWER FRAMES OF THE SAW. Two pins help position the block on the frame. All three parts are held together with a heavy-duty bolt, washer and nut.

In general, a ½-in.-wide hook-tooth blade (2 tpi or 3 tpi) will work fine. I've also had good experience with both the Timberwolf and Wood Slicer® blades.

Beefier Spring Adds More Tension To provide the best possible cut, a bandsaw blade must be tensioned properly. A blade lacking adequate tension is more likely to wander from the cut or produce a bowed cut when resawing.

The source of the blade tension is a compressed spring behind the upper wheel. It's not uncommon for this spring to lack some vitality. When that's the case, the spring can't apply enough tension.

The solution is to replace the original spring with one that has more muscle (see the photo at right). But first check with the

REPLACE A WORN-OUT SPRING. If your cut wanders, chances are that the spring is not providing enough tension to the blade.

The Right Blade for Resawing

Resawing can be next to impossible with the wrong blade. To haul away all of the sawdust created while resawing, you need a blade with big gullets, which means fewer teeth per inch. Also, hook teeth are generally better for resawing.

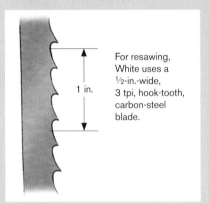

1 in.

For resawing, White uses a ½-in.-wide, 3 tpi, hook-tooth, carbon-steel blade.

supplier to make sure your saw can handle the additional load; otherwise, you might end up with a burned tension mechanism or prematurely worn bearings.

Add an Auxiliary Fence I also made a tall auxiliary fence to support a board during resawing (see the sidebar on the facing page). The fence is short in length but sturdy enough that it remains square to the table when pressure is applied. In addition, it is easy to adjust the fence angle to eliminate blade drift—the propensity for a bandsaw blade to wander from a straight line during a cut. One thing to note: If the factory-supplied fence on your bandsaw is of little value, you'll need to get a better fence before you can add this resaw fence.

My auxiliary fence extends to just past the trailing edge of the blade. There's a reason for this short length. Thick stock

often has a fair amount of tension in the wood, even when carefully dried. When you're resawing, the tension in the wood is released, sometimes causing the offcut to bend or twist into the fence, which means you'll have to push pretty hard to keep the board against the fence. By using a fence that is short in length—much like that on a European-style tablesaw—you can keep the uncut portion of the board firmly against the fence while the offcut is free to bend or twist into the open air.

The fence I installed has two main components: a back piece with a brace that bolts to the original fence and a set of interchangeable faces, each one of a different height. The idea here is to use a face that is narrower than the board to be re-sawn but wide enough to support the board adequately during the cut. That way, both for safety and maximum blade support,

A Versatile Auxiliary Fence

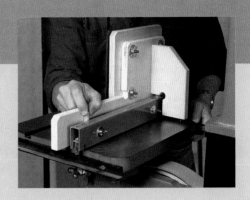

hile being resawn, wide stock has a tendency to tip unless it's supported by a tall fence. Also, the fence has to be square to the table of the bandsaw. White's fence, with three interchangeable faces, offers plenty of support. And it can be tweaked to end up perfectly square to the table. Plus, as shown at right, it's easily adjustable to correct for blade drift simply by adding a spacer between the original and auxiliary fences.

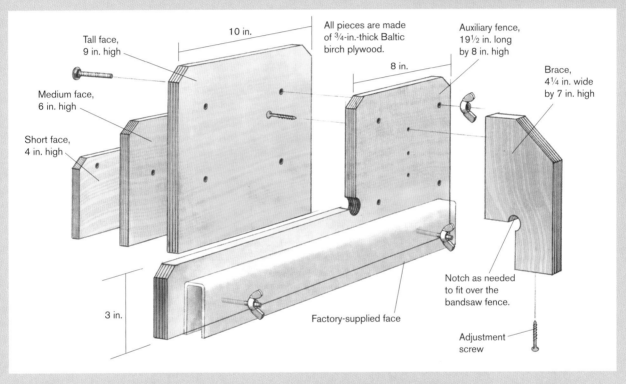

Tall face,
9 in. high

Medium face,
6 in. high

Short face,
4 in. high

10 in.

All pieces are made of ¾-in.-thick Baltic birch plywood.

8 in.

Auxiliary fence,
19½ in. long
by 8 in. high

Brace,
4¼ in. wide
by 7 in. high

3 in.

Factory-supplied face

Notch as needed to fit over the bandsaw fence.

Adjustment screw

the blade guard along with the upper blade guide can be lowered close to the top edge of the board.

With this fence, it's easy to adjust for blade drift by adding spacers between the original fence and the auxiliary fence, changing the angle of the fence relative to the blade. (For more on testing and adjusting for blade drift, see "Bandsaw Tune-Up," p. 176) Dowels or small hardwood blocks work fine as spacers. On some blades, the drift can be considerable. One blade I use

needs a ¾-in.-thick spacer before it cuts straight.

For accurate cuts, the auxiliary fence should be square to the table. Sometimes, however, a factory-supplied fence won't be quite as square as you'd like. To correct for this out of squareness, mount thin shims (I use strips of aluminum flashing attached with double-faced tape) to the back of the fence. The shims should be long enough to bear on any spacer that is added to correct for blade drift. Once the auxiliary fence has been squared to the table, adjust the screw

Shopmade Trunnion-Support Plate Eliminates Table Flex

Delta's 14-in. cast-iron bandsaw has a trunnion support made from cast iron. But most 14-in. cast-iron saws have a cast-aluminum trunnion support. Aluminum castings are usually thinner than the Delta version and tend to flex easily, so anything other than a lightweight board can make the saw table tip a bit. That's not helpful when you want a square cut.

Adding a simple plywood plate to a saw with a cast-aluminum trunnion support will eliminate almost all of the table movement. On the downside, adding the plate sacrifices ¾ in. of resaw capacity, but I feel the trade-off is worth it. The plate is a rectangular piece of ¾-in.-thick birch plywood, with a notch to clear the blade path. It also has a slot to catch an eyebolt that attaches to the back edge of the table. Tightened with a wing nut, the eyebolt locks the table against the 90° stop bolt, virtually guaranteeing that the table stays square to the blade.

The plate dimensions on the facing page should work on most 14-in. cast-iron saws. If you need to revise the dimensions, design the plate so that it ends up 2 in. wider than the trunnion support and projects ½ in. past the back edge of the table.

To locate the holes for the two pins that stick up from the cast-iron saw frame, slide the plate down over the bolts that hold the plate in place and strike the top of the plate with a mallet. Remove the plate and use the dents left by the pins to center and drill the pin holes.

To fully support the trunnion casting, you may have to slip a washer between the plywood and the casting at the two outboard ends of the casting where the bolts that lock the trunnions come through.

To account for the thickness of the plywood, use longer bolts to hold the casting and the blade-guide assembly.

The eyebolt that holds the saw table tightly against the stop bolt slips through a hole drilled in the lip that reinforces the edge of the table. A sharp drill will easily go through the thin cast iron. I cut away a quarter of the loop in the eyebolt to make it easy to fit through the hole. A spacer on the bolt allows the wing nut to clear a flange cast into the top edge of the saw's lower frame.

WEAK TRUNNION SUPPORTS EQUAL TILTING TABLE. Pushing down on the saw table with the heel of his hand, White discovered that cast-aluminum trunnion supports were easily deflected out of square.

A LOOK UNDER THE HOOD. Before the trunnion support can be removed, the table of the bandsaw must be removed.

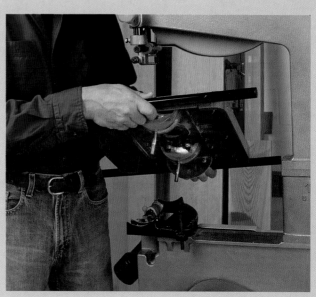

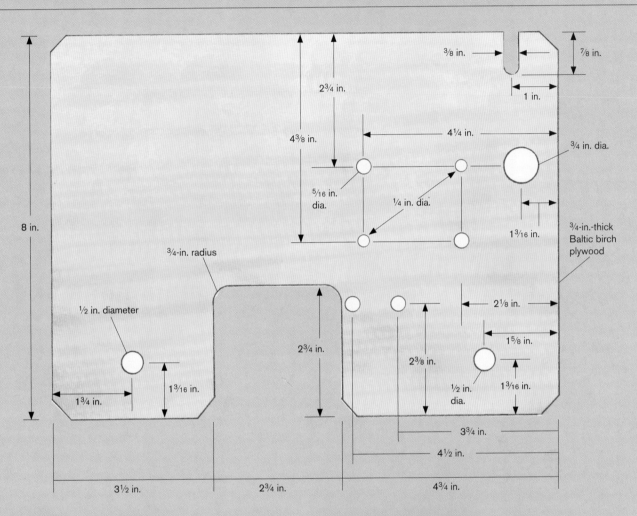

⅜ in.

⅞ in.

1 in.

2¾ in.

4⅜ in.

4¼ in.

¾ in. dia.

8 in.

5/16 in. dia.

¼ in. dia.

1³/16 in.

¾-in.-thick Baltic birch plywood

¾-in. radius

2⅛ in.

1⅝ in.

½ in. diameter

2¾ in.

2⅜ in.

1³/16 in.

1³/16 in.

½ in. dia.

1¾ in.

3¾ in.

4½ in.

3½ in.

2¾ in.

4¾ in.

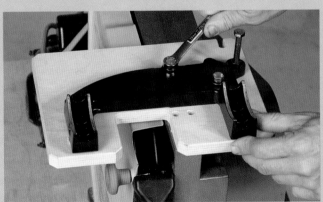

TRUNNION SUPPORT ADDS STRENGTH. A single piece of plywood is all it takes to beef up the aluminum trunnion support. One drawback is that the resaw capacity of the saw is reduced by ¾ in.

EYEBOLT KEEPS THE TABLE PARTS SNUG. A hole bored in the edge of the saw table accepts an eyebolt that slips into a slot in the plywood. Tightening the wing nut keeps the underside of the table firmly against a single adjustable stop bolt.

of the knobs that lock the table trunnions.
The turnbuckles make it easy to fine-
tune the supports to the bandsaw's table
height. The panels rest against stop blocks
on the saw's base. Eyebolts screwed into the
stop blocks help position the piece on the
base. And the support rods just hook over
the knobs. Removing the panels takes only
a few seconds.

To enlarge the stock steel base enough
to accept the infeed and outfeed supports,
add a piece of plywood between the steel
base and the cast-iron frame (or make a
larger base like the one shown on the
facing page and p. 212).

To make a support rod, replace the
right-hand threaded eyebolt on each turnbuckle with a longer bolt that has an eye
large enough to slip around the shank of
the trunnion lock-knob. Once the eyebolts
have been adjusted, add nuts to lock them
in place. Because one of the threads in each
turnbuckle is left-handed, you'll need a left-
handed nut to lock that side. I had no problem finding all of the hardware I needed at
the local hardware store.

The infeed support should tilt at about
a 45° angle. That way, the top end of the
support can't be easily pushed and lifted
by the board it's holding up. The outfeed
support, however, should be installed at a
more upright angle so that you can move
the outfeed table's stop block away from
the saw and clear the cover for the drive
belt. The top end of the support cannot lift
because, on the outfeed end, the drag of the
board pulls against the support rod.

There's a simple way to determine the
length of the supports. Make them longer than necessary. Hold them in position
against a straightedge placed across the saw
table, mark and cut. The top and bottom
edges of the supports are rounded over
with a 3/8-in.-radius router bit.

Make the Base For ripping and resawing, the table of a bandsaw should be close

on the bottom of the brace to give the
fence added support.

Advanced Upgrade

I recommend the advanced upgrade for a
bandsaw being used exclusively for resawing. It adds infeed and outfeed supports to
make it easier to support wide and long
boards. Except for the ones on the Delta
models, the trunnion support is going to
need some beefing up (see the sidebar on
pp. 208–209). Also, the factory-supplied
base is replaced with a shorter, shopmade
base that lowers the saw table to a more
comfortable resawing height.

Add the Infeed and Outfeed Supports
The infeed and outfeed supports are simply
3/4-in.-thick plywood panels that tip out
from the top of the base. The panels are
held in place by support rods made out
of large turnbuckles. The rods attach to
the saw by slipping around the shank

Dedicated Resawer Edition

Anyone doing a lot of resawing should consider adding infeed and outfeed supports along with a lower base. The supports help keep the board from tipping off the saw table, while the lower base places the board at a more comfortable height for resawing and has storage for blades.

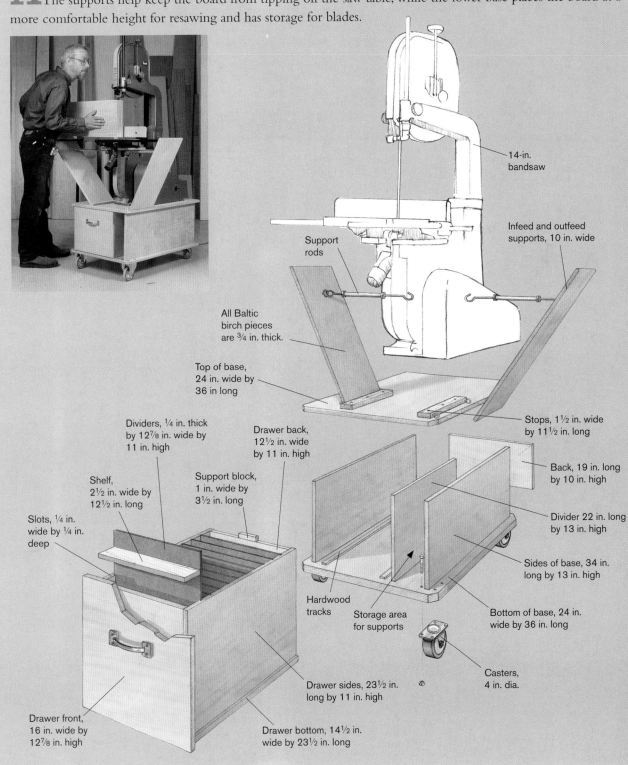

14-in. bandsaw

Infeed and outfeed supports, 10 in. wide

Support rods

All Baltic birch pieces are ¾ in. thick.

Top of base, 24 in. wide by 36 in long

Stops, 1½ in. wide by 11½ in. long

Back, 19 in. long by 10 in. high

Dividers, ¼ in. thick by 12⅞ in. wide by 11 in. high

Drawer back, 12½ in. wide by 11 in. high

Divider 22 in. long by 13 in. high

Shelf, 2½ in. wide by 12½ in. long

Support block, 1 in. wide by 3½ in. long

Sides of base, 34 in. long by 13 in. high

Slots, ¼ in. wide by ¼ in. deep

Hardwood tracks

Storage area for supports

Bottom of base, 24 in. wide by 36 in. long

Casters, 4 in. dia.

Drawer sides, 23½ in. long by 11 in. high

Drawer front, 16 in. wide by 12⅞ in. high

Drawer bottom, 14½ in. wide by 23½ in. long

Dedicated Resawer Edition continued

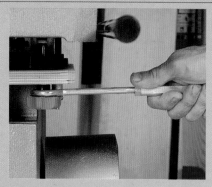

SUPPORTS ASSEMBLE IN SECONDS.
Mounting the infeed and outfeed supports is simple. One end butts against a stop, and the other hooks to the underside of the saw table.

DRAWER OFFERS STORAGE. The single drawer can hold several coiled bandsaw blades, while the shelf in front is a handy place for small parts. The supports slide into the compartment on the right.

to the height of a tablesaw, not the 42-in. to 45-in. height typical of bandsaws on factory-supplied bases. A high table is fine for cutting small stock, but it's awkward for working with large boards being run against a fence. I made my new base as low as possible. The saw's table ended up just shy of 39 in. high, and now it's much easier to handle stock.

The base is a simple box made of Baltic birch plywood and assembled using butt joints and screws. A large drawer provides room for bandsaw blades and miscellaneous small parts. In addition to the drawer, a compartment on one side serves as a place to store the infeed and outfeed supports. The bolts mounting the casters thread into capped insert nuts. The 3-in.-wide gap above the back panel of the box allows access to the motor-mounting bolts.

The motor is simply bolted in place with its pulley in line with the pulley on the saw. The belt tension is adjusted by adding or removing sections from a link belt. Using a link belt eliminates the need for a sliding motor mount. On my saw I was able to reuse the original belt guard. If that's not possible on your saw, make a simple plywood box to cover the belt and pulleys.

The drawer slides on hardwood tracks attached to the bottom of the base. A single hardwood block attached to the top back edge of the drawer prevents the drawer from tipping when extended. The block is slightly oversize and mounted with two recessed screws. Then, for a smooth sliding fit, trim it to size with a block plane.

JOHN WHITE is the author of *Care and Repair of Shop Machines* (The Taunton Press, 2002).

Jointers, Planers, and Shapers

You couldn't call jointers and shapers very versatile tools. However, the jobs they perform are absolutely indispensable for making cabinetry and furniture. These two tools work as a team to dress stock straight, flat, square, and of a consistent thickness. Otherwise, workpieces can become a nightmare of bends, twists, and parallelograms that make it impossible to construct square cabinets and other assemblies.

The job of the jointer is to make workpieces straight, flat, and square. The one thing it can't do, though, is accurately thickness stock, which is where the planer comes in. However, the planer can only thickness stock, it can't flatten it, which is why you need a jointer. To be a successful woodworker, it's critical to understand the teamwork of these two tools and how to use them. Knowing how to tune both machines precisely is also critical, or they simply won't do what they're supposed to.

In this section, you're treated to plenty of excellent advice on tuning, maintaining, and using these shop stalwarts to produce trouble-free workpieces. In addition, you'll find out how a shaper can contribute to your arsenal of tools, performing shaping and joinery maneuvers that are difficult or impossible to do with other machines.

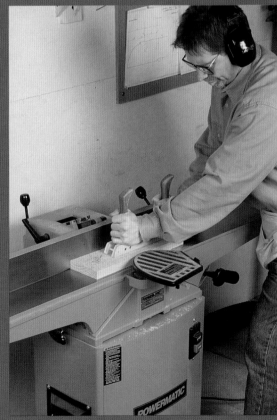

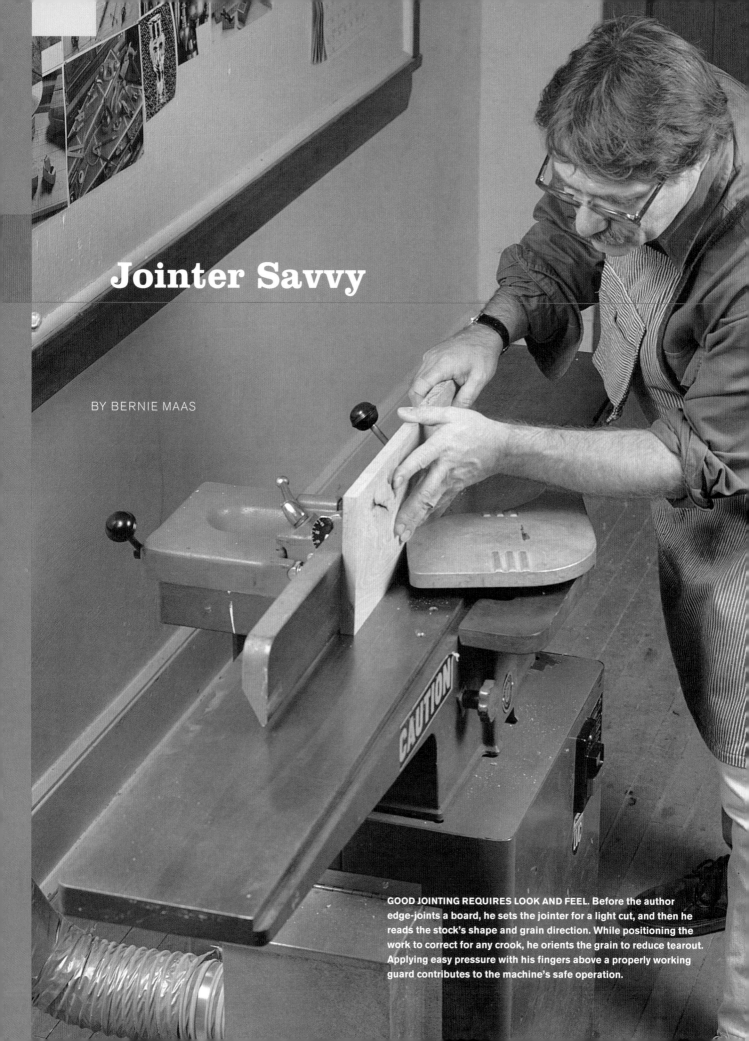

Jointer Savvy

BY BERNIE MAAS

GOOD JOINTING REQUIRES LOOK AND FEEL. Before the author edge-joints a board, he sets the jointer for a light cut, and then he reads the stock's shape and grain direction. While positioning the work to correct for any crook, he orients the grain to reduce tearout. Applying easy pressure with his fingers above a properly working guard contributes to the machine's safe operation.

Like good hand-tool usage, successful wood machining involves working by eye, feel, and intuition. Though fences and motor-driven cutters help, they can't do it all. A squeeze here and a push there—some call it body English—can make all the difference in truing an edge or flattening a surface. These hard-to-describe nuances really boil down to having savvy for the tool you're using.

The jointer is a perfect example of a savvy-demanding machine. To joint cleanly and consistently requires real proficiency. I've run a jointer for 35 years, and while it looks like a set-it-and-forget-it monster, it's not. So to save you from its pitfalls, I'll pass along the jointer pointers I've picked up and now share in my classroom. In addition to describing a jointer's makeup and telling you how I straighten an edge, I'll describe how I read a board's shape and grain, so I joint squarely without tearing wood—all while keeping my fingers safe (see the photo on the facing page).

Jointing 101

Before you begin surfacing a pile of lumber for a project, it helps to be familiar with a jointer's components and how to adjust them. For reference, the drawing on p. 216 shows the machine's basic parts, their purposes and the fundamentals of feeding stock, which are important during both simple and advanced operations (like the ones in "Using a Jointer" on pp. 218–219).

A jointer's main jobs are flattening faces of boards and squaring and straightening edges. These tasks are achieved by adjusting the jointer tables and fence in relationship to the cutterhead. If the fence is set at 90° and the outfeed table is set parallel and exactly to the maximum height of the knives, you can establish a uniform cut by lowering the infeed table by the depth of cut you want. After you have a handle on jointer fundamentals, the most important item is safety.

Safety Comes First There are a few keys to jointing safely. First, be alert and focused. In addition to watching your work and your fingers, make sure your jointer's guard is in place and working properly. Second, work in a warm shop. Cold hands mean numb fingers that are slow and don't grab well. Third, use a push block when surfacing the face of a board. Fourth, don't joint a board less than 12 in. long or under 1 in. thick. Finally, don't white-knuckle it. Feed with just enough force to advance the stock. This way, should the work kick or shatter, your hand won't go flying into the knives. If your fingernails are blue, you're pushing too hard. Either your bite is too big, your stance is off, the blades are dull or your machine is out of whack.

Reading a Board's Grain Ideally, there will be only one grain direction per face of a board. If this is the case, you can easily prevent tearout while jointing. Just feed the stock so that the grain lines run in the direction of the cutterhead rotation—from high to low (see the drawing on p. 216). Of course, life isn't always that pretty: There are knots, and often the grain changes its mind. Sometimes the fibers run in three directions at once (figured cherry is a prime example of this). And it's more likely that tearout will occur the steeper the angle of grain reversal.

So how do you handle recalcitrant stock on your jointer? First, make sure the knives are sharp and protrude equally from the cutterhead, or reserve a sweet spot—a section of the knives dedicated for when you need a razor edge. (I keep a sweet spot in a rarely used space at the rear of the machine.) Second, remember that a fast cutter means a clean cut. Think of your jointer as a lawn mower. When you push the mower into tall grass, the blade lugs down and rips the grass instead of shearing it. To solve this problem, you raise the blade to take a shallower cut, and you go slowly so the

JOINTER ANATOMY AND FEEDING STOCK

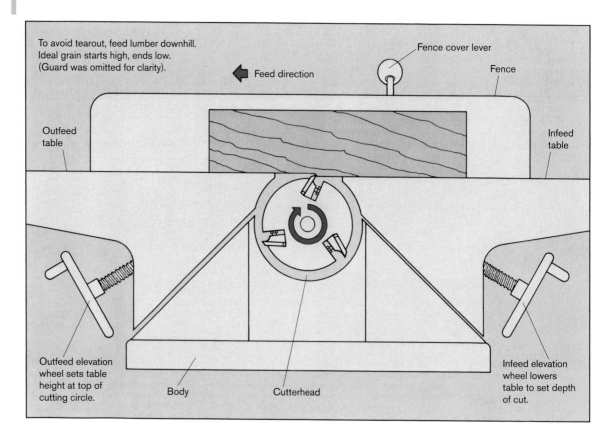

To avoid tearout, feed lumber downhill. Ideal grain starts high, ends low. (Guard was omitted for clarity).

Fence cover lever

Feed direction

Fence

Outfeed table

Infeed table

Outfeed elevation wheel sets table height at top of cutting circle.

Body

Cutterhead

Infeed elevation wheel lowers table to set depth of cut.

engine stays revved. You can joint stock with nasty grain the same way. Reduce the cut to ¹⁄₆₄ in., and then move the problem area of wood slowly over the knives. Keep the knives whirling at top rpms by slowing the feed rate. Although you'll need more than one pass, the cut will be smooth. If you're still having tearout trouble, you may want to back-bevel the knives (see "Using a Jointer" on p. 218).

Squaring Stock When jointing, you should always square an edge to an established face. To do this, joint the face of the board. Then using the newly jointed face as the reference, joint one edge square to it. If your edge is still out of square and you've double-checked your fence setting, most likely the jointer table is guiding the unsquare edge of your work (see the left photo on the facing page). By guiding the

work this way, you're not correcting anything; you're only duplicating the existing angle. To avoid this problem, hold the piece tightly against the proper reference—the fence (see the right photo on the facing page). There should be a tiny wedge-shaped gap between your work and the infeed table. Now feed the work over the knives. The edge should be square.

Correcting a Board's Shape Unless you enjoy having lumber bind up in the tablesaw, you will want to remove any crook in a board before you rip it. (Crook is a curvature that runs from end to end along the edge of a board.) Although crook is common, getting rid of it isn't hard. If your project doesn't require the full length of a board, crosscut it first. Shorter pieces are easier to handle, and they produce less jointing waste. Try to joint with the con-

IMPROPERLY ALIGNED WORK. A beveled edge produces a gap between the fence and the stock's face. In this case, the infeed table guides the workpiece, so jointing will only reproduce the same bevel instead of squaring the edge of the board.

CORRECTLY ALIGNED WORK. Proper pressure and a bit of body English snug this board squarely to the fence. The wedge-shaped gap above the infeed table may point away from the fence, as shown, or toward it, depending on the grain direction.

cave (hollow) edge down. The work should be stable because it'll rest on the ears (ends of the arc) as it passes over the knives.

Sometimes, however, you'll have to joint a piece with the convex edge down. Because it will want to rock, you'll be tempted to hold down the piece tightly to the infeed table as you feed it through the jointer. But if you do this, the board will come out as crooked as when it went in. Instead, set the jointer for a $\frac{1}{32}$-in. cut, and balance the board on a high spot. (The different heights of the two tables should help steady the piece.) Apply moderate pressure, and feed through the knives to create a flat on the edge. Repeat until the work becomes stable as it seats onto the tables. Gradually, you'll even the flat along the entire length.

Straightening Edges and Panels You can modify convex-jointing principles to

straighten a board's edge parallel to its opposite side; in which case, you'll be wasting a small wedge shape. Or you can shave a bit off a panel to make it fit a tight frame. This is great for getting a plywood back to fit an out-of-square carcase that diagonal pipe clamps won't yank back. Start by marking the cut line. I use a fine ball-point pen, which leaves a crisp, dark line that shows up well under shop lights. Make sure you mark the line on the side of the board that will face you as you feed (see the top photo on p. 221). Set the jointer for a light cut ($\frac{1}{64}$ in. to $\frac{1}{32}$ in.), and take a pass. If the taper amount is slight, apply less pressure on the thin end. If you're beginning the cut at the thin end, start with easy pressure, and increase the squeeze as you go. If there's a considerable amount to taper, lift the thin

Using a Jointer: The Advanced Class

BY PETER TISCHLER

Feed rate, depth of cut, knife sharpness, and table alignment all influence the quality of a jointed surface. Too slow a pass can glaze the wood or overheat the knives. Having dull knives or taking too fast a pass causes tearout and often leaves a rough or wavy surface. Too heavy a cut tears up both wood and machine. Too light a pass just wastes time. Misaligned tables lead to inaccuracies in milling. Luckily, you can compensate for many of these operator and machine shortcomings.

Assuming your knives are properly set, there's a refinement called back-beveling, which can improve the quality of the cut especially on figured woods. I'll describe measures to reduce tearout, including how I back-bevel knives. But first I'll explain what down pressure and jointer-table adjustments will do for you.

DOWN PRESSURE AND TABLE SETTINGS

For straight jointing, first apply infeed pressure followed by pressure on the outfeed side, but for a tapered edge, keep pressure on the infeed table only (see the top photo at right). To taper a leg, for example, I mark the taper beginning 1 in. to 2 in. back from where I want it to start. (I straighten the small starting arc with a plane later.) With the leg butting a stop clamped to the infeed table, I take ⅟16-in.-deep passes while maintaining infeed pressure with a push block. I count the number of passes

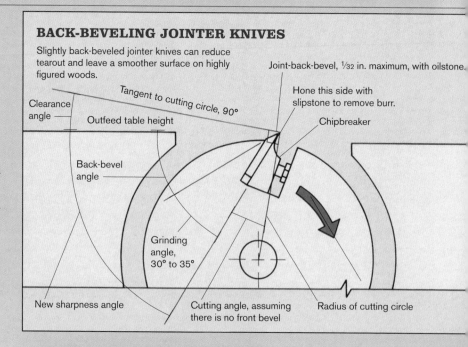

BACK-BEVELING JOINTER KNIVES

Slightly back-beveled jointer knives can reduce tearout and leave a smoother surface on highly figured woods.

- Joint-back-bevel, ⅟32 in. maximum, with oilstone.
- Clearance angle
- Tangent to cutting circle, 90°
- Outfeed table height
- Hone this side with slipstone to remove burr.
- Chipbreaker
- Back-bevel angle
- Grinding angle, 30° to 35°
- New sharpness angle
- Cutting angle, assuming there is no front bevel
- Radius of cutting circle

TO TAPER STOCK, USE PRESSURE ON THE INFEED TABLE. When tapering a leg, clamp a stop on the infeed side to align the start of the cut; then advance the work over the knives (the guard has been removed for clarity).

AN AUXILIARY FENCE SKEWS THE WORK TO LEAVE A SMOOTHER SURFACE on some figured zebra wood. Tischler screwed the plywood fixture together, and then he shimmed and clamped it to his jointer's fence.

so that I can match the taper on all sides of the leg.

To create a "sprung" joint (edges that are jointed with a 1/64 in. or less hollow in their centers to aid in clamping a glued-up panel), I slightly increase downward pressure at the middle of each edge as I pass it over the head. On certain jointers, you can also spring an edge by readjusting the outfeed table. To help me understand table alignments, I consult *Woodshop Tool Maintenance* by Beryl Cunningham and William Holtrop (the book is out of print, so check your local library). The drawing on p. 220, which is adapted from the book, shows what effects various table heights and pitches will have on a jointed surface.

REDUCING JOINTER TEAROUT

When a jointer is running, slight changes can occur in the cutting arc due to distortion in the head or bearing play. As a result, one knife may project farther than the others and tear the surface. The tearout will be most noticeable on figured woods. There are several ways to combat tearout, including skewing the work, proper sharpening, and back-beveling the knives.

Sometimes when I'm jointing wood with difficult grain or high figure, such as bird's-eye or curly maple, I use an auxiliary fence to skew the work (see the bottom photo on the facing page). Skewing, like angling a plane, can reduce

tearout. An auxiliary fence works best on a wide jointer that allows more skew.

The primary bevel on a jointer knife (see the drawing on the facing page) can range from 30° for softwoods, to 35° for hardwoods. To get the angle, I send my knives to a grinding shop because they precisely grind a flat bevel as opposed to a hollow bevel. Occasionally, I'll add a secondary (front or back) bevel myself. This secondary bevel increases the sharpness angle (by adding the back-bevel angle to the grinding angle). But I will do this only if the knives are starting to dull or if I need to surface a run of difficult stock.

It's difficult to grind a front bevel. But back-beveling, as described in Charles Monnett Jr.'s book, *Knife Grinding and Woodworking Manual*, can be done with the knives in the cutterhead. Jointing the back-bevels also removes any cutting-arc eccentricities at the same time (see the drawing on the facing page).

Back-beveling is dangerous and should be done only with the following precautions: The knives must be accurately ground, balanced, and set. The outfeed table should be barely lowered—just until the knives whisper a ticking sound when an oilstone is passed over them as they're rotated by hand. Wrap the stone in paper, so you won't scratch your outfeed table. Finally, clamp a stop across the infeed side near the cutterhead (see the top photo at right) in case the stone kicks.

CAREFULLY BACK-BEVEL THE KNIVES. Clamp a stop block to the infeed table. Then wrap an oilstone with paper. Set the outfeed table, so the stone evenly grazes the knife tips once the jointer is running.

TO REMOVE THE BURR, USE A SLIPSTONE LUBRICATED WITH OIL. With the jointer disconnected, hone the underside of each knife equally, being careful not to cut a finger as you guide the fine India stone.

Once you've safely set up the job, lower the infeed table just below the outfeed table. Start the jointer, and allow it to reach full speed. With a firm (but not monkey-tight) grip, slide the oil-stone across the outfeed table as you dress the knife tips. Turn the machine off, so you can examine the knives. You have ground a proper bevel if there's a thin, straight gleam on the edges. If you didn't get enough back-bevel, lower the out-feed table another .001 or .002 in., and repeat the jointing. Your back-bevel shouldn't exceed 1/32 in.; any more than this will cause the heel of this secondary bevel to pound into the wood.

After back-beveling, hone the knives to remove the burr raised by jointing. To do this, I use a fine India slipstone (see the bottom photo on p. 219). First I unplug the machine. Then I carefully work the oiled stone back and forth across the knife face that protrudes from the chipbreaker. I hone all the knives equally, stopping when I no longer feel drag with the triangular stone. Your patience with this pro-cedure will be rewarded by the cut you'll obtain.

PETER TISCHLER is a North Bennet Street School graduate who runs a chairmaking and cabinetmaking shop in Caldwell, New Jersey.

EFFECTS OF INFEED AND OUTFEED TABLE POSITIONS

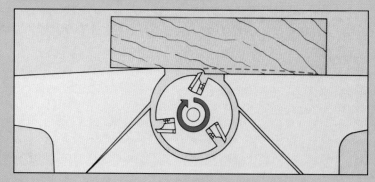

1. Outfeed table high in center results in concave surface.

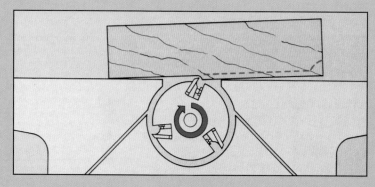

2. Low parallel outfeed table results in heavy cut at back end.

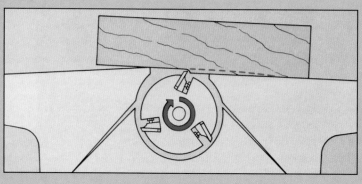

3. Both tables high in center and nonparallel result in con-cave surface.

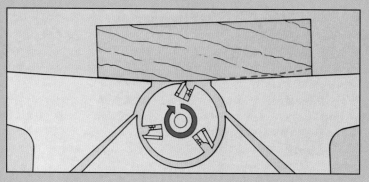

4. Both tables low in center and nonparallel result in convex surface.

end until you can eyeball the line parallel to the infeed table. Lightly joint a flat parallel to the taper line. To get the flat back on target if you've strayed, take partial cuts. Your final pass should run the length of the panel for a clean, smooth edge.

Smoothing Tapers Lots of folks have jigs for ripping tapers on the tablesaw. I've done loads of them that way, but I've always felt that it was a kickback waiting to happen. Instead, I prefer to bandsaw and joint my tapers. I start with rough stock that's about ¼ in. wider than the maximum taper I need. The extra width gives latitude for truing up later. I mark the stock with two lines. The first is the exact taper line. (For safety, I never taper to less than 1 in.) The second line starts ¼ in. below the first. Next I bandsaw as close to the second line as I can. Then I set my jointer for a light cut. Feeding the thick end first with the grain running downhill, I pass the piece over the cutters until I reach my taper line. The best part is that the jointer won't leave ridges and burns as sawblades will. Though somewhat tricky, a few furnituremakers cut tapers using the jointer alone (see the top at right).

Jointing End Grain With care, you can use the jointer to straighten the end grain edge of a panel. If the panel's trailing edge is unsupported, though, it's likely that a ½ in. or so of end grain, which has no structural integrity, will separate from the stock (with a loud whack) as soon as the knives hammer away at it. Luckily, there are several ways to deal with this problem. You can clamp a back-up piece to support the trailing edge before jointing. You can joint half one way and then half from the opposite end. Or you can nick the exiting-end fibers with a utility knife just above the height of the cut. However, my favorite solution came from my eighth-grade shop teacher who simply chamfered his trailing edges slightly above the cut. You can use a rasp, a block plane

STRAIGHTENING THE EDGE OF A PANEL. **To square and straighten panel edges, the author draws an ink line and then shaves toward it with his jointer. After he aligns the work by eye, so the line is parallel to the table, he takes a couple of passes to create a flat. By continuing, he will true up the entire edge.**

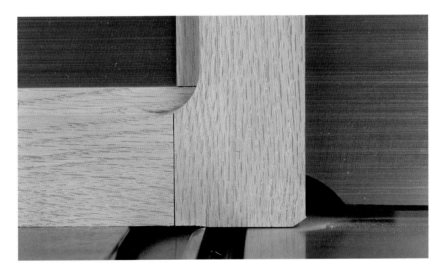

JOINTING END GRAIN. **To avoid splitting the end of a stile, Maas used his belt sander to chamfer the corner before jointing. By carefully easing the frame over the cutterhead, he will flatten each of the four edges. Note that the grain in this rail is running slightly downhill, in the direction of the knife cut.**

or a belt sander to make the chamfer, and the method works equally well on frames, as shown in the bottom photo above. Any chamfer that's left after jointing will feather away when you finish-sand.

Rabbets, Bevels, Chamfers Chances are good that your jointer has a rabbeting arm, which will support a workpiece at the end of the jointer knives. A ledge in the outfeed

CLEAN RABBETS. With the fence set near the jointer's edge, the author slides a piece along the rabbeting arm, taking 1/16 in. at a pass. For clean rabbets, all the knives should project equally toward the rabbeting-ledge end of the cutterhead. A few woodworkers sharpen the ends of the knives to further improve the cut.

SMOOTH CHAMFERS AND BEVELS. A jointer is more versatile than you might think. For decorative table legs, for instance, you can chamfer the corners on the jointer. Or you can precisely bevel staves for a planter. Just angle the fence, adjust for a shallow cut and then feed the work edge over the jointer in several passes

table allows you to plow rabbets because the rest of the board will pass by the cutterhead unimpeded (see the top photo above). The rabbeting feature of a jointer is appealing when you consider the setup time required to do the job on a tablesaw or router table, but be mindful that a jointer's ledge size determines the largest rabbet you can make. Finally, a jointer-made bevel or chamfer adds a nice detail to almost any project. For example, to neatly dress the front of your bookcase shelves, set your jointer fence to 45°, adjust the infeed side for a 1/16-in. cut and then pass each shelf along the fence as you go over the cutter (see the bottom photo above). Without a square edge, the shelf is more pleasing to the eye and to the hand.

BERNIE MAAS is an associate professor of art at Edinboro University of Pennsylvania, where he teaches woodworking and computer-aided drafting. In his free time, he likes to build furniture for his home.

Getting Peak Planer Performance

BY ROBERT VAUGHAN

When it comes to dimensioning stock, a thickness planer is indispensable. That is, unless the knives are dull or the machine's adjustments are out of whack. Dull knives are noisy and strain the motor. Nicked knives produce a molded surface instead of a flat one. Planer maladjustments cause end snipe, tearout, chatter marks, and feed difficulties. Improper planing technique also leads to poor surfacing. Until you are sure that your machine is adjusted properly, it's hard to tell whether your planing problems originate with the tool or with the user.

Fortunately, you don't have to be an experienced machinery mechanic to install knives or troubleshoot your planer. With a little patience and the right tools, you can diagnose and tune up your own machine (see the photo on p. 224). To get predictable results, you'll need two gauging devices, which will let you observe measurements that you may otherwise gain only by trial and error and by feel. First use a gauge that rests on the cutterhead to set the knives. Then use a gauge that rests on the planer bed to measure the relationships between the cutterhead and the machine's other critical parts. These two gauging instruments, which have been used in the woodworking industry for at least 75 years, are simply dial indicators mounted in customized bases.

For up to several hundred dollars, you can buy gauges from various machinery manufacturers or aftermarket sources. But if you need to save your pennies for another tool purchase, I'll show you how to make your own gauges using wood (or plastic, aluminum, or steel), a few nuts and bolts, and an ordinary dial indicator of the proper size with about a ¼-in. plunger range (see the box on p. 226).

Understanding Your Planer

The Parks planer shown in the photo on p. 224, though it is no longer made, contains all the common features found on a thickness planer. Your model may not contain all the components I'll address here. Even so, you should still be able to adapt the same principles to make adjustments to your own machine.

As a board passes through a planer, it is influenced by the relative positions of seven different components: the knives in the cutterhead (above the stock), the bed and bed rollers (below the stock), the infeed roller and chipbreaker (above the stock on the infeed side), and the outfeed roller

and pressure bar (above the stock on the
outfeed side). The drawing on the facing
page shows the relationships of these parts
and the initial adjustment settings. Later, if I
need to, I'll tweak with the adjustments to
fine-tune the planer's cut.

To understand where each of the
planer's seven components plays its role,
it's helpful to follow a board as it's being
planed. First the wood is placed on the

planer bed and fed by hand between the
infeed roller and the front bed roller. The
powered infeed roller grabs the wood and
drives it beneath the floating chipbreaker
and under the rotating cutterhead. Next the
board passes under the pressure bar and out
between the powered outfeed roller and the
back bed roller as it exits the machine. Having any of these components out of whack
will cause problems, so checking each is

ANATOMY OF A PLANER (CROSS-SECTIONAL VIEW)

Setting the Most Important Components

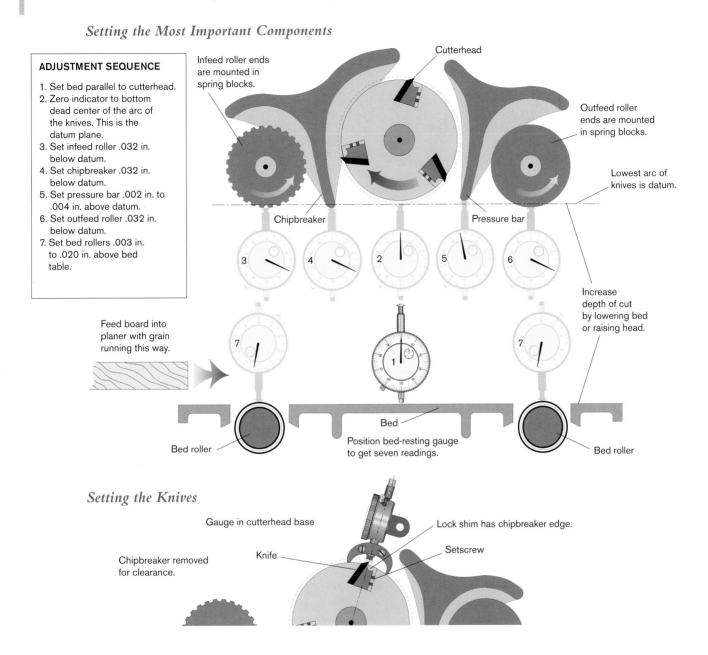

ADJUSTMENT SEQUENCE

1. Set bed parallel to cutterhead.
2. Zero indicator to bottom dead center of the arc of the knives. This is the datum plane.
3. Set infeed roller .032 in. below datum.
4. Set chipbreaker .032 in. below datum.
5. Set pressure bar .002 in. to .004 in. above datum.
6. Set outfeed roller .032 in. below datum.
7. Set bed rollers .003 in. to .020 in. above bed table.

Infeed roller ends are mounted in spring blocks.

Cutterhead

Outfeed roller ends are mounted in spring blocks.

Chipbreaker

Pressure bar

Lowest arc of knives is datum.

Increase depth of cut by lowering bed or raising head.

Feed board into planer with grain running this way.

Bed

Bed roller

Position bed-resting gauge to get seven readings.

Bed roller

Setting the Knives

Gauge in cutterhead base

Chipbreaker removed for clearance.

Knife

Lock shim has chipbreaker edge.

Setscrew

essential. Start by setting the knives in the cutterhead. But before you do anything, prepare the machine, and get the tools you'll need.

Preparation

First, unplug the machine. You'll also want to disconnect the dust boot to gain better access. Then remove the guard for the pulley, so you can advance the cutterhead.

Besides the dial-indicator gauges, you will need a few other tools: an ice pick (or other device to pry up the knives), a wooden block and a mallet to tap the knives down, and Allen wrenches to tighten the lock shim and to turn the jackscrews (if your machine has them). Study your owner's manual so that you will know how to adjust the components on your particular machine and gather the required wrenches.

Shopmade Planer-setting Gauges

My shopmade gauges were adapted from the heavy steel gauges I service planers with in the field. For occasional use, the shopmade gauges give equally precise readings. I devised the gauges so one dial indicator can be interchanged from one base to the other. Because planer dimensions vary, the bases' measurements will also vary. To size them, first get the right dial indicator.

SELECTING A DIAL INDICATOR

A dial indicator is excellent for showing crucial relationships of machine components. One of the inexpensive imported units goes for about $25* (available through Enco Manufacturing®, see Sources). After you thoroughly study the parts of your planer and all its adjustment limits, sketch a full-scale cross section of these (see the top drawing on p. 225). This will help you choose a dial size and also show you how the bases need to be shaped. Select an indicator that will fit easily and can be read clearly in your planer. I use a 1¾-in.-diameter dial with a ⅜-in.-diameter convex replacement tip, like Starrett's® or Mitutoyo's® hardened, chrome-plated type. Convex tips provide better contact over a knife.

MAKING THE BASES

To make the cutterhead-resting base, first make a full-size sketch of your cutterhead (see the drawing on p. 225). Extend a line from the center of the cylinder out over the tip of a knife. Position your indicator over the line with the plunger pointing at the center of the cutterhead. Next draw a base profile with two feet resting on the cutterhead. For two-knife cutterheads, try making an indicator base that has both feet on one side (see the drawing on p. 225). Mark where the plunger stem passes through the base. Then transfer your base profile to a block of wood, and drill and cut to size. Using the hardware shown, assemble the gauge.

For the bed-resting base, make a crow's-foot (tripod) arrangement. The position of the screw feet should be such that the feet won't drop down in the bed-roller slots. Use the planer sketch to locate the indicator tool post. I devised mine so that I can swap the indicator from the front to the back of the post. Finally, round and polish the bottoms of the base's screw feet.

ASSEMBLING THE GAUGES

Cutterhead-Resting Base

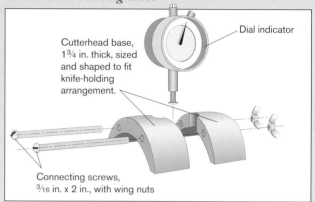

Dial indicator

Cutterhead base, 1¾ in. thick, sized and shaped to fit knife-holding arrangement.

Connecting screws, ³⁄₁₆ in. x 2 in., with wing nuts

Detail: Alternate Base for Two-Knife Cutterhead

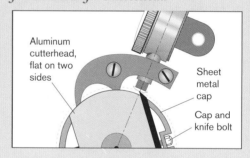

Aluminum cutterhead, flat on two sides

Sheet metal cap

Cap and knife bolt

Bed-Resting Base

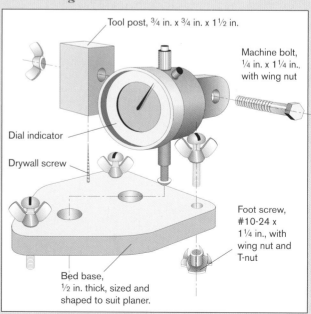

Tool post, ¾ in. x ¾ in. x 1½ in.

Machine bolt, ¼ in. x 1¼ in., with wing nut

Dial indicator

Drywall screw

Foot screw, #10-24 x 1¼ in., with wing nut and T-nut

Bed base, ½ in. thick, sized and shaped to suit planer.

Some metal shims may be handy for fine-tuning adjustments. Depending on what you find once you get into the job, you may also need a file, some emery cloth, and solvent and lubricant. And make sure you're comfortably seated.

Setting the Knives

When setting the knives parallel to the cutterhead, remove and reset one knife at a time to avoid distorting the head. This requires a spare sharpened set of knives. I always have my knives sharpened at a professional sharpening shop. If knives are being installed on an empty cutterhead, then lightly install all the knives, and go from knife to knife, gradually increasing pressure. For maximum support and safety, the knife should be as far down in the slot as practical. There may be differences between cutterheads, too. Some have jackscrews, or there may be two knives in the cutterhead instead of three (see the middle drawing on the facing page).

To check if your old planer knife is a safe size after resharpening, remove the lock shim (also called a lock bar or gib) from the cutterhead, and lay the knife about where it should be. If you see any light through the setscrew holes, reject the knife; it is too narrow and could be thrown from the cutterhead. Don't exert a lot of force on the setscrews, or you'll distort the cutterhead and the screw threads. Apply equal torque on the screws to get uniform pressures and deflections. I get enough leverage from the 6-in.-long leg of my Allen wrench. It's a good idea to lay a rag over the exposed blade to protect your hands in case you lose your grip.

To use the cutterhead gauge, I lightly tighten a knife close to its proper height. This varies from machine to machine, so you should check your owner's manual for the recommended height. I then clamp the dial indicator's ⅜-in.-diameter shaft in the wooden base so that when the base

is rocked on the cutterhead, the dial will move only about .015 to .020 in. At this point, I turn and lock the moveable dial face, so the indicator's hand points to zero when the plunger tip is moved over the tip of the knife (see the photo below). Now the indicator will register the height of the knife edge relative to the cutterhead.

Lightly tighten the setscrews on the outer ends. I usually snug the left side to exact position, go back to the right side and raise or lower that side of the knife to where it should be, and lock it in position. Then working from left to right, over each setscrew, I either raise or lower the knife until I can lock it at the proper height (see the photo on p. 228). Rocking the indicator's plunger over the knife edge shows me the maximum protrusion of the knife edge. Keep in mind that the wood of the gauge base is light and sensitive. Take a few

A CUTTERHEAD GAUGE ENABLES KNIVES **to be set consistently to within one or two thousandths of an inch. The wing nuts on the base allow plunger height adjustment.**

When setting the knives parallel to the cutterhead, remove and reset one knife at a time to avoid distorting the head.

GAUGE HELPS TO ANTICIPATE KNIFE SHIFT. Using the planer cutterhead as a reference, Vaughan reads the gauge over each setscrew to know whether to raise or lower the knives and to anticipate how much each of the knives will shift during tightening.

minutes to get the correct feel of the gauge base contacting the round cutterhead. Repeat the sequence—one knife at a time—for the other knives in the cutterhead.

Setting the Machine

Once the knives are set, install the indicator in the other base with the plunger tip up. Drop the planer's bed until the bed-resting gauge can be easily placed directly beneath the cutterhead. Crank up the bed until the plunger tip just touches the bottom of the cutterhead. Be sure the cutterhead has been rotated so that the knives are out of the way. Then place the gauge at one end of the cutterhead, and rock the cutterhead as you zero the dial at bottom dead center. Zero the other end of the cutterhead as well. Brush the plunger under the center of the cutterhead. If there is a sizable difference (more than .015 in.) between the middle reading and the ones taken from the outsides, then the bed has been worn too much and needs to be remachined.

The Bed The planer bed and cutterhead should be parallel. How to make them parallel varies from machine to machine. Some machines require the table be adjusted and others require the head position be adjusted. For those machines that have no adjustment, the only option is to set the knives in the cutterhead, so they will be parallel to the bed instead of the cutterhead.

Before working with the dial indicator, make sure that the bed has no slop in it as it moves up and down. Most machines have wear shims that can be adjusted. A sloppily fitting head or bed will give poor surface results, such as snipe and washboard.

Defining the Cutting Arc Using the cutterhead gauge again, double-check (over each setscrew) the positions of the knives in the cutterhead. Final setscrew tightening often causes the knife to squirm up a hair. Then position the indicator back in the bed-resting base so that the plunger is at bottom dead center of the cutterhead. Lower the table without disturbing the position of the gauge base. Rotate the cutterhead by hand until one of the knives is at bottom dead center. Carefully raise the table until the plunger tip just touches the knife. Reach in and steady the position of the base while raising the bed just enough to make the knife move the plunger about .015 in. Zero the dial when the knife rotates through bottom dead center of its arc (see the bottom photo on the facing page). This defines on your gauge the lowest point of the cutting circle. This will be your datum. It is this plane that defines the position of the planer's upper internal components. Neither the bed nor the cutterhead positions should be disturbed while making the rest of the upper adjustments on the planer.

The Infeed Roller Straddle the bed roller slot with the feet of the gauge base, and move the indicator in and out under the infeed roller. The position for serrated steel infeed rollers should be about .030 in. to

.035 in. below the cutting arc for most machines. Rubber rollers will be slightly lower. For sectional infeed rollers or chipbreakers, you'll have to average the measurements. Consult your manufacturer's literature to get an exact figure of the correct position in relation to the cutting arc.

When adjusting the infeed roller to the correct position, the face of the indicator may not be in the most convenient spot for viewing. If this is the case, cut a triangular block of wood about 2 in. high, and fasten a mirror to it with double-faced tape to view the results when standing above the planer. This mirror can be used for the other internal components as well.

The Chipbreaker Like the leading edge of a handplane's cap iron, the chipbreaker in a planer prevents long tearouts from occurring. The chipbreaker is often, but not always, set to the same distance below the cutting arc as the infeed roller. Proper alignment keeps long strips of wood from lifting as the top of the board is being cut by the knives. Set the chipbreaker to manufacturer's specifications using the gauge in the same way it was used to set the infeed roller. Some machines have anti-kickback fingers or pawls just ahead of the chipbreaker.

The Pressure Bar The pressure bar is located behind the cutterhead and keeps the newly cut surface from bouncing up into the cutterhead as the stock enters and exits the planer's feeding system. During the cut, it performs a hold-down function when feeding warped stock. If it is set too high, the wood will flutter and a washboard texture will result. And it's likely that end snipe (a slightly thinner section) will occur. If it is set too low, feeding will be impeded. A majority of surfacing problems can be traced to this component, so its position is critical. I normally set a pressure bar about .002 in. to .004 in. above the cutting arc for surfacing face-jointed lumber. For surfacing lumber that is rough on two sides, a slightly higher setting usually works well.

The Outfeed Roller The outfeed roller is usually smooth or rubber-coated, so it won't mark the planed surface. Set the outfeed roller exactly like the infeed roller. It should also be set to the same distance below the cutting circle, unless the manufacturer's instructions state otherwise.

THE PLANER BED GAUGE HAS TO WORK IN DIFFERENT POSITIONS. The base's screw feet are located so the gauge can straddle the bed slots. To check the feed rollers, orient the dial indicator, so it can take overhead readings. To check the bed rollers, flip the indicator on the tool post, sticking the plunger down through the hold in the base.

THE BED GAUGE CHECKS INFEED AND OUTFEED COMPONENTS. It also shows if bed adjustments are needed. By turning the pulley, the author rocks the cutterhead to be sure that his reading bottom dead center of the arc of the knives.

Sources

Enco Manufacturing
5100 W. Bloomingdale Ave.,
Chicago, IL 60639
800-873-3626

The Bed Rollers The bed rollers reduce friction as stock is being fed, and they prevent premature wearing of the bed tables. So, it's important that the rollers turn easily and are aligned precisely. Bed rollers are located in slots in the bed directly below the two feed rollers. The dial indicator will have to be reinstalled in the base with the plunger down to check the position of the bed rollers (see the top photo on p. 229). Adjust the feet so the plunger moves up only about .015 in. when the base sits on the bed. The weight of a wooden base is often not enough to overcome the opposing spring pressure of the indicator's plunger, so hold the base down for accurate readings.

The rougher the lumber, the higher the bed rollers should be set to reduce friction. However, if they're set too high, the workpiece may vibrate, producing a rippled surface. Conventional practice is to set the rollers .002 in. above the bed when dressing faced lumber and about .020 in. when dressing lumber that's rough on both sides. On this machine, I set the rollers to .002 in. and then insert .020 in. shims on those rare occasions when I'm dressing lumber that's rough on two sides (see the photo at right). Machines with no bed rollers don't usually have performance problems related to the lack of bed rollers. But the beds don't stay flat nearly as long either, and the motors work a bit harder.

Helpful Hints to Better Surfacing

The dimensions I have shown are those I use for a starting point when adjusting planers and are far from being written in stone. Other factors such as component wear, wood dryness, wood straightness, and operator preferences can easily dictate that things be adjusted differently.

Adjustment Problems Adjustment screws on planers usually are held in place with locknuts. When the correct settings are reached by turning the adjustment screw, those settings usually alter when the locknut is tightened. It's always a good idea to watch the indicator's hand when the locknut is tightened, so the setscrew can be turned to compensate for the difference.

Spring Pressure Downward spring pressure can sometimes have an effect on planer performance. A heavy spring can emboss infeed roller prints on softwood when making that light final pass. Light pressure can cause roller skidding when rough or warped lumber is dressed. How much is enough? Only the performance of your machine will tell you that.

Safety Because planers pull the wood away from you, loose clothing and jewelry can be a hazard. Noise is also a factor. When knives get dull, they loudly beat off the chips rather than cut them. So always wear

TEMPORARY BED-ROLLER SHIMS MAKE HEAVY MILLING EASIER. When the author wants to do heavy planing, he elevates the bed rollers with temporary shims. This is easier than having to adjust each end of both rollers individually. The shims, tethered on a string for convenience, are removed when it's time to do finer surfacing.

ear plugs in addition to eye and breathing protection. Try to cut out defects such as knots beforehand, and never plane a board that's less than ¼ in. thick or shorter than the distance between the feed rollers.

Any cutterhead that is moderately exposed on the outfeed side should have a shroud over it to prevent easy access to the spinning knives. Drive belts and gears should also be covered, so you don't come in contact with such moving parts. Last, never look into the machine (infeed or outfeed end) when it's running.

Dust Collection Though this machine was not shown with a dust collector, for best planing results, as well as for health concerns, you should have a dust- and chip-evacuation system. Chips can pile up and get pressed into the wood under the outfeed rollers and get dragged around by the knives. This makes for little dents on the wood that will eventually spring back as little bumps when the wood takes in more moisture. Ideally, your planer should produce long, clean shavings (see the photo above).

Planing for Success Planer-operator technique can have as much to do with poor surface quality as a poorly adjusted machine. For example, slower feed rates tend to produce smoother surfaces. And hardwoods generally should be fed slower than softwoods. Also, keep these guidelines in mind when you are planing: Not supporting long stock as it enters and exits the planer will almost always result in a snipe. Trying to surface warped stock will usually cause a washboard surface because the wood is not flat on the planer bed. Taking too heavy of a cut can cause tearout, feeding the wood against the grain will cause tearout, and dressing knotty or highly figured wood increases the risk of tearout. Not taking a light final pass to get to finished dimension can result in a rough surface. High moisture content in the lumber makes the fibers stringy and difficult to cut cleanly. The result is a fuzzy surface. It also will likely be a bear to feed properly. Finally, a planer smooths stock and makes the faces parallel. It will not straighten warped stock.

* Note price estimates are from 1994.

ROBERT VAUGHAN is a contributing editor to *Fine Woodworking*, and he rehabilitates woodworking machines in Roanoke, Virginia.

The Jointer and Planer Are a Team

BY GARY ROGOWSKI

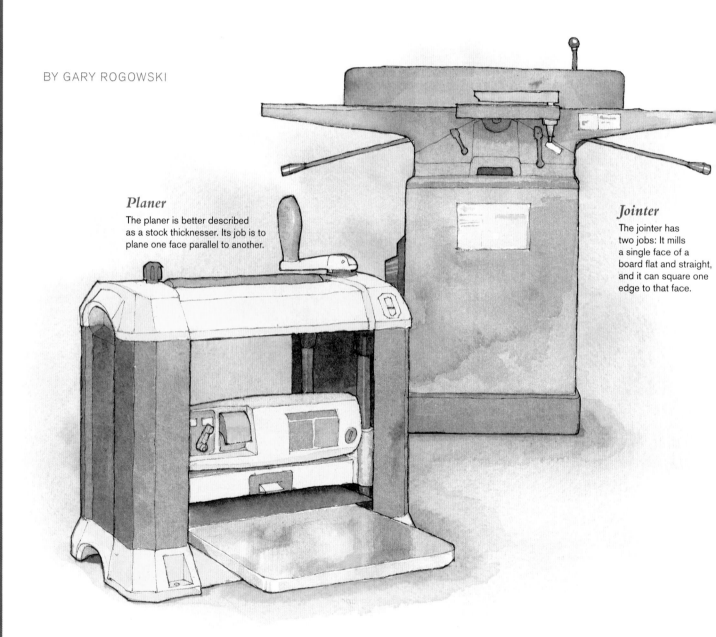

Planer

The planer is better described as a stock thicknesser. Its job is to plane one face parallel to another.

Jointer

The jointer has two jobs: It mills a single face of a board flat and straight, and it can square one edge to that face.

THE JOINER COMES FIRST

This machine planes a flat face on a rough board, using the freshly planed section as a reference surface for the rest of the cut.

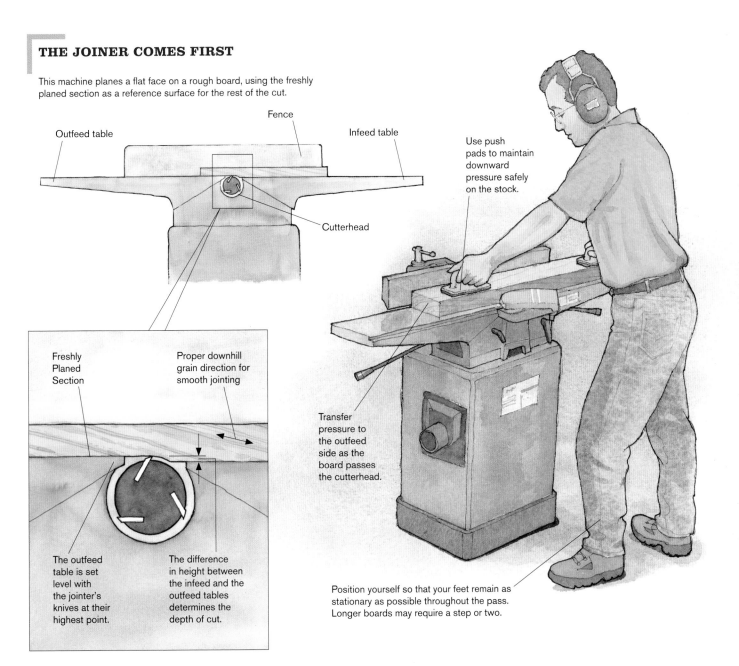

Outfeed table

Fence

Infeed table

Cutterhead

Use push pads to maintain downward pressure safely on the stock.

Freshly Planed Section

Proper downhill grain direction for smooth jointing

The outfeed table is set level with the jointer's knives at their highest point.

The difference in height between the infeed and the outfeed tables determines the depth of cut.

Transfer pressure to the outfeed side as the board passes the cutterhead.

Position yourself so that your feet remain as stationary as possible throughout the pass. Longer boards may require a step or two.

My beginning students often ask me, "Which machine should I buy first, a planer or a jointer?" The answer is both. With a jointer alone, you can't get boards of consistent thickness. And with only a planer, you'll get consistent thickness, but your boards still can come out twisted or bowed.

Perhaps because of these machines' confusing names, many woodworkers don't grasp the separate functions they serve. The European names for these tools—planer (for jointer) and thicknesser (for planer)—are more accurate. The jointer planes a level surface, and the planer simply creates uniform thickness. Because of its American name, some woodworkers think the jointer is only for milling the edges of boards before glue-up.

Together, the two machines form the gateway to serious woodworking, allowing you to mill your own lumber to custom thicknesses instead of being stuck with the surfaced hardwoods available at the local home center. They also allow you to work with rough lumber, which is much less expensive than S2S (surfaced two sides) or S4S stock. Add a bandsaw or tablesaw, and you have the ability to dimension lumber to any width, thickness, and length.

Thicknessing Starts on the Jointer

A jointer works like a handplane turned upside down, with its reference surfaces in line with its cutter knives. Use this tool for flattening one face of a board. If you flip over the board and joint the other side, there is no guarantee the faces will be parallel. On the jointer, each face is cut without referencing the other.

Start by Roughing Stock to Size Before jointing the first face, get your material roughed out to length and width. If a long or wide board is badly cupped or bowed, running it over a jointer until it's flat will waste a lot of wood. You also can rough out around board defects such as knots, sapwood or checks. Use a miter saw or handsaw to rough the stock to length, removing any checked or cracked areas on the ends. Next, rough your stock to width. This can be done in a variety of ways. If the board

is badly crooked, you may need to snap a chalkline on it and bandsaw to the line. Otherwise, run one edge over the jointer or handplane the edge to level it out. Now you can rip the board to rough width.

I highly recommend a bandsaw for ripping rough lumber. It wastes less wood and is much safer because there is no danger of kickback.

Put the Cupped or Bowed Side Facedown It's highly unusual to find perfectly flat stock. That's because wood at a retail lumberyard gets uneven exposure to the air. Here's what to look for: cupping across the width, bowing along the length, and twist or wind in a board's thickness. First, check to see whether the board is cupped across its faces. Use a straightedge or check with your one good eye. It will be easier to run the cupped side down on the jointer table because the board will reference off its two outer edges and not rock. Take off small amounts of wood with each pass until you cut across the entire face and length of the board. Use push sticks or pads to hold the board firmly and safely on the jointer table. Mark the unjointed face with an X.

Twisted wood is deceiving. Use winding sticks to check your lumber or hold a board

WHICH JOINT TO FACE?

Chances are the lumber you are milling will not be flat. Orient the board so that the cupped or bowed side is down to prevent rocking during jointing.

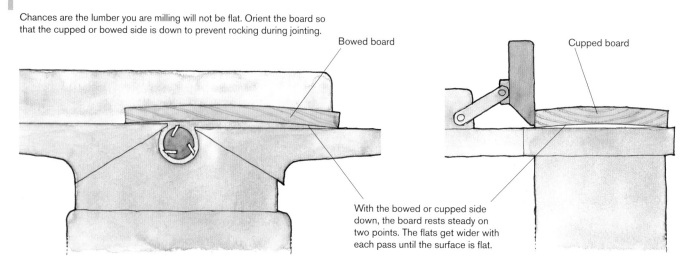

Bowed board

Cupped board

With the bowed or cupped side down, the board rests steady on two points. The flats get wider with each pass until the surface is flat.

ROUGH-CUT STOCK TO SIZE BEFORE MILLING

If you need smaller pieces from a long, bowed board, cutting the board to rough length first will result in thicker stock. The same goes for width.

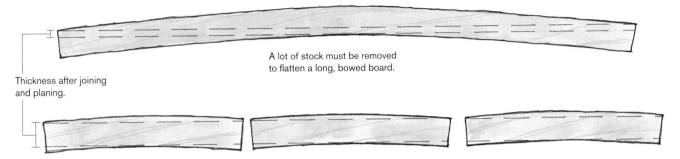

Thickness after joining and planing.

A lot of stock must be removed to flatten a long, bowed board.

You can reduce the waste by cutting a board into smaller lengths or widths before surfacing.

flat on the jointer table and see if it rocks when you push down on a corner. Mark the high corners of one face. On the jointer, start with all of your hand pressure on the leading high corner. As you continue the cut, transfer the pressure to the opposite high corner, trying to prevent rocking to one side or the other. Make multiple passes until the board is flat.

For any of these cuts, check the grain direction of the board before passing it over the jointer. And always keep your feed rate slow, use push pads for protection and to dampen vibration, and take shallow cuts.

The Planer Comes Next

The impatient woodworkers among you may think, let's skip all this bother on the jointer and go straight to the planer. Sorry, it won't work. The planer will take whatever bowed or twisted surface you give it and make a cut parallel to that face. The reference surface on a planer is the bed; the knives are above the stock. So if the board is bowed when it goes in, it will be bowed when it comes out. If it's cupped, the planer's feed rollers may flatten the board slightly, but when it comes out it will pop back to being cupped.

WHY ONE MACHINE IS NOT ENOUGH

Jointers and planers are great at doing the jobs they were designed for, but you can get into trouble by asking them to do too much.

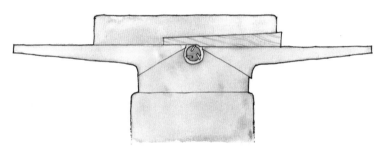

Flat but Not Parallel
If you use a jointer first to plane one side and then the other, you may end up with flat sides but an uneven thickness.

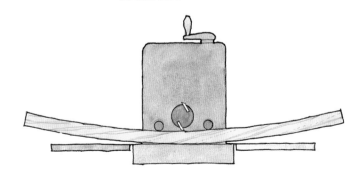

Parallel but Not Flat
If you use a planer tow flatten the first face of a bowed or cupped board, it simply will follow the curve.

THE PLANER COMES NEXT

On this machine, the reference surface (the bed) is on the opposite side of the cutterhead and parallel to it, guaranteeing uniform thickness. Place the freshly jointed, straight side face-down on the bed, and the planed face will come out straight, too.

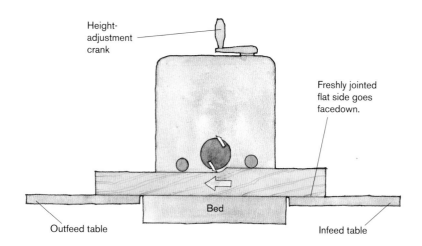

Height-adjustment crank

Freshly jointed flat side goes facedown.

Bed

Outfeed table

Infeed table

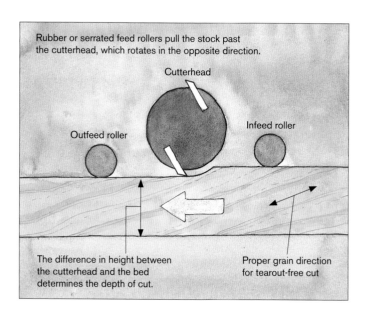

Rubber or serrated feed rollers pull the stock past the cutterhead, which rotates in the opposite direction.

Cutterhead

Outfeed roller

Infeed roller

The difference in height between the cutterhead and the bed determines the depth of cut.

Proper grain direction for tearout-free cut

You must use the jointer first to flatten one face. Then run this straight, flat side facedown in the planer to create a parallel, flat face on the other side of the board.

Arrange all of your boards for grain direction before starting the planer; remember, you're cutting on top of the board now. Make the first pass a light cut. If possible, feed the boards continuously one after the other, end to end, which eliminates the planer's tendency to snipe at the beginning and end of a board. Plane all of the boards down to thickness, leaving them a hair oversize to allow for removing the milling marks. These marks are not a decorative effect.

If you get tearout on a face no matter how you feed the board, dampen a rag and lightly wet down the surface of the wood before planing. This will help soften the fibers and tone down most of the tearout. Also, wax your planer tables.

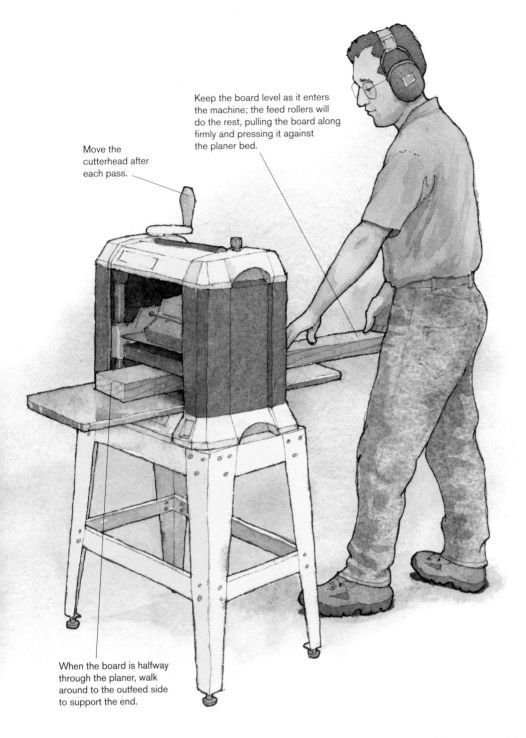

Move the cutterhead after each pass.

Keep the board level as it enters the machine; the feed rollers will do the rest, pulling the board along firmly and pressing it against the planer bed.

When the board is halfway through the planer, walk around to the outfeed side to support the end.

Last, Mill the Stock to Width and Length

After your faces are flat and parallel, work on the edges. Check that your jointer fence is set square to the table just beyond the cutterhead on the outfeed table. This is where your hand pressure should concentrate once the cut is established. Check for crook along each board's edge, and run the crooked edge down to the jointer table. Mark the squared edge and face after cutting.

Rip the last edge to width on the tablesaw or bandsaw. If the cut is rough, you'll want to leave a little extra for one final pass on the jointer. Last, cut the ends to length. Crosscut one end square on all of your boards, using your crosscut sled or miter gauge on the tablesaw. Then clamp on a stop to index the remaining cuts.

GARY ROGOWSKI is a contributing editor for *Fine Woodworking*. He runs the Northwest Woodworking Studio, a school in Portland, Oregon and is the author of *The Complete Illustrated Guide to Joinery* (The Taunton Press, 2001).

Jojnter Tune-Up

BY JOHN WHITE

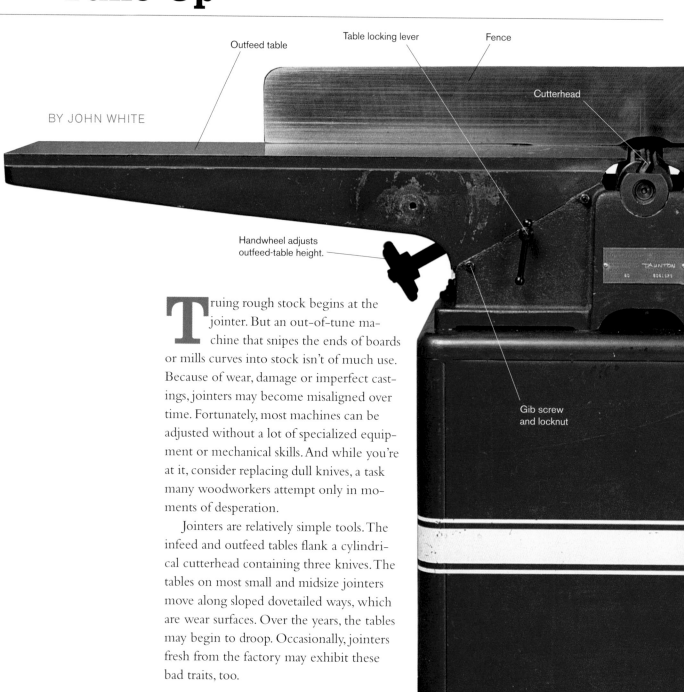

Outfeed table

Table locking lever

Fence

Cutterhead

Handwheel adjusts outfeed-table height.

Gib screw and locknut

Truing rough stock begins at the jointer. But an out-of-tune machine that snipes the ends of boards or mills curves into stock isn't of much use. Because of wear, damage or imperfect castings, jointers may become misaligned over time. Fortunately, most machines can be adjusted without a lot of specialized equipment or mechanical skills. And while you're at it, consider replacing dull knives, a task many woodworkers attempt only in moments of desperation.

Jointers are relatively simple tools. The infeed and outfeed tables flank a cylindrical cutterhead containing three knives. The tables on most small and midsize jointers move along sloped dovetailed ways, which are wear surfaces. Over the years, the tables may begin to droop. Occasionally, jointers fresh from the factory may exhibit these bad traits, too.

The infeed table and fence guide the stock as it crosses the cutterhead. The outfeed table picks up the freshly jointed surface and guides and supports the stock as the pass is completed. The jointed surface is only as straight as the path the wood takes across the cutterhead. If the tables slope, the wood follows the same path. If the tables are misaligned, stock may have a snipe (a deeper cut) or a hump (an uncut section) at the end of the cut or a curve along its length.

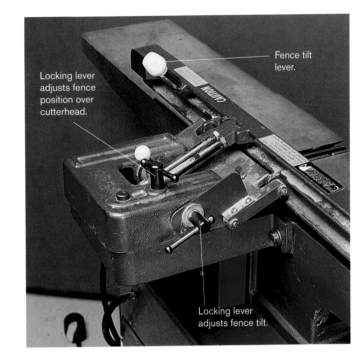

Locking lever adjusts fence position over cutterhead.

Fence tilt lever.

Locking lever adjusts fence tilt.

Fence tilt lever

Infeed table

Handwheel adjusts depth of cut.

The basic tools required for a tune-up are a set of feeler gauges, a small try-square and a good, short straightedge such as the blade of a combination square. A 6-in. dial caliper may come in handy for gauging shim stock, but the job can be done without one. To check the tables for flatness, you'll need a long machinist's straightedge or a test bar (for directions on making and using a test bar, see pp. 242–243) to span the length of both tables.

Unplug the tool before starting. It's also not a bad idea to tape the edges of the knives to protect both you and the knives. It's all too easy to brush a finger or tool across their exposed edges.

Remove Excess Play from the Tables

Each table has an adjustable gib to take up play as the dovetailed ways wear (see the drawing on p. 241). Loose gibs can cause the tables to be out of line with one another. The gibs bear firmly against the dovetailed ways but must slide smoothly. When new,

Four-Step Program

1. ADJUST THE GIBS.
Gibs are located inside the dovetailed ways and do not have to be removed (shown here only for clarity). To ensure the tables move smoothly, tighten the gib screws to remove excessive play.

2. LEVEL THE TABLES.
Use a straightedge (commercial or shopmade) to check that tables are in the same plane. Metal shims can be inserted along the dovetailed ways to correct for tilt.

3. SQUARE THE FENCE.
If the cast-iron fence is warped, attach a piece of plywood or MDF to the fence and shim it flat and square.

4. SET THE KNIVES.
Knives must be parallel to the tables and set to the correct height. Shopmade magnetic holders can assist with the installation.

gibs are coated with grease. Over time the grease wears off. A regular shot of penetrating lubricant will keep things moving smoothly.

Each gib has a pair of gib screws that can be adjusted to take up play as the dovetailed ways wear. The screw nearest the cutterhead has to resist the lifting force caused by the weight of the table's overhang, and it should be adjusted tighter than the lower screw. The third screw on many machines has a handle that serves as a locking mechanism.

Start by backing off the locking lever and the locknuts on the gib screws. Then tighten all screws equally until the table is just locked in place, then back off each of the screws about a quarter-turn. At this point the tables should move with little resistance. Now slowly turn the gib screw nearest the cutterhead while moving the table up and down using the adjusting knob or lever. When the screw is properly adjusted, moving the table should require only moderate effort. Once this adjustment feels right, hold the screw against turning and tighten the locknut. Check and readjust, if needed.

Repeat the procedure with the lower gib screw, but apply slightly less pressure. If your machine has a center screw with a locknut, adjust it last and with only light pressure. Getting the gibs adjusted just right is a matter of both technique and feel, much like tuning a musical instrument. If you're lucky, the tables will now be aligned in a flat plane within .005 in. or less. Check them using the test bar or a long straightedge. If you have an older jointer, chances are that more will need to be done.

Tables Can Be Shimmed Level

Begin by removing the fence. Place a short straightedge across the cutterhead gap and lift both tables until they clear the knives and are in the same plane. Lock them in place. Lay a long straightedge or test bar across both tables. Use feeler gauges to measure any gaps (see the top photo on p. 243).

On an older machine it's a good bet that the tables are sagging. To fix the sag, place thin metal shims along the dovetailed ways to shift one table into alignment with the other (see the bottom photos on p. 243). Flat shim stock may be purchased from machine-shop suppliers. Hobby shops also sell thin pieces of sheet brass and aluminum. Aluminum soda cans will also work; they are about .005 in. thick. Use a feeler gauge to measure how much the outfeed table is out at the far end. If you measure more than .005 in., the table should be shimmed. Anything less than that is probably not worth bothering with for the simple fact that you won't be able to find shim stock thin enough to make the fix.

Shimming is a trial-and-error process. As a rough guide, if your table is out by .006 in., start by cutting two pieces of .002-in.-thick shim stock that measures about 1 in. by 2 in. and apply a light coat of grease on them. To place the shims, back off the outfeed table's gib screws a turn, lift up on the low edge of the table and slip the shims into place on the lower end of the dovetailed ways. Once the shims are in, adjust the gib screws again. Then realign both tables flat to one another and check for flatness using the long test bar or straightedge. The process may have to be repeated a few times.

Jointer tables may be tilted the other way and be dished. Follow the same procedure but place shims at the upper ends of the dovetailed ways on the outfeed table. If you notice that the table is twisted, add thicker shims on the low side. Some small jointers may have a fixed outfeed table, in which case you have no choice but to shim the infeed table. Because the infeed table is adjusted frequently, shims may shift position or tear.

The Fix for a Crooked Fence

A small crown or dip over the length of the fence is tolerable as long as the fence remains vertical to the tables. A twist or

Adjusting the Gibs

Over time the dovetailed ways may wear and cause one or both tables to go out of alignment. Tightening the gib screws removes slack and may correct the problem.

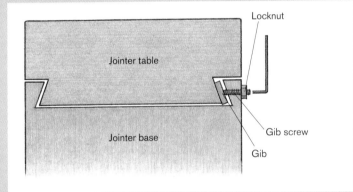

Locknut

Jointer table

Jointer base

Gib screw

Gib

YOU NEED NOT DISASSEMBLE A JOINTER TO DO A TUNE-UP. The narrow, flat bar is a gib, which takes up wear in the dovetailed ways of the infeed and outfeed tables.

THE OUTFEED AND INFEED TABLES HAVE ONE GIB EACH WITH TWO OR THREE ADJUSTING SCREWS. Loosen the locknut and snug up the Allen-head screw to take up any slop. Tighten the screw nearest the cutterhead a tad more than the bottom one.

Leveling the Tables with a Shopmade Test Bar

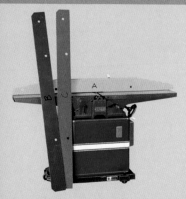

I had hoped that a builder's level would be adequate for tuning up a jointer's tables, but I found it unfit for the task. Machinists use precision straightedges that are meant for just such applications, but at $200* for a 4-ft. version, woodworkers would have a hard time justifying such a purchase.

In search of a shopmade solution, I adapted a machinist's technique for creating precision squares. Technically, the resulting tool isn't a straightedge, because only the three slightly proud screws along one edge are in line. It is more properly called a test bar.

You'll need three bars of the same length and spacing of screws. The screws are adjusted by laying pairs of the bars flat with the screw heads touching. With each pairing, the height of the center screws is adjusted until all three sets of screws touch without either a gap or rocking. This process is repeated several times with different pairings of the bars until all three mate in any combination. When this is achieved, the laws of geometry dictate that the screw heads on each bar lie in a perfectly straight line.

MAKING A TEST BAR

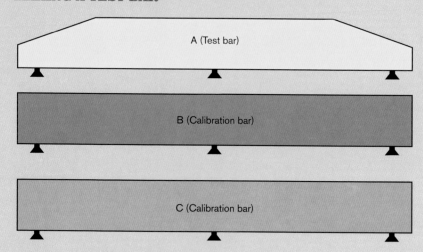

1. Rip three pieces of ¾-in. MDF, each about 5 in. wide and as long as your jointer.

2. Slope the ends of one board (A) to reduce its weight; it will become the test bar.

3. Next, predrill the edges of each board and attach three fine-thread, 1¼-in. drywall screws. Place two screws at the far end and one near the center of each board. File the head of each screw to remove any burrs. Adjust them all so that ¼ in. of screw is exposed.

ADJUSTING A TEST BAR

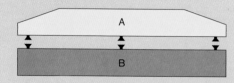

1. Align board A against board B. Adjust only the center screw on board B until all six screws touch.

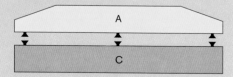

2. Place board C against board A. Adjust only the center screw of board C until all six screws touch.

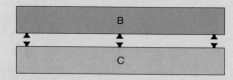

3. Place board B against board C. Adjust both center screws an equal amount (in or out) until all six screws touch.

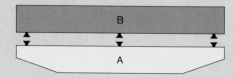

4. Again place board B against board A, but this time adjust only the center screw of board A. Repeat steps 2 to 4 until no more adjustments are needed.

USE THE TEST BAR AND FEELER GAUGES
TO CHECK THE TABLES FOR FLATNESS.
**Tables may sag over time. New machines,
however, may be out of adjustment, too.**

IF THE OUTFEED TABLE SAGS, **insert shims
on each side of the lower section of the dovetailed ways. If the tables are dished (low in the
center), shim the dovetailed ways near the
cutterhead.**

wind, however, will give you fits, because
it will cause stock to rotate as it passes by.
To correct the problem, drill holes in the
soft cast-iron fence and attach a piece of
cabinet-grade plywood or medium-density
fiberboard (MDF) and shim it flat. Once
the fence is mounted back on the jointer,
square it up and take a test pass with a
board that has a flat face. Check the resulting edge with a square, being sure to place
the square against the board surface that
ran along the fence. Adjust the fence stop as
needed to get a square edge on the board.

Sometimes You Have to Replace a Jointer's Knives

Nobody seems to enjoy replacing jointer
knives. That's because it's difficult to keep
the knives in alignment when tightening
the bolts that are threaded into the lock
bars (also called gibs). Patience is required,
no doubt about it. Magnetic knife holders,
either commercially bought or shopmade,
can help.

First Find Top Dead Center Before replacing the knives, top dead center (TDC)
of the cutterhead must be located (see photos 1–4 on p. 244). TDC is a point directly
above the centerline of the cutterhead.
When a knife's edge is at TDC, it is at the
high point of its arc, the ideal spot to align
it level with the outfeed table.

Remove One Knife at a Time Rotate
the cutterhead until the edge of one knife
is at TDC. Lock the cutterhead in place
with a softwood wedge against the infeed
table. Remove the knife and clean all of
the parts, including the slot, of sawdust and
pitch. Smooth the face of the locking bar
and bolts with emery cloth or a stone to
remove burrs, which may cause the knife to
creep when tightened. It's important to remove and replace only one knife at a time
to avoid distorting the cutterhead.

I do a lot of sharpening, but jointer
knives take a lot of time and equipment

How to Get Square, Stable Stock

BY GARY ROGOWSKI

Take a piece of rough wood, fresh off the woodpile or lumber rack. Now transform that coarse stick into a square, flat piece of stock with parallel sides and ends, suitable for your latest project. It seems to take a sort of magic sometimes to make flat and smooth what starts out twisted and rough. The importance of this feat, however, cannot be overstated. If you lay a foundation of accuracy with your milling, then your joinery and assembly have a much better chance of going together smoothly and sweetly.

I am focusing here on milling rough lumber, as opposed to material already surfaced on two or four sides. When starting with rough lumber, you're not bound by the thicknesses that are commonly available in surfaced stock. Also, rough stock is less expensive. And there is no guarantee that surfaced material is truly flat or straight anyway. That leap of faith has gotten many a woodworker into trouble. So proper milling practices are important in any case.

Start with Proper Selection and Storage

Wood is alive. It moves despite our best efforts to keep it flat and square. How can we mill it straight and flat and then keep it

1. Pick good stock and lay out parts

2. Mill the parts oversize and wait

3. Mill the parts to final dimensions

LAY OUT THE PARTS. **The first step in milling is to decide which parts are coming from which boards. Work from a cut list and measure from an end that is freshly cut and free of defects.**

so? Start by learning to read lumber to get a better yield with fewer defects. Learn to recognize end and surface checking, cupping across the width, bowing along the length and twisted sticks. The first step toward having square, flat, stable stock is to leave bad boards at the lumberyard.

Wood movement is dependent on the difference in moisture content from the outside to the inside of the board, so where your lumber is stored along the way also becomes important. Consider the relative humidity of the lumber dealer's facility and

your work area. For example, if the stock is kiln-dried but went from outside storage to your shop, you may need to let it acclimate for a few weeks before milling it.

Rough-Mill to Accommodate Movement

As lumber dries in a kiln or elsewhere, different areas can dry at different rates, and internal stresses can develop that cause the board to move. By the time you get it, the board probably has stabilized, with its internal stresses in balance for the moment.

Rough-Mill and Wait

1. CROSSCUT OVERSIZE

2. JOINT ONE EDGE, THEN RIP

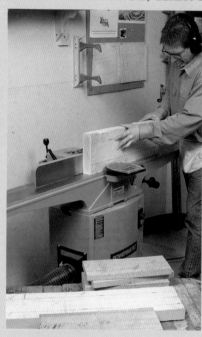

CHECK FOR CHECKING. Take slices off each end of the board until the offcuts are sound. Test for cracks by striking the off-cuts against the table. Then crosscut the parts ½ in. to 1 in. over in length.

JOINT ONE EDGE. It's not important that the edge be square to a face; it just has to be straight and flat. Check grain orientation to get a smooth cut.

RIP TO ⅛ IN. OVER IN WIDTH. The bandsaw is a safer tool for ripping rough lumber than the tablesaw, which is prone to kickback. The bandsaw also wastes less material.

However, when you cut the board into pieces or remove material from the outside, the balance of forces can be disturbed, causing the board to crook, twist, bow, or cup.

In the rough-milling stage, cut the boards a bit oversize and then wait for the stresses to work themselves out again. This may seem like piling more work onto an already big job, but it actually saves time and material. Rough milling won't stop wood from moving, but it leaves enough material to accommodate the movement. If the stock does warp or twist later, you will make it flat and square again when

bringing it down to its final dimensions. You'll lose fewer boards this way and end up with flatter, more stable stock.

Using your power tools effectively also affects your millwork. Each of the tools in your shop is designed for a different part of the milling process.

Length, Then Width, Then Thickness

Start by crosscutting the stock by ½ in. to 1 in. over in length. Look for end checks and honeycomb checks inside the board after you make your first cut. End checks occur as a board dries out faster near its ends than it does in the middle. The wood cracks, or checks, to relieve this stress. It's

3. FLATTEN ONE FACE AND RESAW

MILL TO ROUGH THICKNESS, IF NECESSARY. If the stock must come down more than ¼ in. in thickness, flatten one face on the jointer (left), then resaw or plane to ⅛ in. over in thickness (right).

4. STACK THE PARTS ON STICKERS

STACK IT AND WAIT. Layer parts between stickers to let air circulate. Allow a week or more for the parts to move slightly and stabilize.

very common and no cause for alarm. Plan on losing from 1 in. to 1 ft. of material at each end of a board. Look for checks in the end grain as you cut, but don't trust your eye. Take the offcut and tap it on the saw table or a bench. If the offcut cracks easily, there is still some weakness there. Keep cutting until it doesn't snap easily.

Honeycomb checks are caused by a board drying too quickly on its outer surfaces. This "case-hardening" is often not visible on the surface but can riddle the interior of a board with checks, ruining it for anything but the fire pit. Other times the wood will relieve this stress with one large crack that runs the entire length of the

10-ft. board. Cut away the honeycombing when you find it.

Once the rough crosscutting is done, get your material roughed out to width. If a board is badly cupped across its width or length, running it over a jointer until it's flat can eat up a lot of wood. By ripping pieces to rough width, you work on narrower pieces and can get greater yield. You also can rough out around defects in a board, like knots, sapwood, or checks.

First, joint one edge on the jointer or with a handplane. Just get it flat; don't worry about its being square to any face just yet. When one edge is flat, rip the board ⅛ in. oversize in width on the bandsaw.

WHY ROUGH MILL?

After a kiln-dried board is put into storage, different areas dry and move at different rates, causing internal stresses to develop. When you cut the board into pieces or remove material from the outside, the balance of forces can be disturbed, causing the board to bend or twist. Milling stock a bit oversize in all dimensions leaves enough material to allow you to bring the board back to flat and straight before it is cut to final dimensions. When ripped, lumber tends to go crooked; when resawn, lumber tends to cup or bow.

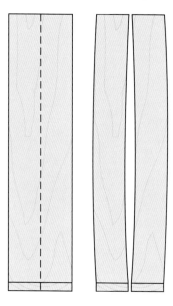

Crook While Ripping

When a board is divided into halves or even thirds, the new pieces tend to bend. Leave at least 1/8 in. extra width to allow for later straightening.

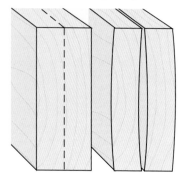

Cup while resawing

Resawing also disturbs the balance of internal stresses, causing the new pieces to cup across their width or bow along their length. Leave at least 1/8 in. extra in thickness so that you can flatten it later.

Bandsaw vs. Tablesaw for Ripping Rough Stock A bandsaw is much safer than using a tablesaw for this ripcut, for a number of reasons: All of the cutting pressure is down into the table instead of at you; there is a smaller kerf and therefore less waste; and if the board closes up on the cut, there is no danger of kickback. (I do not want to recommend that you rough-rip stock on the tablesaw, unless you get a note from your mother.)

Support both ends of the board on a runoff table or adjustable stand. Use a fence on the bandsaw and adjust for blade drift if your saw requires this to make a straight cut. Or just snap a chalkline on the board and make this cut freehand.

If your stock needs to come down more than 1/4 in. in thickness, now's the time to do it. Joint one face flat on the jointer and then square an edge to that face before resawing the stock 1/8 in. oversize on the bandsaw. If your stock is close enough in thickness, rough milling is complete.

Now Stack the Pieces and Wait Next, you must sticker the boards so that air can move around them freely. Don't lay the boards flat on your bench or shop floor and expect them to dry any further. And avoid concrete floors, where boards may in fact absorb moisture and move some. Make 3/4-in.-square by 12-in.-long stickers out of straight hardwood. The pile of stickers I made for my shop some 20 years ago still do their intended job very well.

Let the wood sit for a week or so, depending upon how late your project is running, and allow it to finish moving before milling it to final dimensions.

Use the FEE System for Final Milling

When finish-milling, use the FEE system: Work the Faces, then the Edges, and finally the Ends. This order is exactly the opposite of that for rough-milling.

Mill to Final Destinations

THE FEE SYSTEM

Follow this sequence for final milling.

FACES
EDGES
ENDS

1. Flatten a face of the board and plane to final thickness.

2. Joint one edge of the board and rip to final width.

3. Square one end of the board and crosscut to final length.

1. JOINT AND PLANE THE FACES

JOINT THE FIRST FACE. **Start the finish-milling process by jointing one face flat. Use push sticks or pads to hold down the stock, concentrating pressure just past the cutterhead.**

WITH THE JOINTED SIDE FACEDOWN, RUN THE BOARDS THROUGH THE PLANER. **Once both faces are flat, alternate faces to take off similar amounts from each side until the finished dimension is reached.**

2. FLATTEN AN EDGE AND RIP TO FINAL WIDTH

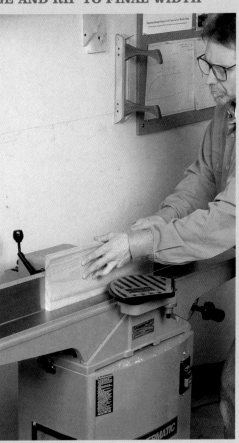

EDGES ARE NEXT. **First, check the jointer fence for squareness (above). Check just past the cutterhead. Joint one edge square, flat, and straight (right), using push sticks or pads when your fingers would pass near the cutterhead.**

MILL THE FINAL EDGE ON THE TABLESAW. **Note that this is the first time the tablesaw has been used during the milling process, and only to remove a small amount of wood.**

3. CROSSCUT TO FINAL LENGTH

ENDS ARE LAST. Use a tablesaw sled to cut the ends accurately. Square up one end first (above), then clamp a stop on the sled to cut the other end (right).

All of the final milling starts with the jointer. (For a better explanation of how the jointer and planer do their distinctly different jobs, see "The Jointer and Planer Are a Team" on p. 232.) Simply put, you must use the jointer first to flatten one face. Then run this straight, flat side facedown in the planer to create a parallel, flat face on the top side of the board. If you flip over the board and joint the other side, there is no guarantee the faces will be parallel.

If the board is cupped across its face, run the cupped side down on the jointer table because the board will reference off its two outer edges and not rock. Take off small amounts of wood with each pass until you eventually flatten the entire face. Then mark the unjointed face with an X. Bowing along a board is just like cup, only it's along the length of the lumber. Again, it's easier to run the concave side down to the table and the humped side up.

For any of these cuts, check the grain direction of the board before passing it over the jointer. The grain should be running down and away from the front end of the board. This will give you a smooth cut with little or no tearout. Also, slow down the feed rate for the best possible results.

A stumbling block you may encounter here is stock that is too wide for the jointer. There are many ways around this but none of them as convenient as having a wide jointer. You can level the first surface with a handplane. You may have to rip your boards to the width of the jointer, then reglue them after milling.

Next, run the boards through the planer, jointed side down. If you get considerable tearout on a face, dampen a rag and lightly wet down the surface of the wood before planing. This will soften the fibers and tone down the tearout. Also, wax your planer

tables to help the machine feed the stock. A runoff table also is handy: It will catch boards for you and minimize snipe, which is the tendency of a planer to overcut at the end of a pass.

After the faces are flat and parallel, work on the edges. Check that the jointer fence is square to the outfeed table just beyond the cutterhead. This is the same point where your hand pressure should concentrate once the cut is established. Check for bowing along each board's edge and run the concave edge down on the jointer table. Arrange the grain direction for the best cut, and mark the squared edge and face after cutting.

The last edge needs to be cut parallel to the newly jointed edge. Again, you cannot just flip over this board and joint the second edge; it will not end up parallel to the first. Use the tablesaw to trim this second edge cleanly. Notice that this is the first time during the entire milling process that the tablesaw has been turned on, and here only to take a sliver off one edge.

With the faces and edges done, you can finish the ends. Crosscut one end square on all of the boards using your crosscut sled or miter gauge on the tablesaw. Then clamp on a stop to index the final cuts.

The reward for all of this hard work will be square and flat stock that should stay that way as you cut joinery and assemble your project.

GARY ROGOWSKI, a contributing editor to *Fine Woodworking*, runs The Northwest Woodworking Studio in Portland, Oregon.

The reward for all of this hard work will be square and flat stock that should stay that way as you cut joinery and assemble your project.

Jobs a Shaper Does Best

BY LON SCHLEINING

I'm convinced that a shaper—more than a router table—should find a home in every active woodshop. Sure, the shaper is well suited for heavy work, like forming deep contours and complex profiles. In fact, I use the machine daily to make custom hand rails, balusters, and other stair parts. But even straight moldings and ordinary light shaping (tasks normally delegated to a router table) can be handled safely and easily by the shaper, and with better results.

I use the shaper for four jobs: running straight molding, raising panels, pattern cutting (see the top photo on the facing page) and doing radius work. Each job requires different tooling and setup. When the machine is molding, for example, you'd hardly recognize it as the same machine that raises panels. Spending time setting up each cut makes the shaper dependable and a pleasure to use.

I've gained confidence with the shaper because I do what it takes to make the machine safe (see the sidebar on p. 257). I haven't skimped on tooling, accessories or jigs. And having an assortment of cutters, guards, jigs, and a power feeder lets me shape items that I would otherwise have to buy from a millwork shop. Jigs, in particular, are great for holding and guiding small or awkward pieces (see the box on p. 259).

Shaper Anatomy: More Solid Than a Router Table

I've tried to do stairbuilding work using a heavy-duty router, but in the middle of a deep profile, I discovered that the router was straining to make the cut. It made me nervous routing with a $2\frac{1}{2}$-in.-diameter bit that weighed several ounces. So I bought a shaper. When I put the same bit in the new machine, the cut was effortless, vibration-free, and just felt a lot safer. A big bit for a router turned out to be a small bit for a shaper. I still use a router from time to time, but the shaper is my tool of choice whenever possible.

Driven by a belt and dampened by lots of cast iron, a shaper just coasts through most lumber. Like a router table, a shaper has a cutter sticking up through a hole in a worktable. And many of a shaper's setups will be familiar to you if you've used a router table. But that's where the similarities end. A shaper is more solid and more powerful than a router table. Though a shaper turns at less than half a router's speed, the shaper produces a superb cut because there is less vibration. There are two reasons for this. First, most shapers weigh almost as much as a cabinet-model tablesaw (about 450 lb.). Second, in most

PATTERN CUTTING IS A SHAPER'S STRONG SUIT. To pattern-shape small parts, the author uses jigs with handles and clamps. Pattern cutting is one of four jobs for which the author says a shaper outperforms a router and router table.

TUNNEL-SHAPED JIG IS BETTER THAN A STANDARD FENCE FOR STRAIGHT MOLDING WORK. Lined with plastic laminate to minimize friction, the jig guides the work smoothly because there is only a few thousandths of an inch clearance. The author's checklist is in the background.

TWO WAYS TO HOLD SHAPER CUTTERS. The spindle with collet (left) holds standard 1/2-in.-shank router bits; the 1-in.-diameter spindle with nut holds stacked wing cutters. The carbide-tipped router bits and two-piece cutter were custom made.

POWER FEEDER IMPROVES STRAIGHT MOLDING. The author relies on a power feeder to run straight molding and hand rails. The feeder makes safe, even cuts. A Plexiglas guard over the cutter lets him see that the chips are being cleared out.

the shaper is that the cutter rotation can be reversed, so cutters may be inverted in certain situations (I'll tell you more about that later). Also, with a shaper, you can move the spindle up and down with a handwheel and then lock the setting. This makes tiny height adjustments easy and precise—something that's difficult to do with a router table.

Accessories and Tooling Increase a Shaper's Capabilities

My Powermatic shaper has a single-phase 220v motor and two speeds: 7,000 rpm and 10,000 rpm. The machine's 30-in.-wide table is thick enough that I can drill and tap holes in it to mount jigs and a power feeder. The shaper came with an adjustable fence with a dust port. The fence is split, so the outfeed and infeed sides can be off-set, like a jointer's tables. This is essential when you're removing the entire edge of your material.

I rarely use the fence alone because I like to bolt on an auxiliary fence for most operations. The machine also came with a miter gauge that runs in a slot, like a tablesaw's, but I never use the miter gauge because I prefer using a fence.

My shaper has three spindles: a solid 1-in. spindle and stub spindles, $\frac{1}{2}$ in. and $\frac{3}{4}$ in. diameter. I use the 1-in. spindle for heavier work, the $\frac{3}{4}$-in. spindle for smaller cutters and rarely, if ever, the $\frac{1}{2}$-in. spindle. Wing cutters (with either three or four wings) or safety cutters (also called anti-kickback cutters) will slide over the spindle. I also can stack a combination of these cutters, spacers (collars) and shims to produce complex profiles. A keyed washer and a locknut hold the cutters on the spindle.

Changing cutters is more involved on a shaper than a router, but you can buy a collet for the shaper (see the bottom right photo on this p. 255), which lets you run $\frac{1}{2}$-in.-shank router bits that interchange

shapers, the cutter is fixed to a 1-in.- or $1\frac{1}{4}$-in.-diameter spindle, which is much more rigid than a $\frac{1}{2}$-in.-diameter router bit shank.

Unlike a router table, where a router is inverted, the shaper is designed to be used with the cutter sticking up. In a router table, the motor sits directly below the cutter where lots of dust goes.

In a shaper, the motor is off to the side. Both my router and shaper are rated at 3 hp, but the router motor will develop the rated horsepower only in a theoretical scenario where power is measured in terms of wattage; the shaper delivers 3 hp at continuous speed and torque.

A shaper's spindle bearings, which are separate from the motor, are much larger than a router's, so the shaper will feel much more solid and stable. Another plus with

With a Shaper, Safety Comes First

ot far from my shop there is a cabinetmaker who wears an oak apron when he's shaping. Even experienced woodworkers are edgy around shapers. But being cautious is wise. A hard thing to learn is taking enough time to be safe. When shaping, I put safety before speed and before cost.

DOUBLE-CHECK THE TOOLING

The biggest fear with a shaper is thrown cutters. I spoke with a guy who had to duck behind his tablesaw when the piece he was shaping kicked a knife loose. As it enlarged the hole in the shaper's top, he said it sounded like a 747 coming in on its belly. Fearing a fire from all the sparks, he slithered back over to the machine to turn it off.

From that story, I've learned to do three things to minimize the risk of loose tooling. First, I don't use slip knives. I use only wing cutters, safety cutters, or router bits. Second, I recheck the tightness of every cutter I install. Third, and most important, I take light cuts while feeding the stock slowly.

MODIFICATIONS ADD A SAFETY NET

I added some extra safety features to the machine when it came out of the crate. I added a cord with a plug and did not wire the machine directly to a circuit. I keep my shaper unplugged, except when I'm running it. When I'm changing cutters or have my hands in the shaper's innards, I drape the disconnected cord where I can see it.

I made a foot-operated kill switch, which is a hinged paddle that contacts the off button (see the photo above). I can hit the paddle while keeping both hands in position, my body upright and my eyes on the cutter. Another improvement was tensioning the shaper's belt, so it will slip if a workpiece gets jammed.

USE THE RIGHT SETUPS AND STAY FOCUSED

Making the job comfortable is one shaper-safety item that's frequently overlooked. Besides wearing eye and ear protection, I make sure I have good footing. I collect old rubber door mats to use as non-skid pads.

A KILL SWITCH OFFERS SECURITY, SO THE AUTHOR BUILT THIS FOOT-CONTROLLED OFF SWITCH. **He also keeps the spindle-reversing switch taped, so he doesn't change the cutter rotation inadvertently.**

I always pick the appropriate spindle speed for the cutter diameter (large cutters require slower rpms). Where possible, I shroud the cutter with a guard or a power feeder. If I'm using the fence, I keep the gap in it as small as practical, and I use a table insert ring sized to the cutter.

When shaping, I keep my hands well out of the cutter's reach. Because I always use either a jig or a starting pin, I am never free-handing work into the cutter. When feeding stock, I shape end grain first. I work against the cutter rotation (unless I'm climb-cutting with a feeder), and I stay out of the line of a kickback. I do not shape stock that has knots or pieces that are too short or too thin.

During shaper setup and use, I keep the shop door locked and the phone answering machine on. When my attention is drawn away from my work, I write down the next step and tape the note to the machine before I take care of the problem. When I return, I take a few extra moments to refocus, and I don't hesitate to postpone a tricky or unfamiliar job if something doesn't feel right. That's usually when I'm about to make a mistake.

readily. Despite the shaper's slower speed, I've found that router bits run fine. You also can use cutterhead tooling, or insert tooling, in a shaper, where the knives are locked in the head by a setscrew, an alignment pin or a V-groove. With cutterhead tooling, you can replace and swap knives, and you can grind a blank to make a custom profile. For my work, however, I'm only comfortable shaping with wing cutters, router bits and safety cutters.

In my shop, the shaper sits alongside a central work station, so I have ample infeed and outfeed area. I built a platform for the shaper, so it is at the same height as the work station table. Because I don't use the miter gauge, I rotated the machine 90° clockwise from its conventional position. This orientation offers better access to the controls and makes changing tooling easier.

> *For most shaping, I use a series of light cuts, which are easier on the machine, and they get me used to the process.*

USE JIGS FOR SAFE AND CONSISTENT SHAPER WORK. Schleining built a jig to shape a profile on the side of a handrail piece. Secured vertically in a holder, the piece is rotated with a handle past the cutter. The shaper is turned 90° from its normal position.

I also bolted the machine to the floor and to the work station to reduce vibration. With the shaper secured, I can apply pressure without worrying that it will move. To keep the work area and my lungs clear, I have a 1,000-cu.-ft.-per-minute (cfm) dust collector that keeps up with most of the waste. For every jig, I make a dust pickup boot from a coffee can or standard metal heating duct.

Checklists and Other Precautions

Pilots use checklists every time they land an aircraft or take off in one. I also use checklists when shaping (see the bottom left photo on p. 255). Remembering to tighten the spindle nut, just like remembering to drop the landing gear, is too important to leave to memory alone. In a quiet moment, I write down the sequence of an operation. I include everything from locking the height adjustment to counting the pieces after a run. Each time I make a setting that I plan to use again, I make sketches and jot down the dimensions in my notebook. When I quit for the day, I mark where I have left off.

Make Light Cuts, and Take Your Time

A shaper is capable of cutting in a single pass, but I only do so when I'm using a power feeder and forming relatively modest profiles. For most shaping, I use a series of light cuts, which are easier on the machine, and they get me used to the process. Instead of taking a chance of ruining a piece by hogging all the way in one pass, I take an initial pass and then clean up with light subsequent passes.

My shaper fence adjusts outward for progressively deeper straight-run cuts (see the photo on p. 256). For raised panels, I elevate the cutter into the piece in stages. When pattern cutting and doing radius work, I also increase the depth of cut in steps. First I bandsaw close to my lines to minimize how much the shaper has to cut. Then I use a flush cutter followed by the profile cutter. Graduated bearing sizes let me make deeper and deeper cuts.

Straight Runs: Shape with a Fence and a Power Feeder

For straight shaping runs, I always use a power feeder. To me, a shaper isn't complete without one. The immediate benefit of the feeder is that the stock moves past the cutter at a constant rate. Chatter and burn marks are gone because the stock feeds without hesitation due to changes in hand positions, which are harmful, repetitive motions anyway.

A power feeder offers other advantages. When the feeder is set slightly askew, the stock will hug the fence. Because the wheels apply constant down pressure, there is little chance of a kickback, and boards that are bowed stay flat on the table. The power feeder hovers over the cutting area, so it shields me from flying chips (see the photo on p. 256). Most important, though, is that a power feeder keeps my hands far away from the cutting action.

The jig I use to form straight molding (see the bottom left photo on p. 255) resembles a tunnel. Its opening is two or three thicknesses of paper wider than the stock I'm running. This allows .010 in. to .015 in. clearance, so the stock slides without binding. I line the tunnel with plastic laminate, and I lubricate it with TopCote. The key here is to have all the blanks milled consistently. I use a portable planer to thickness the stock, and I mill a couple of pine blanks at the same time so that I can test the shaper's setup. The roof of the jig is the power feeder.

Panel Raising

The conventional way to raise panels on a shaper is to run the panel face up (see the drawing on p. 260). Panel-raising cutters

Shaper Jigs Put You in Control

Shapers require more hold-downs, guides, and stops than other machines. I've spent half a day setting up an operation that takes just a few minutes.

To build jigs, I use Finnish birch plywood because it wears well and is strong. I use ¾-in. plywood to make jig bases. To hold a workpiece, I prefer toggle clamps because they grasp and release easily, and the tension can be adjusted. I integrate a cutter guard and a dust hookup into most jigs.

For small pieces, I make the jig oversize and put handles on it (see the photo below). I also make the part longer than it needs to be. To keep the work from being yanked out, I screw the end of the piece where it won't be near the cutter.

I never get tired of seeing perfect contours emerge from jigs. When I'm done with a jig, I hang it on the wall, where it's always handy.

INVERTED PANEL RAISING IS SAFER. Because Schleining likes to keep work between his hands and the cutter, he prefers to raise panels with the bevel facing down. The auxiliary table and guard also shield the cutter.

Working with Machines

Woodworking machines produce great projects if you know how to use them correctly. Unfortunately, they also produce plenty of dust and noise. Many of us who have been working wood for 25 years or more used to be a bit cavalier about these hazards, but everyone has pretty much wised up these days. There's no excuse to expose ourselves and our families to harmful dust and noise when good protection is available.

In this section, you'll see that there are plenty of affordable dust collectors and air filters for the modern small shop. The science of noise protection has also progressed, with the marketplace offering no shortage of solutions for maintaining our hearing (and neighborly relations) for years to come.

Because woodworkers are notorious tool junkies, the subject of working with machines implies the subject of buying machines. Fortunately, you can often minimize damage to your pocketbook by buying used equipment. The trick is knowing what to look for, and how to put the fix on any problems that do surface. You'll find great advice on all these topics in the following pages.

Taming Woodworking Noise

BY JACK VERNON

Those tools that we most need to use are the very ones that offer the greatest potential danger to our ears. Common woodworking machines such as routers, planers, and tablesaws can cause permanent hearing damage. The good news is that there are easy ways to protect your hearing while continuing to work wood with power tools. But first it helps to understand the problem.

Hearing-Damage Basics

Loud sounds damage hearing in much the same way that earthquakes damage buildings. Loud sounds simply shake apart the delicate inner-ear structures called hair cells. These hair cells are highly specialized nerve endings designed to receive sound energy and convert it into neural impulses. In turn, those neural impulses produce our ability to hear. Sound waves strike all parts of our body, but only the hair cells of the inner ear can convert that sound energy into what causes us to hear. Once destroyed, the hair cells are gone forever.

Open a pea pod, and take out one pea. That is about the size of your inner ear, and amazingly, it contains 30,000 hair cells and approximately the same number of nerve fibers leading away from the hair cells up to the brain. You can easily appreciate that the inner ear is not only a very delicate structure, but it is compacted into a very small space.

Measuring Woodworking Noise

As might be imagined, damage to the ears produced by loud sounds is a combination of the intensity of the sound and the length of time to which one is exposed to that sound. Sound measurements of what we commonly call loudness, which actually measure the sound pressure level (SPL), are expressed in decibels (dB). Decibel units represent a logarithmic scale because the human ear can perceive such a large range of different intensities. Logarithmic notations are expressions of ratios; for example, if one sound is twice as intense as another sound, it is 6 dB more intense. If one sound is 10 times more intense than a second sound, the first sound is 20 dB more intense.

The federal Occupational Safety and Health Administration (OSHA) standards limit industrial workers to 90 dB SPL for an 8-hour day. For sound levels of 95 dB, only a 4-hour work day is allowable. At a sound level of 100 dB, the allowable

263

PROPER EAR PROTECTION HELPS PREVENT HEARING DAMAGE. Common woodworking machines, like this table-mounted router, can quickly damage hearing unless you protect your ears. LeRoy Schmidt, foreman of the carpenter shop at Oregon Health Sciences University, wears ear muffs during tests conducted by the Oregon Hearing Research Center.

THE EAR IS AN AMPLIFIER. Using this miniature microphone inserted into the ear canal, researchers measured sound levels right at the ear drum. The findings showed the ear canal amplifies woodworking noise on average by about 7 dB over conventional readings taken at ear level.

workday is 2 hours, for 105 dB, 1 hour, 110 dB, 30 minutes, 115 dB, 15 minutes and so on.

To study how woodworking machines affect hearing, members of the Oregon Hearing Research Center staff measured the intensity (loudness) of the sound in the conventional manner, at the ear level. But we also used special equipment—a miniature microphone—to measure sound intensity inside the ear canal at the eardrum itself (see the photo at left). The chart on the facing page lists our measurements of typical woodworking machines under appropriate and normal operating conditions. Keep in mind, however, that tools vary from maker to maker, with some being louder than others.

The sound measured at the eardrum is significantly louder than that same sound measured at ear level. In practical terms, that means that the ear canal leading to the eardrum produces some amplification of the sound intensity. For example, the noise generated by the 15-in. planer was 9 dB more intense at the eardrum than when measured at the ear level. On average, the sound produced by the machines we measured was increased by the ear canal about 7 dB (and remember an increase of 6 dB is a doubling of the sound intensity). In other words, sounds are more than twice as loud at the eardrum.

Another problem with woodworking power tools is that when we hold them, we stimulate our ears by bone conduction (sound traveling through the body), as well as by airborne sounds. Ear muffs and ear plugs block out sound coming to the ear through the air. When bone conduction of sound is involved, it would be desirable to use the power tool in short bursts to minimize any accumulation effect (see the left photo on p. 266). Anti-vibration gloves may also help, but we have not tested them.

Warning Signs of Hearing Damage

When other parts of our bodies are damaged, the warning signal is pain. But for the ear, the warning signal is tinnitus (ringing in the ears). Ringing in the ears after exposure to a woodworking tool means that tool was too loud for your ears and that you should always wear ear protection in the future when using that tool. Don't be guided by the actions of others. Some people have tough ears, and some people have tender ears, with all grades in between. You may have noted that Norm Abram of *The New Yankee Workshop* seldom wears ear protection. I would assume that Mr. Abram has tough ears.

The way in which hearing impairment starts can be deceptive, so deceptive as to go unnoticed initially. Imagine the inner ear

Type of Machine	Sound Intensity	
	At Ear Level	At Eardrum
Nail Gun (6d 2-in. finish nail)	104 dB	110 dB
Chop saw	102 dB	108 dB
Router	104 dB	107 dB
15-in. planer	96 dB	105 dB
10-in. tablesaw	95 dB	103 dB
Palm sander (quarter sheet)	96 dB	103 dB
Panel cutter	95 dB	102 dB
Dust collector	93 dB	99 dB
Bandsaw	92 dB	98 dB
Shop vacuum	90 dB	97 dB
10-in. tablesaw (with Silencer® blade)	86 dB	93 dB
6-in. jointer	80 dB	90 dB

HOW LOUD ARE WOODWORKING MACHINES?

laid out like a piano keyboard, the low frequencies to the left and the high frequencies to the right, with each frequency systematically spaced in between. It is the high frequencies that are damaged initially by loud sounds, so one can sustain a considerable amount of damage before the ability to hear the lower pitches becomes impaired. The sounds to which we pay attention and which we commonly use are restricted to the low-frequency portion of the ear, starting with about 4,000 Hz (cycles per second) and moving to lower pitches.

The typical course of hearing loss is something like this: With the initial hearing loss, the person has no difficulty hearing and understanding speech as long as the person is in a relatively quiet place. But when there is background noise present (in a restaurant or at a cocktail party, for example), the person will hear speech, but he or she will not be able to understand it. This condition is an early warning of hearing loss. Moreover, that kind of hearing

loss often can be compensated by a pair of properly fitted hearing aids.

Ear Protection

There are two common forms of ear protection: ear muffs and ear plugs. In extreme cases, it is advisable to use both types at the same time. Much has been made of ear plugs as a protective device, and it is true that ear plugs work about as well as ear muffs. Ear plugs such as the foam EAR brand plugs available in most drugstores, are good protective devices, and they are inexpensive. A disadvantage of ear plugs is that they can be difficult to insert correctly. And it takes time to get them inserted. In addition, the ear plug is vulnerable to jaw movements, which can break the sound seal. Place your finger in your ear and move the jaw, as in chewing or talking, and note the amount of ear canal movement. It is this movement that can make ear plugs less effective.

Properly selected ear muffs offer as much sound protection as do custom-fitted ear plugs. More important, ear muffs are easier to put on and take off, provided they are available at each noisy machine. If the muffs are on the other side of the shop

TAKE OFF THOSE NOISY SAWBLADES AND REPLACE THEM. Several manufacturers, including Freud®, CMT®, and Everlast (not shown) now offer special sawblades designed to cut down on noise. Changing to one of these blades may reduce saw noise by up to 7 dB. The blades have laser cuts that dampen noise and vibration.

from the tool being used, there's an inclination to say, "This is a very brief task; I don't really need ear protection." We recommend that a pair of ear muffs be placed on each machine capable of producing ear-damaging loud sounds. The ear bows of safety glasses can break the sound seal for some ear muffs, but our research showed the cuffs on the Thunder 29 ear muffs available from Safety and Supply (see Sources) are sufficiently pliable that they can be worn over glasses without any loss of sound protection.

Quieting Woodworking Machines

In addition to ear protection, it is possible to reduce the amount of sound generated by certain machines. Several manufacturers are marketing so-called quiet sawblades (see the right photo on the facing page). We tried the Silencer 10-in., sawblade available from Everlast Saw and Carbide Tools, Inc. (see Sources), and we found it reduced table-saw noise level by 9 dB when compared to a regular carbide blade. Remember that reducing sound intensity by 6 dB means cutting the intensity in half; a reduction of 10 dB means a reduction of three times. Thus the 9-dB sound reduction provided by the Silencer blade is significant.

Many machines, such as the bandsaw, produce some of their noise by the resonance of their metal panels. Attaching pieces of plywood to these panels helps reduce the sound generated by the saw. For example, the noise produced by a 16-in. Grizzly^{SM} bandsaw was reduced from 92 dB to 89 dB by loading its panels with plywood. Mounting tools on rubber isolation blocks or wood mounts can reduce sound levels (see the photo at right).

Keep tools in good working order. Dull tools tend to make more noise than do sharp ones. Misaligned belts and pulleys can generate excess drive-train noise. Worn or poorly lubricated bearings will add to noise.

Think about your hearing when you purchase woodworking equipment. Some designs and individual tools are louder than others. Machines with universal motors tend to be louder than those with induction motors. Gear-driven tools are usually louder than belt-driven or direct-drive tools.

In general, shielding, insulating and muffling can reduce machine noise. The degree to which these procedures are effective depends in part upon the conditions of the individual shop, such as size, shape, surface of the walls, ceiling construction, and ceiling

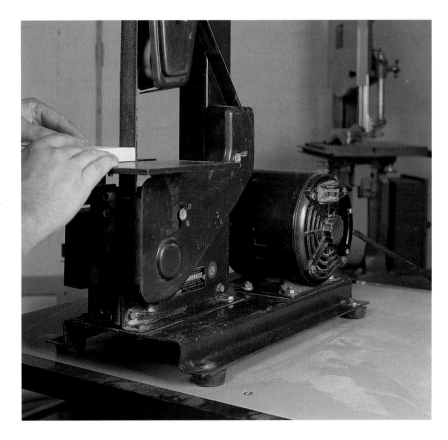

RUBBER MOUNTING PADS CAN CUT MACHINE NOISE. Mounting machines on antivibration mats or on rubber foot pads, such as those on this 1-in. belt sander, can cut down on woodworking noise by isolating or dissipating the vibration that causes noise.

height. Each situation requires individual attention. But the point is to look for ways to reduce sound levels, and you will find them.

It's important to prevent permanent damage by protecting your ears from harmful noise any way you can. Remember: If after exposure to a noise your ears ring, even briefly, then the sound was too intense for your ears, and in the future, use ear protection.

JACK VERNON is director of the Oregon Hearing Research Center at Oregon Health Sciences University in Portland. Jim Nunley and Jonathan Lay, also members of the research center, contributed to this article. All three men are active amateur woodworkers. Those who already may be suffering from tinnitus can contact the Oregon Hearing Research Center (see Sources) to learn about relief procedures for tinnitus.

Sources

Safety and Supply
595 N. Columbia Blvd.
Portland, OR 97217
503-283-9500

Everlast Saw and Carbide Tools, Inc.
9 Otis St.
West Babylon, NY 11704
516-491-1900

Oregon Hearing Research Center
3515 S.W. Veterans Hospital Rd.
Portland, OR 97201-2997
503-494-8032

Dust Collection
for the One-Man Shop

BY ANATOLE BURKIN

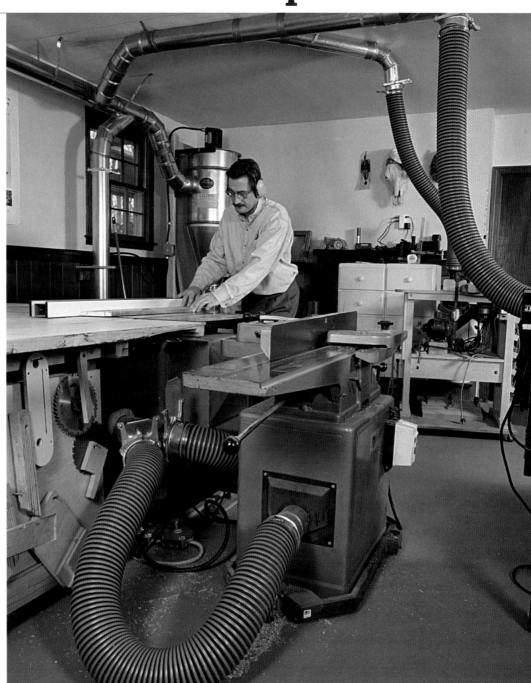

D on't throw away the broom just yet. Even the best dust-collection system won't eliminate the need for occasional sweeping. A good system, however, will keep the broom and your lungs from wearing out prematurely.

There are two main points to consider when choosing a dust collector. First, figure out the air-volume requirements of the machines in your shop (see the chart on p. 273). Next, decide on what kind of hookups you are going to use: flexible hose, PVC pipe or metal duct.

To see what size and type of collector would best suit a one-man shop, I gathered a sampling of machines, from 1-hp single-stage units to 2-hp two-stage collectors, including one cyclone: Delta (1½ hp single stage), Dust Boy (2 hp two stage), Jet (2 hp single stage), Oneida® (1½ hp cyclone) and SECO UFO-90 (1 hp single stage). I used the collectors with my tools, which include a 10-in. cabinet saw, a 15-in. planer, an 8-in. jointer, and a 16-in. bandsaw.

The horsepower rating is a fairly reliable guide to the performance of a dust collector (see the chart on p. 272). Hookups, however, are everything. Too much flexible hose will rob even a big collector of power. PVC pipes, in short runs, work fine with a sufficiently powered collector, 1½ hp or more. Metal duct, not unexpectedly, performs best. Even an 8-year-old, 1-hp collector can collect chips from machines 25 ft. away when hooked up to a properly designed system. Using a 1-hp collector this way may seem misguided, like putting a racing exhaust system on a subcompact car, but the experiment illustrates how you don't have to spend a fortune to get decent results. Every shop is different, of course, and your results may vary, so use my findings as guidelines, not absolutes.

A 1-hp Single-stage Collector Can Handle Any Machine in My Shop

The biggest sawdust producer in my shop is a 15-in. planer. And even a 1-hp single-stage dust collector can handle that machine, hooked up with about 6 ft. of 4-in.-diameter flexible hose. I borrowed a new UFO-90, same as my old collector, to see if anything had been changed. It's still the same machine, rated at 650 cu. ft. per minute (cfm) by the manufacturer, but when hooked up to 6 ft. of flexible hose, it moves about 420 cfm. That's slightly less than the 500 cfm recommended for a 15-in. planer, but 90 percent of the time the 1-hp collector can handle it because I rarely plane 15-in.-wide stock.

One-hp single-stage collectors cost about $200★. Some woodworkers buy two units and station them strategically in their shop. At 82 decibels (measured at 8 ft.), a 1-hp dust collector isn't much noisier than a vacuum cleaner, and each one takes up about 3 sq. ft. of shop space.

I also used the 1-hp collector with a PVC duct system (4-in.-diameter pipe and fittings) and measured the moving air volume at the tablesaw–jointer connection, which is at the end of about 25 ft. of pipe and hose. At that distance, because of

1-HP COLLECTORS. Small, portable collectors are easy to move around the shop. Make connections to one tool at a time using a short piece of flexible hose.

Three Styles of Dust Collectors

The most economical and biggest-selling dust collectors are the two-bag, single-stage models. Single stage means the dust is sucked through the impeller (fan) and dumped into the lower bag. The upper bag collects fine sawdust and lets the exhaust air back into the shop.

Two-stage collectors are the next step up. The motor and impeller sit atop a barrel. Chips enter the barrel and are directed downward, although the swirling air inside may occasionally move smaller chips upward. A filter bag hangs off to one side and collects the finest dust.

Two-stage cyclones are at the top of the evolutionary chain. The motor and impeller sit atop a cone-shaped canister, the cyclone, which is connected to a trash can below.

Chips or other large debris enter the cyclone and swirl downward, avoiding the impeller. The longer the cyclonic chamber, the greater its effectiveness at slowing down and separating large particles. Air is filtered either by a pleated internal cartridge or by one or more felt bags hanging off to the side of the machine. Internal-cartridge cyclones use the least amount of floor space. The upper bags or cartridge filters of all collectors must be shaken out occasionally to remove fine dust.

DANGERS OF SINGLE-STAGE COLLECTORS

Debris entering a single-stage collector passes through the impeller, many of which are made of steel. Even a small bit of metal, such as a screw, can cause a spark when it hits a steel impeller. Dust-collector explosions are rare, but the potential is there. Debris, metal or otherwise, not only makes a racket when it hits an impeller but also imparts stress on the bearing and will shorten its life. I heard of a wood-worker whose collector's sheet-metal housing was punctured by a screw that entered the impeller.

One way to reduce the risk of fire is to choose a single-stage collector with a plastic or aluminum impeller. Although the impeller itself won't cause a spark, metal debris striking the steel housing may have the same effect. Steel impellers are fine, however, if you avoid using the dust collector to sweep up miscellaneous debris off the floor or workbench.

Single Stage
Sawdust must first pass through the impeller (fan) before being separated.

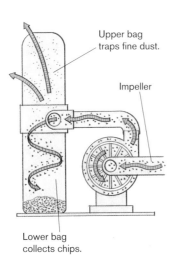

Upper bag traps fine dust.

Impeller

Lower bag collects chips.

Barrel-Style Two Stage
The larger chips entering a two-stage collector tend to drop out before they have a chance to strike the impeller.

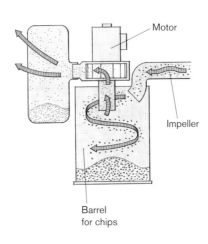

Motor

Impeller

Barrel for chips

Two-Stage Cyclone
The shape of a cyclone is most efficient at slowing down the speed of debris, allowing most of it to settle out before reaching the filter.

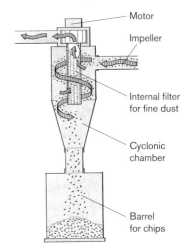

Motor

Impeller

Internal filter for fine dust

Cyclonic chamber

Barrel for chips

increased resistance, the air volume drops to under 300 cfm, less than recommended for woodworking tools. In reality, however, one can live with that. But if I'm face-jointing wide boards, the collector can't always handle the volume, and chips jam the jointer's dust port. Maybe 80 percent of the time it works okay.

When I hooked up the 1-hp collector to a newly installed metal duct system, with my tools in the same configuration as before, I was really surprised. The air volume was back up to 360 cfm, very acceptable. Then I hooked up my old 1-hp collector, which is outfitted with oversize felt bags (available from Oneida Air Systems) that improve airflow and capture fine dust (see the sidebar at right), and I measured almost 400 cfm. That's a significant gain.

A 1½-hp Collector Can Be Hooked Up to Longer Runs of Hose or Duct

As you might imagine, hooked up to one machine at a time, a 1½-hp collector does not have any trouble removing chips, even with a long (12-ft.) run of hose. Delta rates its 1½-hp collector at 1,200 cfm, a number that is derived in a lab, not under real shop conditions (for more on manufacturer specs, see the sidebar on p. 273). Hooked up to a 6-ft. run of 4-in.-diameter flexible hose, I measured about 500 cfm with the Delta and 470 cfm using an Oneida Air Systems 1½-hp cyclone collector. Cyclones and two-stage collectors have slightly more internal air resistance; hence the lower cfm reading. That's about what you can expect from any 1½-hp collector hooked up to 4-in.-diameter hose.

I also hooked up the 1½-hp collectors to two machines running simultaneously. Performance ranged from good to so-so, depending on how much sawdust was being spit out by my tools. The best way to

1½-HP COLLECTORS. Although collectors in this power category may occasionally be used with two tools simultaneously, for best performance, use blast gates and run one tool at a time.

Go With Felt Bags

The standard bags issued with most dust collectors are good for capturing particles of 25 microns to 30 microns or bigger. A micron is $\frac{1}{1,000,000}$ of a meter in length; looked at another way, the paper this book is printed on is about 25 microns thick. Fine dust blows right through filter fabric, back into the shop. Dust particles under 10 microns in size are the most harmful because they can get past the respiratory tract and enter your lungs. Unless you wear a dust mask while woodworking, toss out the stock bags and replace them with felt bags rated at 5 microns or less.

FABRIC VS. FELT. A fabric bag, left, has less thickness and is more porous. Felt, right, does a much better job of filtering out very fine dust.

Determining Your Dust-Collection Requirements

MEASUREMENTS WERE TAKEN WITH A DIAL-GAUGE MANO-METER (A PRESSURE GAUGE) AND PITOT TUBE. The chart below compares the performance of a few dust collectors when using hose, PVC pipe, and metal duct.

PERFORMANCE OF DUST COLLECTORS UNDER VARYING CONDITIONS

Horsepower	6 ft. from collector, 6-in.-diameter straight metal duct*	6 ft. from collector, 4-in.-diameter flexible hose	6 ft. from collector, two runs of 4-in.-diameter flexible hose	25 ft. from collector, at jointer hookup, 4-in.-diameter PVC pipe	25 ft. from collector, at jointer hookup, 5-in.-diameter metal duct
1 hp single stage	550 cfm	Excellent	Fair	Fair	Excellent
1½ single stage	825 cfm	Excellent	Good	Good	Excellent
1½ hp cyclone	700 cfm	Excellent	Good	Good	Excellent
2 hp single stage	980 cfm	Excellent	Excellent	Excellent	Excellent
2 hp two stage	825 cfm	Excellent	Good	Good	Excellent

Fair: under 300 cfm   Good: 325 cfm to 500cfm   Excellent: more than 350 cfm

*Bags or filters attached with a light coating of sawdust present.

METAL

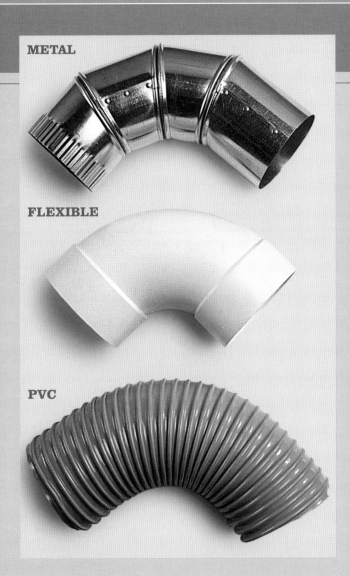

FLEXIBLE

PVC

MATERIALS THAT AFFECT AIR-FLOW. The metal elbow, which is designed for central dust-collection systems, has a gentle sweep, which lowers resistance to airflow. Plastic PVC pipe has a tighter-radius bend and restricts airflow more. Ribbed flexible pipe also disturbs airflow, up to three times as much as metal.

AIR VOLUME REQUIREMENTS OF MACHINES	
Tool	**CFM Needed**
10-in. tablesaw	350
6-in. or 8-in. jointer	300–450
12-in. planer	350
15-in. planer	500
Drill press	350
14-in. or 16-in. bandsaw	350
Radial-arm saw	350–500
12-in. disc sander	350
12-in. to 24-in. drum sander	300–500
Oscillating spindle sander	350
Floor sweep	350

MAKING SENSE OF MANUFACTURER SPECS

There's a fair amount of misleading marketing specs on dust collectors. When an ad says a collector is rated at 1,200 cfm, what does it mean? Not much, really. Cfm stands for cubic feet per minute, a measure of the volume of air moving past a point of reference. The cfm figure needs to be put in the context of the amount of resistance, or friction, present (called static pressure, or SP). Air moving through duct or hose encounters resistance, just as a person would slipping down a water slide. The more bends and bumps, the slower the ride or the lower the air velocity and volume. Many manufacturers rate their machines without bags or duct attached.

While trying out a number of dust collectors, I measured their performances under real working conditions, using flexible hose, PVC pipe or metal duct in my 420-sq.-ft. shop (see the chart above). The resistance readings ranged from 3 in. to 5 in. I also measured collectors hooked up to a straight piece of 6-in.-diameter metal duct, just to get a baseline, highest-possible performance figure.

Collectors ranging in size from 1 hp to 2 hp have impellers (fans) sized from 10 in. to 12 in. in diameter. All things being equal (motor speed and impeller design), a bigger impeller coupled with a bigger motor will move more air than a smaller pairing. There are some differences among collectors; to learn more, ask a manufacturer for an impeller performance chart.

As soon as any collector is hooked up in the shop, performance declines in relation to the length and type of hookup. That's why smooth-walled metal duct, with wide-radius elbows and wyes, is better than PVC pipe.

2-HP COLLECTORS

SINGLE STAGE. Many 2-hp collectors can handle two tools at once. Although 4-in.-diameter PVC pipe is not the best duct material, satisfactory results can be obtained when connected to a 2-hp collector.

BARREL-STYLE TWO STAGE. A 2-hp collector has enough power to handle larger machinery, such as this 18-in. planer (right). This collector by Dust Boy is a two-stage model with a 55-gal. drum.

direct maximum airflow to the tool being used is to attach a blast gate to each hose.

Hooked up to a PVC duct system (a run of about 25 ft. of pipe), both the Delta and Oneida collectors captured most of the sawdust when running one tool.

A 1½-hp Delta collector costs about $350★. A two-stage unit such as the Oneida costs almost twice as much. Penn State Industries also sells a cyclone collector. (For more on the advantages of two-stage collectors vs. single-stage units, see the sidebar on p. 270.)

Both 1½-hp collectors performed exceptionally well when connected to metal duct and used with one tool at a time. With two blast gates open, the air volume dropped and was insufficient to operate two big machines at once.

The larger-volume bags or canisters of 1½-hp collectors hold a lot of material, about 30 gal. worth, which means fewer trips to the compost pile, a big advantage over the 1-hp machines that hold about half of that. A 1½-hp single-stage collector

takes up about 7 sq. ft. of shop space. But a vertically stacked two-stage cyclone such as the Oneida takes up only 3½ sq. ft. of shop space, a big plus in a small shop. More horsepower does mean more noise; both registered 85 decibels at 8 ft. The Delta comes wired for 115v but can be switched over to 230v. The Oneida comes without cable or switch. It can be wired to run on either current.

A 2-hp Unit Can Sometimes Handle Two Machines at Once

Hooked up to two 6-ft. runs of 4-in.-diameter hoses, a 2-hp single-stage collector draws over 350 cfm from each port, plenty for many woodworking machines. The 2-hp two-stage Dust Boy didn't match the power of the 2-hp single-stage Jet machine, although it has other qualities that may be preferable (see the sidebar on p. 270). When I connected the 2-hp units to the PVC duct system, they too were robbed of considerable power, but one machine could be operated at a time with satisfactory results.

When connected to a metal duct system, the Jet collector really moved a lot of air, 570 cfm at the tablesaw–jointer connection (after about 25 ft. of duct). With two blast gates open, the air volume was reduced to less than 300 cfm, still acceptable for some operations. The Dust Boy produced slightly lower readings but still had more than enough power to run one tool at a time in any configuration. If you regularly operate more than one machine simultaneously, it would be wise to look at 3-hp or bigger dust collectors.

The 2-hp machines are no noisier than the 1½-hp collectors. They cost more, however. The Jet is priced at $400★; the Dust Boy sells for about $650★. Most 2-hp collectors come wired for 230v. The Dust Boy can be run at either 115v or 230v.

Choosing Among the Options

On the matter of choosing a dust collector, a two-stage cyclone gets my top vote. A small cyclone collector takes up less room, is easy to empty, and runs very clean. For example, on all of the single-stage units, even after running them for only 1 hour, fine dust appeared on the machine and in the area around it. That's because it's difficult to get a perfect seal between the bag and housing. The Oneida cyclone, outfitted with an internal filter, rubber gaskets and wide metal ring clamps, seals better.

Two-stage units such as the Dust Boy (Delta also makes a two-stage collector) are also nice and compact. The Dust Boy takes up 6 sq. ft. and less vertical space than most collectors. The Dust Boy (as does the Oneida) comes with a Leeson® motor and cast-aluminum housing and impeller (fan), and the sturdy plastic barrel holds a lot of debris, 55 gal. worth. Before it can be emptied, however, the heavy motor and housing must be lifted off.

Removing the lower bag of a single-stage collector is an easy matter of loosen-

ing a band clamp. The real fun begins when you try to reattach it. If you've ever had to put your pants on with an arm in a cast, you'll get the idea. The lower bag must be wrapped around the metal waist of the machine and held in place before the clamp can be cinched. Some manufacturers, such as Jet, add an elastic band inside the lower bag to facilitate reattachment somewhat.

Woodworker's Supply tried to solve the lower-bag problem with a clamp-on skirt accessory. The skirt and a standard 30-gal. trash can replace the lower bag. Because the skirt remains attached to the collector's housing, it's easy to cinch the lower belt that attaches the skirt to the trash can. I just wish the skirt were made of felt rather than the more porous woven fabric. This setup

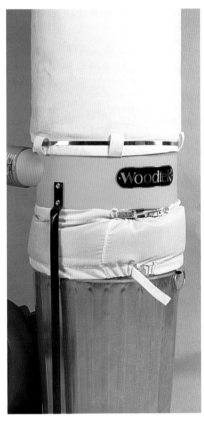

BETTER CONNECTIONS. The Oneida cyclone collector's trash barrel is connected by a large metal ring, which simplifies reattachment (left). Woodworker's Supply sells a clamp-on skirt accessory that is used with a 30-gal. trash can (right). The skirt is easier to reattach than a standard lower bag.

Designing a Central Dust-collection System

NO SCREWS OR RIVETS NEEDED. Quick-Fit duct pipe from Nordfab is assembled using gasketed clamps. Photo by Anatole Burkin

Oneida Air Systems designed my ductwork, which is very typical for a one-room shop under 500 sq. ft. The ductwork begins with a 6-in.-diameter pipe connected to the collector. At the first wye (split), the duct reduces to 5-in.-diameter branches. The 5-in.-diameter pipes serve the biggest tools (jointer, tablesaw and planer), even though they all have 4-in.-diameter dust ports, which ensure good air volume to the machines. Also, you can change the dust port to a 5-in.-diameter connection for better performance. A 5-in.-diameter to 4-in.-diameter reducer is used to make the transition.

The 4-in.-diameter branches that split off the 5-in.-diameter line serve smaller tools, such as the bandsaw and router table. Blast gates are installed at each tool. The final connections were made with flexible hose, which allows me to move my tools around.

I used 24-gauge (mostly) snap-lock pipe, spot-welded fittings, and aluminum blast gates, which are available from many companies. (Avoid lighter-gauge metal duct designed for heating or cooling systems; it can collapse under vacuum.) A higher-quality system will employ 22-gauge spiral pipe and welded fittings, which are stiffer and more airtight, and yes, they cost more. Quick-Fit® duct supplies from Nordfab® are also premium priced, but the components go together easily and don't require duct tape or caulk.

Although individual 24-gauge components aren't that expensive (a 5-ft. run of 5-in.-diameter snap-lock pipe costs about $8*), it all adds up. A very basic three-machine setup may be had for a few hundred dollars. A system for half a dozen tools and a floor sweep may cost $500* or more.

To help illustrate the photos in this chapter, an orange and black flex hose was used to make connections from pipe to tools; black flex hose, however, works fine. It's best to use a minimum of hose because it produces about three times the friction of metal pipe. Friction will reduce the performance of the system. All pipe seams and connections must be sealed with caulk or duct tape. Clear silicone caulk is a good choice because it's virtually invisible and is easy to remove.

DESIGN HELP IS AVAILABLE

Designing the ductwork for a central dust-collection system can involve a lot of calculations. For those of us who skipped math class, there's help available.

- Air Handling Systems of Woodbridge, Conn., has an on-line duct calculator program (www.airhand.com). The company outlines the concepts of duct design in a four-page brochure.

- Oneida Air Systems of Syracuse, N.Y., will design a duct system free of charge for its customers (www.oneida-air.com). All that's required is a shop drawing showing the types and locations of woodworking machines.

- Nordfab of Thomasville, N.C., manufacturers of the Quick-Fit line of duct and fittings, offers a free design service. The company has a downloadable program (www.nordfab.com), but you need a CAD program to run it. The company also offers a peel-and-stick shop layout kit for analog woodworkers.

- If you wish to tackle duct design yourself, all of the necessary information can be found in *Woodshop Dust Control* by Sandor Nagyszalanczy (The Taunton Press, 1996).

Sources

Air Handling Systems
(800) 367-3828
Duct supplies and duct
design

American Fabric Filter Co.
(800) 367-3591
Custom-made dust bags

Delta
(800) 438-2486
Dust collectors

Dust Boy
(800) 232-3878
Dust collectors

Highland Hardware
(800) 241-6748
Dust collectors

Jet
(800) 274-6848
Dust collectors and supplies

Kraemer Tools
(800) 443-6443
Dust collectors and supplies
(Canada)

Leneave Machinery
(800) 442-2302
Dust collectors

Nordfab
(800) 532-0830
Quick-Fit duct supplies

Oneida Air Systems
(315) 476-5151
Dust collectors, duct supplies and duct design

Penn State Industries
(800) 377-7297
Dust collectors and supplies

Powermatic
(800) 248-0144
Dust collectors

Sunhill Machinery
(800) 929-4321
Dust collectors and supplies

Woodworker's Supply
(800) 645-9292
Dust collectors and supplies

Wilke Machinery
(800) 235-2100
Dust collectors and supplies

NO SCREWS OR RIVETS NEEDED.
**Quick-Fit duct pipe from Nordfab is
assembled using gasketed clamps.**

will reduce the air volume (the collector "breathes" through both bags) when using the stock upper bag. With a larger upper bag, I found that the cfm readings were not compromised. But if you happen to vacuum up any offcuts, they will make quite a racket rattling around in a metal trash can.

Although many woodworkers, myself included, have used PVC drainpipe for duct without mishap, experts warn against using the material. The connectors (elbows and wyes) restrict airflow, and the material builds up a static charge, which may cause a spark and set off an explosion. (Running

grounded copper wire inside the pipe reduces the hazard.) Use PVC at your own risk. Metal duct and fittings are obviously better and will also last longer. I've broken half a dozen plastic blast gates in as many years. If you're on a tight budget, go with flexible hose or build a metal duct system in stages, starting with only a couple of hookups. Your collector will work more efficiently, and so will you.

* Note price estimates are from 2000.

ANATOLE BURKIN is a senior editor of *Fine Woodworking.*

Credits

The articles in this book appeared in the following issues of *Fine Woodworking*:

Photos: p. iii by Jonathan Binzen, courtesy *Fine Woodworking*, © The Taunton Press, Inc., p. iv top left by Paul Anthony courtesy *Fine Woodworking*, © The Taunton Press, Inc., top right by Boyd Hagen, courtesy *Fine Woodworking*, © The Taunton Press, Inc., p. 1 top left by Vincent Laurence, courtesy *Fine Woodworking*, © The Taunton Press, Inc., top right by Michael Pekovich, courtesy *Fine Woodworking*, © The Taunton Press, Inc. p. 2 top by Matt Berger, courtesy *Fine Woodworking*, © The Taunton Press, Inc., bottom by Asa Christiana, courtesy *Fine Woodworking*, © The Taunton Press, Inc., p. 3 top by Steve Scott, courtesy *Fine Woodworking*, © The Taunton Press, Inc., bottom by Vincent Laurence, courtesy *Fine Woodworking*, © The Taunton Press, Inc., p. 4 by Paul Anthony courtesy *Fine Woodworking*, © The Taunton Press, Inc., p. 40 by Mark Schofield, courtesy *Fine Woodworking*, © The Taunton Press, Inc., p. 88 by Michael Pekovich, courtesy *Fine Woodworking*, © The Taunton Press, Inc., p. 148 by Anatole Burkin, courtesy *Fine Woodworking*, © The Taunton Press, Inc., p. 175 by Tom Begnal, courtesy *Fine Woodworking*, © The Taunton Press, Inc., p. 213 by Alec Waters, courtesy *Fine Woodworking*, © The Taunton Press, Inc., p. 262 by William Duckworth, courtesy *Fine Woodworking*, © The Taunton Press, Inc.

p. 5: Biscuit Basics by Tony O'Malley, issue 165. Photos by Asa Christiana, courtesy *Fine Woodworking*, © The Taunton Press, Inc. Drawings by Jim Richey, courtesy *Fine Woodworking*, © The Taunton Press, Inc.

p. 14: Choosing and Using a Scrollsaw by Paul Schürch, issue 177. Photos by Asa Christiana, courtesy *Fine Woodworking*, © The Taunton Press, Inc.

p. 22: Oscillating Spindle Sanders, issue 137 by Bernie Maas. Photos by Dennis Preston, courtesy *Fine Woodworking*, © The Taunton Press, Inc., except p. 24 courtesy Clayton Machine Corp.

p. 25: A Circular Saw in the Furniture Shop? by Gary Williams, issue 143. Photos by Jonathan Binzen, courtesy *Fine Woodworking*, © The Taunton Press, Inc.

p. 32: Jigsaws in the Woodshop by Paul Anthony, issue 125. Photos by Paul Anthony, courtesy *Fine Woodworking*, © The Taunton Press, Inc.

p. 41: Mortising with a Router by Gary Rogowski, issue 121. Photos by Vincent Laurence, courtesy *Fine Woodworking*, © The Taunton Press, Inc. Drawings by Jim Richey, courtesy *Fine Woodworking*, © The Taunton Press, Inc.

p. 50: All About Router Bits by Jeff Greef, issue 116. Photos by Jeff Greef, courtesy *Fine Woodworking*, © The Taunton Press, Inc., except p. 51 top & pp. 54–55 by Scott Phillips, courtesy *Fine Woodworking*, © The Taunton Press, Inc. Drawings by Bob La Pointe, courtesy *Fine Woodworking*, © The Taunton Press, Inc.

p. 58: Template-Routing Basics by Pat Warner, issue 125. Photos by Strother Purdy, courtesy *Fine Woodworking*, © The Taunton Press, Inc. Drawings by Vince Babak, courtesy *Fine Woodworking*, © The Taunton Press, Inc.

p. 65: No-Frills Router Table by Gary Rogowski, issue 123. Photos by Vincent Laurence, courtesy *Fine Woodworking*, © The Taunton Press, Inc.

p. 71: The Ultimate Router Table by John White, issue 153. Photos by Asa Christiana, courtesy *Fine Woodworking*, © The Taunton Press, Inc. Drawings by Bruce Morser, courtesy *Fine Woodworking*, © The Taunton Press, Inc.

p. 81: Five Smart Router Jigs by Yeung Chan, issue 177. Photos by Mark Schofield, courtesy *Fine Woodworking*, © The Taunton Press, Inc. Drawings by John Hartman, courtesy Fine Woodworking, © The Taunton Press, Inc.

p. 89: A Tablesaw Primer: Ripping and Crosscutting by Kelly Mehler, issue 167. Drawings by Jim Richey, courtesy *Fine Woodworking*, © The Taunton Press, Inc.

p. 92: Weaving Shaker Tape Seats by Glenn A. Carlson, issue 121. Photos by Charley Robinson, courtesy *Fine Woodworking*, © The Taunton Press, Inc., except p. 93 bottom by William Duckworth, courtesy *Fine Woodworking*, © The Taunton Press, Inc.

p. 98: Tablesaw Tune-Up by Roland Johnson, issue 179. Photos by Steve Scott, courtesy *Fine Woodworking*, © The Taunton Press, Inc., except p. 101 bottom left by Michael Pekovich, courtesy *Fine Woodworking*, © The Taunton Press, Inc. Drawings by Jim Richey, courtesy *Fine Woodworking*, © The Taunton Press, Inc.

p. 110: Tablesaw Kickback by Garrett Hack, issue 139. Photos by Joe Romero, courtesy *Fine Woodworking*, © The Taunton Press, Inc., except p. 113 by Matthew Teague, courtesy *Fine Woodworking*, © The Taunton Press, Inc.

p. 114: Tablesaw Splitters and Blade Covers by Kelly Mehler, issue 152. Photos by Asa Christiana, courtesy *Fine Woodworking*, © The Taunton Press, Inc. Drawings by Jim Richey, courtesy *Fine Woodworking*, © The Taunton Press, Inc.

p. 124: A Tablesaw Sled for Precision Cutting by Lon Schleining, issue 128. Photos by Strother Purdy, courtesy *Fine Woodworking*, © The Taunton Press, Inc. Drawings by Michael Pekovich, courtesy *Fine Woodworking*, © The Taunton Press, Inc.

p. 130: Safe Procedures at the Tablesaw by Howard Lewin, issue 132. Photos and drawings by Michael Pekovich, courtesy *Fine Woodworking*, © The Taunton Press, Inc.

p. 138: Taming Tearout on the Tablesaw by Steve Latta, issue 168. Photos by Matt Berger, courtesy *Fine Woodworking*, © The Taunton Press, Inc. Drawings by Kelly J. Dunton, courtesy *Fine Woodworking*, © The Taunton Press, Inc.

p. 143: One-Stop Cutting Station by Ken Picou, issue 107. Photos by Vincent Laurence, courtesy *Fine Woodworking*, © The Taunton Press, Inc. Drawings by Michael Gellatly, courtesy *Fine Woodworking*, © The Taunton Press, Inc.

p. 149: Jigs for the Drill Press by Gary Rogowski, issue 140. Photos by Anatole Burkin, courtesy *Fine Woodworking*, © The Taunton Press,

Inc. Drawings by Vince Babak, courtesy *Fine Woodworking*, © The Taunton Press, Inc.

p. 155: Best Practices for Drilling by Ernie Conover, issue 170. Photos by Matt Berger, courtesy *Fine Woodworking*, © The Taunton Press, Inc.

p. 160: Using a Hollow-Chisel Mortiser by John West, issue 116. Photos by William Duckworth, courtesy *Fine Woodworking*, © The Taunton Press, Inc., except p. 165 by Boyd Hagen, courtesy *Fine Woodworking*, © The Taunton Press, Inc.

p. 167: Choose the Right Drill Bit for the Job by Brian Boggs, issue 138. Photos by Jonathan Binzen, courtesy *Fine Woodworking*, © The Taunton Press, Inc., except pp. 168 right, 169, 170 top, 171 top, 172 top right, 173 top right, & 174 left by Michael Pekovich, courtesy *Fine Woodworking*, © The Taunton Press, Inc. Drawings by Vince Babak, courtesy *Fine Woodworking*, © The Taunton Press, Inc.

p. 176: Bandsaw Tune-Up by John White, issue 157. Photos by Erika Marks, courtesy *Fine Woodworking*, © The Taunton Press, Inc. Drawings by Jim Richey, courtesy *Fine Woodworking*, © The Taunton Press, Inc.

p. 186: Resawing on the Bandsaw by Ronald Volbrecht, issue 122. Photos by Dennis Preston, courtesy *Fine Woodworking*, © The Taunton Press, Inc., except p. 193 by Scott Phillips, courtesy *Fine Woodworking*, © The Taunton Press, Inc.

p. 194: All About Bandsaw Blades by Lonnie Bird, issue 140. Photos by Lonnie Bird, courtesy *Fine*

Woodworking, © The Taunton Press, Inc., except p. 195 by Michael Pekovich, courtesy *Fine Woodworking*, © The Taunton Press, Inc. Drawings by Vince Babak, courtesy *Fine Woodworking*, © The Taunton Press, Inc.

p. 203: Soup Up Your 14-in. Bandsaw by John White, issue 159. Photos by Tom Begnal, courtesy *Fine Woodworking*, © The Taunton Press, Inc., except p. 204 by Michael Pekovich, courtesy *Fine Woodworking*, © The Taunton Press, Inc. Drawings by Melanie Powell, courtesy *Fine Woodworking*, © The Taunton Press, Inc.

p. 214: Jointer Savvy by Bernie Maas, issue 102. Photos by Alec Waters, courtesy *Fine Woodworking*, © The Taunton Press, Inc. Drawings by Mark Sant'Angelo, courtesy *Fine Woodworking*, © The Taunton Press, Inc.

p. 223: Getting Peak Planer Performance by Robert Vaughan, issue 107. Photos by Robert Vaughan, courtesy *Fine Woodworking*, © The Taunton Press, Inc., except p. 224 by Alec Waters, courtesy *Fine Woodworking*, © The Taunton Press, Inc. Drawings by Matthew Wells, courtesy *Fine Woodworking*, © The Taunton Press, Inc.

p. 232: The Jointer and Planer Are a Team by Gary Rogowski, issue 160. Drawings by Jim Richey, courtesy *Fine Woodworking*, © The Taunton Press, Inc.

p. 238: Jointer Tune-Up by John White, issue 142. Photos by Anatole Burkin, courtesy *Fine Woodworking*, © The Taunton Press, Inc. Drawings by Vince Babak, courtesy *Fine Woodworking*, © The Taunton Press, Inc., except p. 242 by Michael

Pekovich courtesy *Fine Woodworking*, © The Taunton Press, Inc.

p. 246: How to Get Square, Stable Stock by Gary Rogowski, issue 165. Photos by Asa Christiana, courtesy *Fine Woodworking*, © The Taunton Press, Inc. Drawings by Michael Pekovich, courtesy *Fine Woodworking*, © The Taunton Press, Inc.

p. 254: Jobs a Shaper Does Best by Lon Schleining, issue 112. Photos by Alec Waters, courtesy *Fine Woodworking*, © The Taunton Press, Inc. Drawings by Kathleen Rushton, courtesy *Fine Woodworking*, © The Taunton Press, Inc.

p. 263: Taming Woodworking Noise by Jack Vernon, issue 141. Photos by William Sampson, courtesy *Fine Woodworking*, © The Taunton Press, Inc. Drawings by Kathleen Rushton, courtesy *Fine Woodworking*, © The Taunton Press, Inc.

p. 268: Dust Collection for the One-Man Shop by Anatole Burkin, issue 141. Photos by Anatole Burkin, courtesy *Fine Woodworking*, © The Taunton Press, Inc., except p. 268 by William Duckworth, courtesy *Fine Woodworking*, © The Taunton Press, Inc., & p. 273 by Michael Pekovich, courtesy *Fine Woodworking*, © The Taunton Press, Inc. Drawings by Vince Babak, courtesy *Fine Woodworking*, © The Taunton Press, Inc.

Index

The New Best of Fine Woodworking Series

A collection of the best articles from the last ten years of Fine Woodworking

OTHER BOOKS IN THE SERIES

Designing Furniture

The Best of Fine Woodworking
From the editors of FWW
ISBN 1-56158-684-6
Product #070767
$17.95 U.S.
$25.95 Canada

Small Woodworking Shops

The Best of Fine Woodworking
From the editors of FWW
ISBN 1-56158-686-2
Product #070768
$17.95 U.S.
$25.95 Canada

Working with Routers

The Best of Fine Woodworking
From the editors of FWW
ISBN 1-56158-685-4
Product #070769
$17.95 U.S.
$25.95 Canada

Building Small Projects

The Best of Fine Woodworking
From the editors of FWW
ISBN 1-56158-730-3
Product #070791
$17.95 U.S.
$25.95 Canada

Designing and Building Cabinets

The Best of Fine Woodworking
From the editors of FWW
ISBN 1-56158-732-X
Product #070792
$17.95 U.S.
$25.95 Canada

Traditional Finishing Techniques

The Best of Fine Woodworking
From the editors of FWW
ISBN 1-56158-733-8
Product #070793
$17.95 U.S.
$25.95 Canada

Working with Handplanes

The Best of Fine Woodworking
From the editors of FWW
ISBN 1-56158-748-6
Product #070810
$17.95 U.S.
$25.95 Canada

Working with Tablesaws

The Best of Fine Woodworking
From the editors of FWW
ISBN 1-56158-749-4
Product #070811
$17.95 U.S.
$25.95 Canada

Workshop Machines

The Best of Fine Woodworking
From the editors of FWW
ISBN 1-56158-765-6
Product #070826
$17.95 U.S.
$25.95 Canada

Workstations and Tool Storage

The Best of Fine Woodworking
From the editors of FWW
ISBN 1-56158-785-0
Product #070838
$17.95 U.S.
$25.95 Canada

Traditional Projects

The Best of Fine Woodworking
From the editors of FWW
ISBN 1-56158-784-2
Product #070839
$17.95 U.S.
$25.95 Canada

Hand Tools

The Best of Fine Woodworking
From the editors of FWW
ISBN 1-56158-783-4
Product #070840
$17.95 U.S.
$25.95 Canada

Spray Finishing

The Best of Fine Woodworking
From the editors of FWW
ISBN 1-56158-829-6
Product #070875
$17.95 U.S.
$25.95 Canada

Selecting and Drying Wood

The Best of Fine Woodworking
From the editors of FWW
ISBN 1-56158-830-X
Product #070876
$17.95 U.S.
$25.95 Canada

The New Best of Fine Woodworking Slipcase Set Volume 1

Designing Furniture
Working with Routers
Small Woodworking Shops
Designing and Building Cabinets
Building Small Projects
Traditional Finishing Techniques

From the editors of FWW
ISBN 1-56158-736-2
Product #070808
$85.00 U.S./$120.00 Canada

The New Best of Fine Woodworking Slipcase Set Volume 2

Working with Handplanes
Workshop Machines
Working with Tablesaws
Selecting and Using Hand Tools
Traditional Projects
Workstations and Tool Storage

From the editors of FWW
ISBN 1-56158-747-8
Product #070809
$85.00 U.S./$120.00 Canada